FORWARD

BOOK 5: THE EVENTING SERIES

NATALIE KELLER REINERT

Forward

By Natalie Keller Reinert

Cover Photo: iStock

ISBN: 9781095581520

Books by Natalie Keller Reinert

Show Barn Blues Series
Show Barn Blues

Horses in Wonderland

The Eventing Series
Ambition

Pride

Courage

Luck

Forward

The Alex and Alexander Horse-Racing Series
The Head and Not The Heart

Other People's Horses

Claiming Christmas

Turning For Home

Heroines on Horseback Historical Romance Novels
Miss Spencer Rides Astride

The Genuine Lady

The Honorable Nobody

Short Stories
Horse-Famous: Stories

Deck the Stalls: Horse Stories for the Holidays (Editor)

"Doesn't matter, FORWARD, FORWARD!
Now, that is good."

- Isabel Werth, Olympic Equestrian, teaching a
dressage clinic
As quoted in *The Chronicle of the Horse* forum

CHAPTER ONE

The day I fought with Pete, the light streaming through the skyscrapers was a brilliant gold, gilding every leaf and every blade of grass and every stray pebble knocked by careless feet into the pathways of the park. No one turned and looked at us, because we were civilized people and it was too awful, too embarrassing: the young woman with the tear-streaked face and sun-touched hair falling from a once-sleek bun; the young man with the piercing eyes leaning on the well-worn crutches. No one turned and looked at us, but they all heard us, and we didn't care, we didn't stop, until we both wanted to and it was too late and we had turned away from each other.

The day I fought with Pete, New York was a film set, the kind of New York everyone sees in the movies and never finds in real life. Just moments before, the day had been gray, rain-spattered, diesel-scented, like a tractor left running in the barn aisle on a soggy December morning. As riders from cleaner climates, we'd looked at each other from our vantage points atop our horses and asked: *why would anyone live here?*

Then, suddenly, without warning, the clouds parted and the sun sprang up from the rooftops of Manhattan and the people came pouring out of their apartment doors like bees swarming from their hive. Just like bees, they buzzed straight to the park, to bury their noses in the sweet clover of the lawns, and when they saw us already there, in our breeches and our boots, leading our gleaming horses to the arena set up at the Wollman Rink, even the most jaded New Yorkers paused to give us a second glance. We were alien and lovely, and we towered above them even on the ground, even when we were fighting.

The day I fought with Pete, the mayor shook our hands and told us we were favorites of his niece, and did we see her showing at the Winter Equestrian Festival in West Palm back in January? We did not; we were not WEF people and we knew his niece had never heard of either of us, but we smiled back and said we'd look for her this coming winter, and he smiled and said she'd love that—she'd be the girl on the white pony, with pigtails. The governor was there, too, but we didn't meet him; he didn't like horses and he kept to himself, sitting aloof on the platform where the dignitaries were enthroned, pretending they knew what was going on in the arena before them.

The day I fought with Pete was the best day of my life, for at least ten hours or so.

***

The craziest thing was that the show had to go on. Pete swung away on his crutches and disappeared into the crowd. I began stalking back to the holding tent where the day's competing horses were stabled, but I suddenly stopped short, a cold hand clutching my heart, and spun around to catch him. I had to stop him; I couldn't let him go away angry over something so foolish. We were a team. We had to face our problems together.

The crowd was buzzing now that the shouting had stopped, and as my eyes swept over their gossiping ranks I thought Pete would stand out to me. But I only saw the ridiculous scene of a horse show dressed up as a society party: women in expensive sundresses and strappy heels; men in linen shirts and madras shorts and pastel-colored loafers. It was the weekend after Labor Day and the city was suddenly warm with summer's last hurrah, and I had made everyone's party much better with the gift of my public temper.

Lacey was waiting for me in the doorway of the tent, her eyes round and her pale face flushed. A full summer in Florida hadn't yet restored the deep tan and multitude of freckles she'd boasted before she'd gone back to Pennsylvania. A year bent over textbooks had transformed her back to the white-skinned Irish-American girl she'd been born. Three months running my eventing barn had put steel back in her spine and sharpened her cheekbones, but at this moment she looked more like a frightened child than an unflappable barn manager. With her chestnut hair knotted in tight pigtails, she reminded me of an overgrown Pippi Longstocking. I braced myself for the sharp questions she'd lob at me the moment I was within hissing distance. I had grown tired of her immediate *Mom and Dad are getting a divorce* reaction every time Pete and I had a fight.

This time, though, it might not be an overstatement.

"Is Dynamo ready to go?" I asked, pushing past her before she could say a word, before she could burst out with a torrent of emotion which would be overheard and gleefully passed onwards by the entire aristocracy of English riding (and yes, there were a few actual aristocrats in the bunch), before she could make me cry. I *wasn't* going to cry. Not here, not now, not in front of the world, or that part of the world which mattered to my future. "We need to be warmed up in the next half an hour or he won't have his shit together for the first round. And there's no second chances tonight. We go in and kill, or we sink the team and we lose the big check."

Lacey could only watch me sail by, her mouth gaping open, at a loss for words. I wasn't surprised. No one could tamp down her emotions like Jules Thornton. Maybe I'd softened over the years, but when I needed to pull on my old persona, it was still there. I reclaimed my guise as the brittle, ice-cold queen of eventing, and it would take more than a fight with my boyfriend to put me off my game with just an hour until the Central Park Arena Eventing Challenge.

I stalked past the other horses, the other grooms, the other riders, to the stall in the center of the tent where Dynamo was leaning over a blue rubber stall guard, his chestnut mane bound up in tiny round plaits and his halter on over his bridle. At least Lacey had, indeed, been tacking him up as I'd requested. While I'd been outside blowing up my world, she'd been busy doing the simple work that made it go on spinning.

"Let's go, Dyno-saur," I murmured, running a hand down his shining neck. It was rather short, bulging with hard muscle from crest to wither—Dynamo didn't have the graceful swan's neck so many successful event horses possessed. His low, heavy sprinter's body wasn't built for dressage, which made our warm-ups that much more important. I needed all the time I'd been granted to get his body curving together, coaxing his hindquarters and shoulders and spine and neck into working in unison, and I couldn't spend a single second trying to figure out what I'd just done with the rest of my life.

Only the competition mattered. Only the *horse* mattered.

I led him out of the stall and through the tent.

My fellow competitors parted before the two of us like the waters of the Red Sea, arms full of custom-made saddles and sheepskin half pads and girths built with NASA technology. For the first time in my career, I knew I was their equal, not just in raw talent and drive, but in the material things as well. My horse might be an off-track Thoroughbred I'd rescued from a kill pen when I was a teenager, but he was decked out in the latest tech, just like the six-figure warmbloods who had been shipped across the Atlantic via first-class equine air. Once my name had been added to the Eventing team roster, Rockwell couldn't get me new clothes and tack fast enough. I brushed imaginary leaves of alfalfa from my dove-blue riding jacket, the very picture of a modern major champion, and led my childhood horse, blinking in the light, into the golden city evening.

No one really knows their breaking point.

We all talk about it as if we do. "I'm at my breaking point." "He's pushing me to my breaking point." "Another blow and I'll reach my breaking point."

What happens when we *do* get there? It's different for everyone.

Every time I thought I reached my breaking point, I kept going. Every time I thought one more catastrophe would send me reeling, back to my parents' house with my tail between my legs, I found a way to keep going.

Tonight was no different.

And if the evening's events passed by me in a fog, if I only remember it in snatched fragments, like a movie I wanted to watch but couldn't quite stay awake through, that was for the best. That was how I didn't reach my breaking point. Because if I'd truly remembered that night, I don't know how I could have kept going the way I did. The only possible answer was that Pete didn't matter to me the way I'd thought he did, and I knew then and I know now, that wasn't true.

I remember the glaring LED lights shining down on the odd-shaped arena, and the cross-country jumps casting shadows across the groomed white sand. I remember thinking it was the most bizarre thing I'd ever seen, because who had ever seen a cross-country course lit up for night riding, or coops and picnic tables and coffins set up on harrowed footing? I remember Dynamo's head craning to take in the crowds all around him, more humanity than we'd ever experienced, and the sensation of all those eyes beneath all those skyscraper lights, like being in a fishbowl at the bottom of the Grand Canyon.

I remember his hooves brushing the potted ferns surrounding the looming corner fence as we made a tight turn, my legs jammed into his sides, my hands high, my body upright, willing him to make the short distance to the eye-popping arch of the apple-shaped keyhole fence. I remember thinking that I didn't know what fence came next, and still my body curved naturally to the left, guiding him over a fat, maxed-out table designed to look like a squat country cottage. As if we'd grown so big here, jumping cross-country fences in a converted ice-skating rink instead of out in the actual country, that even the farmhouses shrank beneath our stature.

I remember thinking this wasn't eventing, no matter what they wanted to call it, but it was fast and it was trappy and it was fun.

Yes, I remember having fun.

The mayor congratulated me and Lacey took Dynamo's reins while I smiled for the flashing cameras. The other riders melted away after we shared the award ceremony for the top team, and I stood alone to celebrate my individual win. I thought about the horse this check would buy me as I stood there, with a grin plastered in place long after its natural expiration date, my lips curling above my teeth, my cheeks aching, as cameras clicked and flashed. I curled my toes inside my custom boots, delirious with pleasure. Lacey held Dynamo nearby, wearing a cooler stitched with a New York City skyline, as if he had become the city's now, as well.

Then, suddenly, as if hours were erased from my memory, I was alone on the street.

What street? I was lost. I didn't know the street names— the numbers, rather. The biggest city I'd been in before this week was Tampa. I was walking under trees, crossing shadows from the gleaming white streetlights, past the wrought-iron gates of narrow mansions built of pale marble. The night was sticky-hot, as if a blanket had been laid over the city the moment the sun went down. Right now in Ocala, there would be a soft breeze playing through the live oaks, and lightning glinting in the distance from a storm which had passed earlier in the day. No such luck in Manhattan.

Somehow I got turned around and found myself back in the bright lights of Midtown. The mansions and brownstones gave way to delis and smartphone stores and luggage emporiums, and then I was under the canopy of our hotel and then I was in the lobby bar and there was Pete, his crutches leaning against the dark wood paneling in the far corner, his gaze trained out the window at the passing yellow cabs and city buses, exhaustion etched in every line of his face.

I stopped so long in the wide doorway between the lobby and the bar, the doorman came over and asked if I needed help. I felt his eyes on my riding jacket, now rather rumpled from allowing Dynamo to give me a couple good face-rubs before Lacey haltered him and rescued me. My white breeches were smudged in a few spots thanks to my own horse-dirty hands. When I brushed the sharply-dressed doorman away, I saw him step over to the front desk, where the woman behind the counter pointed at her computer screen and scolded him; he went slinking back to the heavy revolving door at the entrance, and I knew she'd told him that the dirty, livestock-scented men and women in the hotel this evening were actually honored guests.

In the corner, Pete gazed out the window.

I don't know how long I stood there, waiting for him to look up. He was looking for me, obviously, but why didn't he know I was there, just across the room? Shouldn't someone who loved you know that? Shouldn't he have spun around, his eyes widening, and immediately fumble for his crutches, quickly growing frustrated that he couldn't rush across the room to me? Shouldn't I have pushed the other bar patrons in their teetering heels and gleaming oxfords aside, meeting him more than halfway?

Why didn't it happen?

Earlier today, New York had been a movie, but now it was just a noisy, clattering, sweaty city again, and I wanted to go home, breathe in the humid Ocala air, settle down on my own couch in my own living room, and send Amanda an email I'd had in my drafts for months, telling her I was ready to buy that horse.

Pete would be there. He lived there, too. It was his living room, too.

And with that strange, simple logic, I turned around and went upstairs. I looked at my reflection in the gold-flecked mirrors of the elevator, and I walked through the heavy brass doors when they opened, and I went into my room and I slipped out of my show clothes and fell into bed and when I woke up in a gray dawning morning, I was intensely aware that I was still all alone.

CHAPTER TWO

Four months before, in the pollen-heavy Florida spring, you never could have told me I'd wake up alone in a Manhattan hotel room. I mean, you could have *told* me, but you couldn't have made me believe it. I would have laughed you out of the room. For one thing, what would I be doing in New York City? In September, when I should be prepping my horses for the fall season—to say nothing of my barn full of students who needed to get ready for their own seasons? Not a chance I'd feel like I could go on a jaunt up to Manhattan, a place I'd never been before and really had no reason to ever visit.

Of course, four months before *that*, you never could have convinced me I'd have a barn full of students who were on my mind night and day. But life is strange, and equestrian life is strangest of all.

So it was that at the start of the summer, New York and its discontents were far from my mind. I had other problems, and at the time, I really thought they were big enough. There were the usual worries of running a barn: hooves which were too flat, or too soft, or too brittle; tails which would not grow; the horse who was going through some sort of refusal renaissance and couldn't get through a course without stopping at half the fences; hives popping up on the neck of a warmblood which might be succumbing to the insect allergies which ended bright Florida show careers; a tween student facing the dreaded breaking point of choosing either boys or horses; a missing set of bell boots somewhere in the biggest pasture on the farm.

Then there were the little extra concerns which came with trying to establish oneself as a rider at the top of one's sport, as a kind of bonus: things like finding most of your division at your next event were riders already competitive at the four-star level, while you were just starting to tackle three-star, or puzzling over how to keep your racing-fit horse from turning the extended canter into an extended hand-gallop in the next dressage test. Although the last time Dynamo had done this, everyone had applauded politely. He had a very nice gallop.

I was reliving the moment we'd hurtled up the long side of the dressage ring, driving towards the little white chain that separated us from the knot of spectators, taking in the alarm on their faces from a place somewhere outside my body, when a female voice startled me back to reality.

"Are we having summer camp, Jules?"

I looked up from the bridle I had been taking apart

before my daydream stilled my fingers. Jordan, fourteen and coltish, took a look at the mess in my lap and recoiled. I couldn't blame her.

I had picked up the dusty, cob-sized black bridle from a spider-webbed corner of the feed store in High Springs, hoping it would fit the tiny face of Tomeka's little Arab-Hanoverian cross—I know, I can't understand who makes these kinds of breeding decisions either—and the whole thing needed to be soaked in vinegar or bleach or hydrochloric acid. There was green mold blossoming beneath the brass fittings, spreading its powdery fingers under the leather keepers. And beneath the mold, there was a layer of greasy filth, coexisting with the surface algae bloom in a disgusting natural alchemy which belied years of forgotten neglect in the back of someone's AC-free tack room.

"I hope this actually *is* black leather and not just a layer of grime on a brown bridle," I muttered, surveying the filth on my fingers.

"Jules," Jordan said urgently, getting back on topic with her usual practicality. "Everyone's asking. Last week, you said you'd tell us by Monday. It's Saturday."

"What's that, Jordan? I'm sorry." After a couple of months living at Alachua Eventing Co-op, I still had to remind myself to pay attention to the barn kids. My prior life's philosophy had included tuning out children, but I couldn't do that anymore. These kids weren't some other trainer's problem anymore—they were my problem, signed and delivered. I had agreed to take on an entire pack of barn rats, who, freed from their hunter/jumper barn constraints, were gradually growing feral right in front of me. I'd seen one of them riding in shorts the other day. "Start over again. I'm listening now."

"Okay, Jules, remember the summer camp? We were talking about it after lessons the other night. Everyone really wants you to do one." Jordan pushed the pale wisps escaping from her skinny braid behind her ears and grinned nervously. Tall and thin, with a pointy chin and wide brown eyes, fourteen-going-on-fifteen Jordan was usually the anointed messenger of the barn kids' demands, mainly because she didn't know how to say no to anyone. Heaven help her in a year or two when she got her driver's license and ended up driving everyone around.

I turned back to the bridle while I considered her question, but without much luck. The last buckle on the bridle was defying my demands. I wrenched at it and my hands just slid across the greasy leather. I should have just bought something new from Rockwell with my discount, but old penny-pinching habits die hard. "I haven't even thought about summer," I finally admitted. "I was thinking about fall events, mainly." Fall events for *my* horses, no less— when I had more than a dozen students out there who expected to be on track with their own eventing careers by the end of summer.

I kept trying not to think about that.

"Next week is May first," Jordan pointed out. "We get

out of school in less than four weeks. You should have that on your giant calendar."

We both looked through the tack room door, across the barn aisle, to the massive calendar hanging on the closed office door, where I wrote out training intervals and event dates in bold, decisive Sharpie. I lived and died by my giant calendar, and everyone in the barn knew it.

But the dates on it still belonged to my event horses, as little as my string was these days. I could read their names from here: Mickey, Jim Dear, Dynamo. Flip through the calendar and my summer was actually already written there. I had gallop days, dressage lessons, cross-country schools, and events, all the way through October. The events were circled in red.

It was an ambitious calendar, but I had three good horses who could make it all a reality, barring hoof abscesses and soft-tissue injuries. With Dynamo running at Advanced, Mickey at Preliminary, and Jim Dear moving up from Training to Prelim once we got his dressage jitters ironed out, I had a chance to make some solid connections this year, and possibly bring in some new horses to compete next year. I had resigned myself to thinking very long-term about my competition goals, because the job of trainer at Alachua meant I was supposed to be focusing on my students first.

Putting myself second was not a philosophy I was completely resigned to yet.

Jordan was still looking at me expectantly.

"In my defense, this is my first year working around a school calendar." I slid my eyes back to the bridle, giving a decisive wrench to the leather in my hands. The cheekpiece I'd been wrestling with popped free and went flying across the tack room, flopping to a halt against the lockers against the wall. I sighed. "Can you get that for me?"

Jordan obediently chased after the errant cheekpiece.

"I can add the dates to the calendar," she offered humbly as she returned the greasy piece of leather. "I can do it right now, before our lesson. I'll add our last school day, and our first day back in August. Oh! And the evening jumper shows at Woodland... we all really like those." She pulled out her phone and started consulting a show listing website. "Is one show a month okay?"

"Keep the writing small," I suggested. "I need room for extra things like unplanned farrier visits to go on there. Or I'll never be able to keep track of appointments *and* all of your riding lessons."

"I'll put them at the very bottom of each date," Jordan promised, and galloped off to update my sacred calendar with the dates she deemed important to the barn kids.

The barn kids! My entire life now was keeping track of barn kids. Their schedules, their riding goals, their squabbles, their missing saddle pads, their poorly-chosen bits, their inability to pick up the left lead without leaning into the left stirrup, their hopes, their fears. Honestly, it was a *lot*.

I shook my head at myself, and then the bridle's last

buckle finally ripped loose, its brass pin slipping unwillingly from the dirt-encrusted hole it had rested in for years, and dropped the whole mess on the floor. The bridle pieces scattered across the linoleum at the toes of my paddock boots, which honestly didn't look that much better. *Everything* needed cleaning.

Well, that's a good use for summer camp, I thought, trying to look on the bright side. Amusing a dozen kids aged between twelve and seventeen for hours on end? I could set all of them to tack-cleaning an hour a day and we'd have the whole place polished by fall.

I'd just file that idea away to bring up with Pete later, although he was so busy with his string of horses at the moment, I doubted I'd see much of his face during any summer camp sessions. Pete seemed to spend as much time as possible in the saddle, riding his horses for impossibly long training sessions. When he wasn't in the arena, he was holed up in the office he'd set up in the second bedroom of the house, where he was constantly on the phone with current and potential owners, going over training schedules, or talking with vets and farriers, or brooding over books.

He really had been cultivating a Big Name Trainer vibe these days, which showed a bit of inflated ego in my opinion, considering he only had a half-dozen horses under him, and only two of them were running higher than Training.

Still, I was starting to feel like the wife of a successful trainer with a barn-full of kids.

It wasn't exactly the look I'd been going for.

I sighed and shook it off. Then I picked up the jug of ammonia and tipped some into a small plastic bucket at my feet, wrinkling my nose at the stench. This bridle was going to need a full strip-job.

The sound of shod hooves dragging on the cement aisle made me look up from my smelly task a short while later. I stripped off my rubber gloves as I straightened slowly, feeling joints creak and pop their way into working order, then headed into the barn aisle to meet Pete and his horse.

They made a sorry pair as they approached me, both of them dripping with sweat and looking miserable. Here we were in the last week in April and these two were already halfway to dying of sunstroke. *Again.*

I wasn't happy with the way this partnership was going so far. Pete had been riding Rogue since midwinter, when he'd been a young girl's problem horse at a hunter/jumper barn. He'd only been at our barn for the past two weeks, purchased for Pete by a new player in the eventing game, Rick Delannoy.

I didn't like Rick. He wanted to show up at events and point to his champion horse to impress women, but that wasn't my problem with him. As long as an owner was paying the bills, their motivation was their business. What mattered was that they stay out of the kitchen, and Rick Delannoy wasn't just sending back every dish Pete plated, he was going into the kitchen and telling Pete how to cook.

None of us had foreseen how domineering Rick would be: calling every day, demanding regular progress reports, questioning Pete's every decision. He didn't know the first thing about horses, but he seemed to know quite a lot about absorbing unsubstantiated training theories from the Internet. Yesterday, Pete had come out of the barn office sweating, his face red and his jaw clenched, and said that Rick had ordered a full training rig to be sent to the barn, so Rogue could be lunged every day in it and brought to a "full state of engagement more quickly than riding could do it," according to the blog post Rick had been reading.

"What are you going to do?" I'd asked quietly, because Pete had not been as forceful as someone like, say, *me* might have been in telling Rick where to stick his gadgets and gimmicks.

"Tell him it never came and blame it on the post office, I guess."

Pete walked Rogue into the wash-rack and turned him around. The horse stood still without being asked, his sides heaving, sweat dripping onto the concrete floor.

For a moment, I considered taking the high road. I could just help Pete untack Rogue quietly, without picking on him about the state his horse was in. Then I discarded that notion. Pete needed to hear the truth, and I was just the girl to give it to him.

"That horse is exhausted, Pete. You need to give him a week off. *You* need a week off. You both look like wrecks."

Pete didn't even look at me to acknowledge my

thoughtful critique of his training methods. He just stripped
the saddle, half-pad and saddle towel off together with the
dangling girth and flung it all onto the nearby rack. Then he
shouted down the aisle for one of the kids to come grab him
and cool him out.

It was Lindsay who came running, seventeen and
already acting like she ran the barn, her hands outstretched
to take the lead rope from me. She looked the horse over
and made a quick decision. "I'm going to walk him until he's
a little cooler, before I put any water on him," she said
briskly, glancing at me for approval.

"Sounds good," I agreed. I'd been giving Lindsay hints
about horse care for the past few weeks, thinking she might
make a good working student or even an event groom in the
future.

She'd only walked the dripping horse a few steps down
the aisle before Pete had disappeared into the barn office,
carelessly leaving the door hanging open behind him. As the
cold air-conditioned breeze swept my hot cheeks, I heard
him barking at his phone to call Rick Delannoy.

I should have closed the office door and kept both the air
conditioning and the phone conversation inside, but I didn't.
Instead, I left the door open and busied myself just outside,
tidying up the tack discarded there, wiping Rogue's white
hairs and sweaty foam from the straps of the bridle and
breastplate, all the while listening to Pete describe every
step of the ride, and what he was expecting from the horse
tomorrow.

This daily check-in was a strange requirement which had cropped up the moment the ink was dry on their contract—Delannoy wanted constant reports on the horse's progress as he transitioned from jumper to eventer, and set strict goalposts he expected Pete to meet with the horse each week. I'd never heard of such a thing, and I was pretty sure it was going to end in tears. It was demoralizing, for one thing, and it eroded Pete's authority as the trainer, for another. That was what Rick liked about it, I was sure. The check-ins let him micro-manage Rogue's training, and ensured Pete knew exactly who was boss.

But Pete was the expert. Pete was the trainer. Pete should have been the boss.

At first, I'd fought Pete's acquiescence on this. I'd told him to threaten Rick with ending the partnership. Push him, I'd said—he'll give in.

Pete said he wasn't willing to risk it. I'd backed down. I knew he loved Rogue.

But what was happening now: these over-the-top training sessions, that sweaty horse dragging his hooves down the aisle as Lindsay murmured coaxing encouragement to him? That wasn't love. Or if it was, it was a funny way of showing it.

I sighed, wiping the sweat from Pete's dressage girth. "You'd be no better," I reminded myself.

The truth was, we were both driven by demons.

As soon as I heard Pete end the call, I ducked into the tack room with the saddle over my arm and acted as if I'd been putting things away the entire time: tossing laundry into the bin next to the old green washing machine, hanging the drenched bridle onto the hook for cleaning later, once the sweat had evaporated from the abused leather, sliding the saddle onto its carpet-lined rack. By the time Pete came into the room, his face clouded, I was back on my stool, already sporting my yellow dishwashing gloves, rinsing the ammonia bath from the dirty black bridle as if I hadn't heard a thing.

Not that it mattered; Pete barely looked my direction before he started digging around in a black enameled tack trunk, unearthing a heavy canvas tote bag. I recognized it as his bit bag, a collection of mouthpieces he'd acquired over the years or inherited from his grandfather. It was a strange assortment; we'd pawed through them before, eyeballing the wicked curves of the segunda and the heavy beads of the Waterford. The bit bag was more of a conversation piece than anything. Despite his impressive collection, Pete usually used one bridle and bit to school all of his horses: a battered, butter-soft padded bridle with a loose-ring French link snaffle. He just adjusted the cheekpieces for each horse as he worked through the day. While he occasionally upped the bit power for cross-country, Pete believed every horse should go in the lightest bit possible, and he worked hard to live up to that ideal.

Now, though, Pete was pulling out bits and holding them up one by one, studying their respective merits. None of the choices looked like anything he'd ever put in a horse's mouth.

"What's that?" I asked, unable to stop myself, as he paused and considered a particularly odd-looking curb bit, with a high port and large, round rings for the reins and cheekpieces.

"Just some kind of gag," Pete said, looking at it without pleasure. "For precision. For very tough customers."

"Well, it's gross-looking. Put it away before one of the kids sees it and gets the wrong idea."

He stood up from the tack trunk, his knees cracking, and slipped the bit over a free hook on the tack-cleaning hanger.

"That's the opposite of putting it away," I said, a feeling of alarm rising. "You aren't going to *use* that thing, are you?"

"He's being a bull out there, even when we're schooling on the flat." Pete sighed, his eyes not leaving the complicated bit. "He wants to race around the fences and the way he's going, one foot wrong and someone's going to get hurt. I've used this on jumpers before and it's gotten the message across. I just need him to *listen*."

I looked more closely. The bit had rings *for* its rings, for heaven's sake, and a curb chain besides. It was meant to exact immediate obedience from a horse. In fact, it might even require the horse to be some sort of clairvoyant to avoid punishment. I wasn't against a strong bit on a strong horse in theory, but I couldn't help but think this was some kind of quick fix, meant to help Pete meet his owner's impossible demands. And there was also the problem of the aesthetics. A bit with rings the size of appetizer plates was not what we'd sold to the parents of all those impressionable children running around the barn. They'd set me up in business with the expectation of a more wholesome environment than what they'd seen their children experience at their big show barns. They'd come here *because* of our French link snaffles and our slow training philosophy.

"It looks awful," I announced, in the understatement of the year.

"He's been allowed his own way for too long," Pete replied. "It wasn't just the bucking issue costing him in the jumper ring. He's so hell-bent on taking charge out there, it could cost us rails, even time penalties, if I've got to take the long way just to keep him under control. He was never meant to be a teenager's horse and she just let him have his own way to prevent fights, so now that he's fit, we're having those fights, constantly. And don't forget, if I don't have him in hand and he gets a bad distance, we'll just crash out there and die."

I shook my head, annoyed with that old argument. "Yeah, yeah, I get all that. But you and I both know you don't fix control issues with a bit, Pete. This is a shortcut. And I've never, ever seen you take a shortcut. Why start now?" *When we're surrounded by children?* I added mentally. I didn't want to make Camp Jules-and-Pete the scapegoat for every situation I thought called for a critique, or I'd have said it aloud, too.

Pete raked his hand through his coppery hair, fastening

his gaze on the bit for a few moments. "It'll be okay," he said finally. "It's still *me* on his back. A bit is only as harsh as a rider's hands."

"You know that's just a saying." I stood and flicked the extra rings on the bit's loose-rings, where the rope of the gag would be threaded. You could have the hands of an angel, but a gag was still called a gag for a reason. There was no use sugar-coating reality. A harsh bit only worked better than a soft bit because of its threat. I decided it was time to bring in the *think of the children* argument. "And how are we going to explain this to the kids? We're supposed to teach them to find solutions to their problems, not use gadgets."

On cue, Jordan stuck her head into the tack room. "Guys, we are mounting up for our lesson, okay?" Her helmet was already buckled under her pointy chin.

"I'll be right there," I promised. "Just get everyone stretched out."

"Will do," Jordan nodded and disappeared again. Outside the tack room, I heard hooves sliding sluggishly over concrete—her aging warmblood Sammy, in no hurry to start work. I *had* to get that girl on a new horse, I thought for the hundredth time. Then I focused on Pete again.

"She didn't see the bit hanging there," I warned him. "But they're all going to, especially since you're using them all as a revolving set of working students, and you're going to have to tell them that sometimes riders take their training orders from their owners. Which is a *terrible* lesson to teach them, Pete." I moved to the door, ready to start teaching the six o'clock lesson.

"Why don't you just lay off?" Pete growled, pulling a spare bridle off a wall hook and throwing it onto the rack alongside the gag bit. "I'm sorry I'm not living my entire professional life up to your specifications, Jules. I'm sorry that sometimes I have to make tough decisions in order to keep this business going."

I paused in the doorway and looked back at him. He was tugging at the buckles on the bridle's cheekpieces, ready to remove the normal, everyday snaffle hanging from them and replace it with the gag. "I think you mean *your* business," I said softly, not wanting my voice to waft down the barn aisle, where eager teenagers would pick up on our domestic dispute with glee. "My business is going just fine without having to pander to dick-head owners."

And I went out to teach my class.

There was a gap between us on the couch that night.

Of course, Marcus was more than happy to fill it, slinking up onto the vacant middle cushion and spreading out, a splayed-out pillow of happy tricolor beagle, his tail on Pete's thigh, his nose on mine. I slipped my hand over his long, silky ears, pulling at them softly, and felt quietly triumphant that I was still Marcus's favorite, even after two years of living with Pete. Even after Pete saved his life, pulling him out from under my mobile home in the eye of a hurricane. If Marcus had at some point shifted allegiance, that would make nights like this even tougher to handle. But I had the head; Pete had the tail. I was still tops in Marcus's book.

Pete was typing furiously on his phone, an unending series of blue bubbles flooding its screen every time he put it down long enough to pick up his beer from the scratched glass top of the coffee table. I sipped at my own beer and watched him surreptitiously, outwardly pretending to watch a rerun on TV.

Any other woman might have been excused for feeling jealous. I might have invented a trip into the kitchen or to the barn so I could glance over his shoulder, get a glimpse of his texts. But Pete's face was not the face of a man sexting with a crush. He looked harried and angry, and every time he put his phone down, it crashed a little harder on the glass. I knew the person on the other end was Rick.

I felt for him, but not enough to apologize for the things I'd said earlier, or to push Marcus out of the way to bridge the gap between us. Pete was going to have to get out of this one on his own, and in his own time... as long as his decisions didn't threaten my business and the relationship I had with the students, and their parents.

I actually had a good thing going here, even if I was still struggling with the career shift from trainer to coach, and I wasn't going to let something as minor as a long-term relationship with another human ruin it.

Okay, I told myself. *That was probably going a little far.*

But at the same time, I argued with myself, would I have thought it if I hadn't meant it? Things were a bit of a mess right now, and maybe we were at a crossroads we just hadn't recognized yet.

The exciting partnership we'd had before was gone. Team Briar Hill felt long ago, as if we'd left it behind in that rented field where we'd huddled inside our horse trailer, waiting for better things to come.

The better things had come, but not the way either of us had expected. And maybe we should have waited for something else. Maybe I'd settled when I'd accepted the co-op and the riding coach life. Had it been the wrong decision for me, or for Pete? I didn't know anymore. It had been a shot at an address without wheels, a nice barn and a riding ring and a steady income, and it had felt like we were being saved.

I looked over at Pete, withdrawn into himself, as far away on the other side of the couch as if he was in another room, another house, another county, and I wondered if I had only saved myself.

CHAPTER THREE

Most of the time, though, we just kept working through our days as though nothing had changed between us. There wasn't a lot of downtime in our days, and it was those quiet moments, when we were left alone with our thoughts just a little too long, that let the doubts creep in.

The next morning, we went about our day as if there'd been no space between us on the couch. We went out at six-thirty, we brought in the horses from night turn-out, we fed them breakfast, we got on with things. I had already ridden two horses and had led Jim Dear out to the arena, walking alongside Pete and Barsuk, when I felt my phone buzz and saw I'd gotten my ride times from May Days Horse Trials.

It was the first time I was taking students to an event and I was eager to see how the schedule would work out, so I pulled up Jim Dear to take a closer look at the email. Pete paused as well, watching with interest.

I furrowed my brow at the message. "Well, this *can't* be right."

Pete looked over my shoulder and cupped a hand over my phone, shielding the screen from the blazing morning sunlight. "Oh, those are close together," he said, without a trace of sympathy.

"How are my Training Horse times up against the kids' Beginner Novice times?"

"They're running two dressage rings." Pete pointed at the notes under the times. "See? One is in Ring A and the other's in Ring B."

"But they have to know that riders in the higher levels will have to coach kids riding in the lower levels. That's like, how this business *works*. Or that's what everyone has been telling me for years, anyway."

Pete kissed me on the cheek, as if his affection would make all of my problems disappear. "Making it work is part of the fun," he said cheerfully.

I shoved him off, startling both Jim Dear and Barsuk, but I wasn't sorry. "Says the person who shows up, teaches his one dressage lesson per group, and walks away. As if you had any idea how much trouble I'm having scheduling my life around these kids! You spend *all* of your time on *your* horses. I get less than half of that time to spend on mine!"

Pete didn't say anything to that. He just led Barsuk on into the arena.

I looked at Jim Dear for a moment, the plain bay Thoroughbred waggling his ears as he took in the steamy mid-morning scene.

I sighed and slid my phone back into the pocket of my breeches. It was Tuesday; all I needed from life right now was an offended Pete in my way while I tried to make it through another week of barn chores, riding, lessons, a farrier visit, and everything else crammed into my schedule. I considered catching up with him and apologizing, telling him I was just feeling pre-event jitters with all of these new factors crowding around in my head. It had been nerve-wracking enough to consider an event when I just the rider —adding students to the mix, and junior students at that, was almost too huge to contemplate without an infestation of butterflies fluttering around in my stomach.

But—*no*, I decided. I wasn't going to apologize. He'd ceased to be my partner, but he hadn't had the grace to tell me he was backing out. Sure, Pete helped with running the barn. He gave two dressage lessons a week, one to the more advanced riders, one to the others. He wasn't contractually obligated to do that much. If that was all he was going to give, fine, but I wasn't going to grant him some sort of amnesty from my moods just because he thought he was immune to helping with the lesson program. He was doing the bare minimum, as far as I was concerned.

I led Jim Dear into the arena, closed the gate behind us, and mounted up. Time to get to work. For forty-five minutes or so, everything except riding could just disappear.

Later that morning, I went into the office and found Pete

settled deep in the old green desk chair, making slashing marks in a training diary I'd never seen before. He glanced up as I threw myself in one of the battered chairs kept for visitors and swung the swivel-seat around to snag a Diet Coke from the rusting fridge growling to itself in the corner.

"Did you want one?" I asked, waving a can in the air.

"Not if you're going to shake it up like that."

I sighed and pushed the can across the desk anyway. "Take it. You need the caffeine."

He took the soda and sipped at it between additions to the diary.

"What are you writing?" I asked eventually.

"Everything," Pete said. "I think the only thing not recorded here are the astrological houses we pass through during each ride."

"This is for Rogue?"

He nodded, turning a page.

"Pete, this is an abusive relationship."

"What do you want me to do about it?"

"Tell him you're done. None of this was in your contract. You don't have to do it. You're being told to record, in detail, the ways in which you're pushing a horse too hard. Pete," I whispered, leaning over the desk and placing a hand on the diary. "Do you realize this could destroy your career? If something goes wrong with Rogue and this somehow goes public, people will tear you apart. You'll never get another horse."

"That's quite a conspiracy theory," Pete grumbled, but I

watched his expression shift towards concern, and I knew I'd hit home.

"In the age of the Internet, nothing's too crazy to be true." I took my hand from the diary and stretched my palm over his hand, pushing it down until he opened his fingers and let the pen fall. "Let's go ride in the pasture. You need to relax. Rogue needs to relax."

He paused, lips pursed as if he had something more to say, then simply nodded.

Sometimes, riding is the only thing that can save you. Even as a professional, as a person who had to ride horses for money long after the thrill was gone from most basic training sessions, I understood that.

So even though a long ride along the fences of our pastures, while the hot May sun blazed down on us, did not sound particularly enchanting, once we got out there, we were glad we'd done it.

The horses picked their way down the steep hillside of the west pasture, Mickey's nose hovering over Rogue's tail. By the time we reached the flat ground along the furthest fence, seeking the narrow strip of shade from the longleaf pines on the far side, we were riding side by side, our stirrup irons clanking when the horses swayed together.

"This is going to be a tougher summer than I'd thought," Pete said eventually. "But I really am going to push back on Rick—some. Not on everything. I can't risk losing this horse, Jules." He ran a hand along Rogue's neck, stroking him beneath his short white mane. I could still see the blunt edge where the mane had once been cut, jumper-style, rather than thinned with a pulling comb the way most event riders trimmed manes.

"You can ride him the way you want at home," I pointed out. "There's no one with a camera on you, Pete. Prove your way works. You can lie on the phone, and win at the events. Rick will never know. He isn't going to come out here and babysit you."

"But what if we aren't fast enough? What if he's not ready this fall? Rick will pull him. He's told me as much already." Pete's voice was rough with despair.

I knew what he was going through. I'd just spent the last few months in an agony created by this very scenario, and I really couldn't recommend it.

But no one had ever asked me to push Mickey beyond his limits, beyond what we thought fair as horse-people, into actions which some of us might think abusive. I thought overwork and harsh bits were abusive training, and I didn't want it in my barn, let alone coming from Pete. He had to see he was wrong in this, but if I pushed him, he'd get defensive again, and the conversation would be over.

"You're going to have to do what's right," I said finally. "But I think doing what's right includes a lot of gray areas."

Pete chuckled despite himself. "I thought right and wrong was supposed to be black and white?"

We turned at the end of the fence and made our way up the hill. There was a wooden coop about halfway up, and the ground around it was leveled into a little flat terrace, so that even the novice kids could jump into the next pasture. The horses saw the jump coming even though they weren't pointed at it. Mickey jigged sideways in anticipation, and Rogue imitated him, cavorting like a carousel horse about to break free from his brass pole. Pete sat easily in the middle of the saddle, his toes turned up and his chin turned down, letting all that equine energy rise and fall in front of him. There was never any use in trying to tamp down high spirits, we both knew that.

I looked between Mickey's black-tipped ears, white forelock blowing through them with the breath of a distant sea breeze. Here we go, twins on two white horses, I thought. We must look like superheroes. So virtuous. Always knowing the difference between right and wrong. Imagine if equestrian life could really be that simple! Our questions should not have been so impossible to answer. To have to ask ourselves, was it really worse to use a gag on a horse who needed more groundwork, than it was to insist on the extra work, only to see the horse go to someone who might use the gag, and who knew what else, ruthlessly? Was a threat less punishing when it came tempered with love? Or was it a betrayal one hundred times worse?

"Nothing's black and white," I said. "Nothing's that simple."

Pete hopped Rogue over the coop, sat down quickly and pushed the naughty horse through the hump in his back, then drew him to a halt as Mickey followed him over. I pressed my hands to Mickey's hot neck and let his dainty parabola lift me from the saddle—just enough to leave his back, the way I had been drilled throughout my childhood, to never give more effort than was necessary, to dole out energy in carefully measured spoonfuls. Riding was a series of subtle gestures and corrections, a great trainer—not Laurie, my childhood instructor, but a clinician I'd worshipped—had told me. We chose a trajectory and stuck to it, but we tweaked on the way. A half-halt, a counter-bend, that funny lip-fluttering sound which never failed to get a horse's attention, a wiggle of the outside rein, a touch of the inside heel a few inches behind the girth—and there you had it, three nice strides. Just a thousand more to go.

By late afternoon, the sun and heat had grown intense, smothering all of the farm residents under a sweaty blanket which couldn't be kicked off. Pete and I retreated into the house at lunchtime, but when four o'clock rolled around, bringing the after-school crowd, I went back outside with Marcus at my heels, wearing some very unprofessional cut-offs and a loose tank-top instead of breeches and riding shirt. I did a walk-through of the barn, making sure everyone knew I was there and on the watch, then slipped back outside, escaping the pre-lesson din. Who knew kids were so *loud*, all the time?

I leaned against the front pasture fence and gazed out across the sunburned field, hiking up one foot on the bottom board. Marcus was rummaging around in some deep grass that the horses had been grazing around for some indecipherable horse-reason, only his wagging tail visible above the thick greenery. I could hear him snuffling, deep contented beagle-sounds as he sought out some sort of vermin I probably didn't want to know about.

"Marcus," I called, watching his tail go from waving happily to paddling madly when he heard my voice, "please don't catch anything poisonous or endangered."

Marcus poked his head above the grass and turned towards me with a toothy grin, his pink tongue dangling, as if to assure me that he was *definitely* getting into trouble today, and then he went back to his sniffing.

"Has Marcus ever just followed a scent right off the property?"

It was Lindsay. She came up beside me and placed one booted foot on the bottom fence board, leaning her forearms over the top and clasping her hands in a perfect imitation of me. Or maybe it was just how we all stood when there was a nice three-board fence handy for leaning on. "No," I said. "But he's microchipped and tagged, because one day he will. It's inevitable with a beagle. Is everything going okay in there?"

Lindsay shrugged. She had changed from her school polo into a tank top, and her shoulders were tan and muscled. Helping around the barn was doing her some good. Her mother had been enforcing a workout schedule at home for a little while, but soon realized that all she had to do was drop Lindsay off and the stall-cleaning, jump-setting and hay-stacking would handle all of her daughter's health club needs. "Everyone is just tacking up. Except for Maisey and Ricky. They're in the tack room fighting over a saddle pad."

"That seems like a nice, normal thing to do."

"Imagine having a sibling," Lindsay mused, as if such a thought had never occurred to her before.

"No, thanks."

There was a shriek from inside the barn, and Marcus popped up from the grass again, his ears perking towards the sound. He liked drama. I was not so fond of it. I pushed back from the fence unwillingly. "I'm not their babysitter," I told Lindsay, and she just shrugged again, following me into the barn.

Inside, chaos had spread from the tack room into the barn aisle. The Battle of the Saddle Pads was intensifying by the second, and had already reached the point where groomed horses had been returned to stalls so that the screaming match could take place without fear of spooking anyone in the cross-ties. Jordan was cuddling an armful of orange-striped Barn Kitty, her back against Sammy's stall door, her face shocked. Heather and Tomeka had gone for the peacemaker roles and were tugging at Maisey and Ricky, respectively, trying to get them to tone it down. The rest of the crew were hissing urgently to one another, an undercurrent of whispers and gasps and shocked giggles.

All of this had happened before and would happen again, so I wasn't too concerned—Maisey and Ricky were expected to share tack, something no reasonable equestrian would ever expect of a pair of children, let alone siblings, and they were bound to battle over it—but I was startled to see Pete, standing in the office door with his phone in one hand and Rogue's new bridle in the other, staring at the scene with a tense air of disbelief.

"Enough!" I bellowed, with the kind of tone that brings rearing horses to the ground. The buzz of whispers switched off immediately, although the fight did not.

"I hope you *fall off* and *break* your *neck!*" Maisey screeched into the sudden silence. Then she looked around. "Oh," she said in a much smaller voice.

"Well, *you're* not riding today," I said calmly. "Go and sit in the tack room until your parents get here."

"Our parents aren't coming back until after seven," Ricky said plaintively, pushing back his shaggy brown hair. "They went to Gainesville to look at sofas."

"Going to be a long evening, then," I replied without pity. "I hope you brought your homework."

They retreated into the tack room, exchanging dirty looks with each other.

I checked the time on my phone. "We have fifteen minutes until the four-thirty lesson, so if you're in it, better get tacked up right now. If you're not in it, I'm giving a conditioning ride in the pasture at six, but none of you are invited unless the tack rooms are *spotless.*"

The aisle burst into frantic activity. The Tuesday four-thirty was a group lesson for the younger kids, who were trying to transition their hunter-ring skills into the strengths they'd need to get through a novice dressage test and around a cross-country course: a more secure leg for flatwork, a stronger core to maintain galloping position for a full course, and the like.

Two of them, Tomeka and Julia, were making their Beginner Novice debut at May Days next weekend (apparently, they would be doing so at the very same time I was riding Jim Dear in Training Horse).

It was early in their eventing careers to make a start, but May Days had a delightfully simple BN course, and they'd schooled nicely over the Novice fences at my friend Haley Marsh's course. Add in their impressive show miles for children of their ages, and remarkably steady horses, and I had thought it would be a fun little coming-out party for Alachua Eventing.

If they could hold it together. The mood here was pretty tense, and I had a feeling there was more to it than the latest battle between Ricky and Maisey. I watched them bounce around their horses with tense expressions on their faces, tightening girths and strapping on splint boots.

"I thought these hunter show kids were professionals," I muttered to Lindsay, who had stuck by my side.

She shrugged. "They're still little kids. Their nerves are catching up to them. You don't see *me* competing next weekend, do you? No way I'm ready for that. I know better."

"Meanwhile, your mom is ready to kill me for the

extended delay. Thanks for that, Miss Cautious."

Lindsay crossed her arms over her chest. "Hey, how do you know eventers are crazy? They get mad at you for exercising caution in dangerous situations."

"Jules," Pete called, interrupting our giggles. "What the hell was all that about?"

I turned on him with a withering look. "You were literally *in the barn* when it broke out, Pete. Maybe you should know more than me."

Pete went back into the office.

"Shit." Lindsay's tone was admiring. "That was ice-cold."

"I'm really done," I said thoughtfully. "He's been a total jerk about, oh, everything."

"But Mom and Dad, you *can't* get a divorce."

I cuffed Lindsay on the shoulder. "I don't want a divorce, you idiot. I just want him to get his head out of his ass."

"I feel like it's more likely you'll get a divorce. Wait— you're not married. What are we even talking about?"

"We're not talking about anything."

"But—"

"This conversation never happened," I said. "Pete and I are *fine*. Things have been a little testy between us, but we're just figuring out our new jobs."

"If you say so," Lindsay said mockingly, strutting off to oversee the tack room clean-up, and I had to stop myself from chasing her down so that I could convince her she was wrong.

That had to be it. We were just trying to work out our new roles in life, and it was complicated. We'd been through so many big changes over the past two years; our life had been a non-stop roller coaster. Now, things had stopped, abruptly, with the promise of a long-term job and a farm to go with it. This stability gave us time to stop and think about what we'd been through, and there was drama in there to be dealt with.

I could barely deal with my own internal drama sometimes; asking me to take on Pete, with all of his barely-unpacked baggage, was just not possible all of the time. So there would be some spats.

Right?

I wandered down the aisle to the far end, where our horses were stalled. Mickey pushed his nose over his stall door, hoping I'd brought him a surprise dinner. I flicked my finger along the top of his door, and he reached a long, whiskered lip up to push at it. His pink tongue was quick to follow. I gave it a little squeeze and he slurped it back into his mouth.

"Let's count our blessings, Mickey," I said. "Number one: you. And the rest of our little crew." I looked down the aisle, where Dynamo and Jim Dear had popped their heads out as well, ears pricked, ready for attention.

Blessing number one: I had my horses. It was a miracle that I had Mickey at all. Everything that had gone into trying to crowdfund the money to buy him from Michelle, her refusal to sell to me, and the ultimate sleight-of-hand trick when the co-op purchased him for me: this was the stuff of family movie nights.

Blessing number two: my students loved me. That was an understatement; I could seriously say I had god-like status with my students. This was such a nice state of affairs, I really should have taken up teaching long ago. Why hadn't anyone told me how pleasant it was to have a built-in fan club which followed you everywhere and mucked your stalls in exchange for your attention and brought you Diet Cokes whenever you asked?

My only complaints were the silly, nagging ones you dragged up when there was nothing big left to worry about. There was our distance from Ocala, the heart of the Florida horse world, for example.

And there was Pete's lack of interest in the business I'd thought we would run together.

For example.

CHAPTER FOUR

Saturday afternoon, three o'clock, everyone from human to horse hiding in the barn from the blistering sun, and all I wanted was a nap.

"I *hate* May," I grumbled, flinging myself into my desk chair so hard it swung around in a reluctant half-circle, knocking my knees into the wall.

Pete came into the office hot on my heels, his dark t-shirt wet with sweat. He'd been out looking for a lost shoe in the front pasture, and he tossed his battered trophy onto the desk before flinging himself onto the old brown couch sagging against the wall, resting his ankles on one arm so that his sandy boots dribbled a miniature haboob on the dark cushions. I looked away before I said something sharp and unnecessary. It was a *barn* sofa, I reminded myself. The kids were on it half the time anyway, and they never thought twice about kicking their dirty boots all over it. To say nothing of Marcus and his muddy paws.

"We know you hate May," sighed Pete, who clearly had no issues with needling *me*. "All May, you say, 'I hate May.' Also, all of April."

"Well, what's not to hate about it?" I held up my phone to show him the temperature from the nearest weather station, which, admittedly, was located over an hour away in Gainesville. "It's eighty-nine degrees without a cloud in the sky and no chance of rain! May is everything terrible about summer, times ten. May is accursed."

"It'll rain next month," Pete said comfortably, closing his eyes. "And then you'll complain about the footing. And the thrush. And the rain rot. And the lightning."

Pete was right, so I tamped down the rest of my complaints. *Still*, I thought to myself, a wet arena was better than one so hot I worried about the horses' frogs burning when they touched it. The white sand of our arenas made them into giant oval mirrors, so bright in the midday sun they could be hard to look at. I looked at my phone, flicked through my email, found nothing exciting, and sighed. Sleep was nipping at my heels. The air conditioner was droning its comforting murmur just inches from my head, and the white noise was hypnotizing. Maybe if I tipped my head back at just the right angle, I could fall asleep for a few minutes...

"Jules!" Jordan burst into the office, sending both Pete and myself shooting upright.

"Good lord, Jordan," Pete grumbled.

"What's going on?" I was halfway out of my chair already, hands scrambling for what I might need—my pocketknife, a twitch I'd left on the desk a few days ago, a syringe and needle from the stash I kept in the top drawer. Equine emergencies could come in many shapes and sizes. Where were the wire cutters? I didn't have any wire fencing, but that was irrelevant. When it comes to injuries, horses always find a way.

"Did you decide on the summer camp dates yet? It's only because my mom needs to know and Maisey's mom told her she's got to be out of the house between eight and five every day because she knows Maisey and Ricky will destroy the house if they're left alone together and—"

I sank back down into my creaking chair. From the couch, Pete flung an arm over his eyes and laughed soundlessly. I wasted a minute or two glaring at him, but he never looked up. Jordan cleared her throat. A girl who took everything seriously, she stood ready to take my marching orders back out to the troops in the barn aisle.

"Go look at the calendar," I said weakly. "Camp is every day there's no school and no horse shows. Will that work?" They were going to be here all day, every day, anyway. Why not call it camp?

"Even weekends?"

"No. On weekends you should go places with your parents. Weekends are family time. I'm taking weekends off." This, at least, seemed inspired. Why did the kids need to be here on Saturdays and Sundays if they were harassing me Monday through Friday? Blessedly quiet weekend days, punctuated only by chores and naps, suddenly loomed in my mind's eye. How many weekends were there between June and mid-August? How many of them had horse shows? Probably too many. My daydream wavered a little. "No riding on weekends," I repeated, trying to retain my bubble of optimism. "Everyone will need a break."

"Except for horse shows," Jordan clarified, as this was a sticking point for all of them. Had I been so obsessed with showing when I was a kid? Of course I had. I still was.

"Except for horse shows," I agreed.

"Got it." Jordan turned for the door, paused, looked back at me. "Do you know how much it will cost?"

"Cost? Oh..." I glanced at Pete, hoping for input, but he was still hiding his face from the world. Naturally, he would tap out right when I needed his help. I hated doing any sort of numbers, and coming up with a charge for summer camp would be a tricky thing, since the regular group lessons were part of the dues each parent paid to the co-op. I had rates for additional lessons spelled out in my contract, but we'd never talked about camp or clinics. "I'll have to work that out with your parents," I said finally. "I'll send an email."

"Thanks!" Jordan dashed out of the tack room.

I slid my appointment book across the desk and wrote "summer camp email" under the laundry list of things to do tomorrow. I knew I wasn't getting to it tonight. I still had to make a hay order, teach the five o'clock group lesson, evening chores, and add vet bills to board invoices before the day was over. I tapped my phone. 3:12 PM. I flipped it over, the glass clattering on the chipped laminate of the desk. "Shit," I sighed. "Shitty shitty shit."

"What's wrong?" Pete asked from under his arm.

"Everything," I said pointlessly. "Just too much to do, not enough time to do it." I closed my appointment book and pushed it away from me. It slid against a stack of colored folders, each one filled with health records, reminding me that I had to go through them and check the expiration dates on Coggins tests. Since the kids had come from a few different barns, their horses' test dates were all over the place, an annoyance I was planning to temper by getting half the barn's annual bloodwork done in spring, and the other half in fall. That way no one could complain that they'd just had a test done in the past few months.

Running a barn had always been a balancing act, but add in all of these separate personalities, and the little shortcuts I'd taken over the years to keep myself sane, like keeping every horse on the same vaccination and bloodwork schedule, suddenly became more difficult to implement than I'd ever expected. Boarding barn life was no joke. I had a newfound respect for all the barn managers out there, making their twenty or thirty or sixty-stall barns click over like clockwork every month.

"You need an assistant. You can't run this barn, and teach all those kids, without some help," Pete muttered, without any apparent recollection that we had been full partners before. "Ask the board to get you money for the salary and hire someone."

"I won't need an assistant this summer, with kids to do

all of the chores as part of camp," I pointed out.

"They already do half of the work around here," Pete said, "and you're still wiped out. They do evening feed, they turn out, they even muck out until the minute their parents get here, and there's still plenty left to do."

I pushed back from the desk. We'd both had assistants in the past; I'd had Lacey, and Pete had Becky running his old barn... after things between Becky and I blew up. But they'd both left us for school, looking for bigger things than mucking out and tacking up.

When I thought of them, I'd always felt like I'd broken two aspiring trainers in succession. They'd looked at my life and thought, *nope, that's not what I want.*

"Maybe we should just hire a groom," I suggested. "Someone to muck stalls and turn out, under supervision. That would be cheap."

Pete sighed, as if I was being extremely unreasonable and he didn't have time for it. "You just said the kids will be doing that all summer. If that's all you want, you might as well wait until fall."

I shrugged and went into the barn aisle, leaving behind the budding argument. The truth was, I was afraid to go to the board and ask for more money. Maybe the fear was silly, but it didn't make it any less real.

The parents who ran the co-op board were kind, friendly people. They paused for conversation on weeknight evenings when they came to pick up their kids. They hung around on sunny weekends and were not afraid to break out cheap chardonnay or canned margaritas if I was taking the kids out on a field ride and they didn't have to lean on the arena rail pretending to know what was going on during their lesson. They brought us thoughtful treats: decadent little cakes from the bakery in High Springs, or cases of Diet Coke for the tack room fridge. Maisey's mom didn't like her high-energy kids to have caffeine, so she kept bringing fruity sparkling water and fixing notes on the fridge door with messages like "everyone try this flavor!!" As a result, we were all slowly getting addicted to the seltzer's strange, fruit-suggestive flavoring, something more like drinking water infused with a scented candle than a soda. Which sounds horrifying, until you consider how mouthwatering some scented candles could be. I wouldn't even allow those sugar cookie-scented ones in my house. I'd be forever thinking I had cookies on hand and getting disappointed.

But if I mentioned one evening that I could really go for some sugar-frosted cookies, chances were one of the moms would stop for a box of them on the way to the barn the next day.

The affection was evident, so why couldn't I just go to them with my problems? What I couldn't get past was that these parents held my entire life in their hands. Our relationship was based on an annual contract the attorneys amongst them had drafted and I had dutifully signed without truly understanding: a thick packet of documents which promised me the rent on the house, an allotment of stalls in the barn, the right to run the barn as I saw fit, and a monthly salary. If in a little less than a year, I'd proven to be a bad investment in their eyes, I could find myself back on the streets—no house, no stalls, no students, no income.

The thought of such an end to this experiment was too terrifying to contemplate, so every time an issue came up which might rock our gently bobbing boat, I distracted myself with some undone chore. The minute Pete said, "take it to the board," whether I was lamenting a leak in the feed room ceiling or wishing I could get a bigger rig to take all of these horses and kids to shows, I changed the subject and got busy in the barn. I found a mane that needed pulled, or buckets that needed scrubbed, or stall bars which needed dusting. Anything which could drive my little discontents out of my head before I was foolish enough to bring them up to the people in charge. Anything to avoid dealing with that back-of-the-mind fear of being cast out of a barn a third time.

Green Winter. Briar Hill. My old homes were ghosts following me from farm to farm. Camping out alongside a rented pasture in High Springs, I'd felt, for a moment, liberated from their memories. I didn't *need* a barn, I'd thought for a few heady months. I didn't *need* a house. I didn't *need* anything but my horses.

Back under the secure roof of a sturdy concrete-block barn, with arenas and pastures and a house which didn't sway in a thunderstorm (to say nothing of a few extra digits in my bank account) and I was back to worshipping land with the fierce devotion of Scarlett O'Hara—except that if I knelt down and picked up a handful of Alachua County sand, I'd end up with half a dozen fire ant bites. I *couldn't* go back to the itinerant life. My horse trailer's living quarters had been packed full of eventing and horse show gear again. I couldn't even *find* the bed, let alone consider sleeping in it.

The barn aisle stretched to either side of me, horses pushing at their stall guards and pulling at their hay-nets, my only anchor in a vast world constantly on the verge of tilting too quickly for me to keep my balance. If I lost this place, if it all happened again, I knew I'd snap. I wouldn't even wait to see what Pete thought we should do. I wouldn't ask advice of friends. I'd just leave. I'd load Mickey, Dynamo and Jim Dear into my trailer and start driving. We'd end up somewhere out west and make a new life for ourselves amidst the ponderosa pines and the mountain goats. I would be that crazy lady who lived in the cabin with her three horses. It was not the future I was gunning for. It was just something I knew was lurking there, waiting to pounce.

I cast my gaze about for something which needed fixing and spotted Lindsay, lounging on a hay bale left in front of her horse's stall, looking at her phone and occasionally reaching up to tease William, her warmblood gelding, with a few strands of timothy hay. Lindsay did not necessarily need fixing (her mother might disagree, but I thought the level of snark she displayed was impressive) but that hay bale shouldn't be there. I had a rule about leaving things— anything—in the barn aisle. There were simply too many people and horses running around to let anything sit for more than a few minutes. A pair of splint boots here, a grooming kit there, and before you knew it the whole place looked like that horsey garage sale the Tack Shack held twice a year.

Plus, barn kids have naturally sticky fingers. Tack lockers had been one of the first things added to the barn when we'd moved in. I didn't need to arbitrate constant "I was just borrowing it!" scandals in addition to everything else on my plate. As it was, I still got a few per week.

"Lindsay," I called, "can you please throw that hay bale into a wheelbarrow and give everyone a flake?"

Lindsay gave me an appraising look. "It's not time to feed," she said eventually, once she had decided I was not in a threatening mood. "I'll feed it to them at five," she added, as if we were in negotiations.

"They can't eat at five because there's a lesson at five," I countered. "They'll eat at six-thirty tonight, once everyone's back in the barn, unless they were in the lesson, and then they'll eat at seven-thirty."

"That seems..." Lindsay lifted an eyebrow, reminding me so strongly of Pete's signature expression that I felt my temper start to rise. "That seems kind of late."

"That's how it has to work when half of you are riding and the other half have gone home, and I am in the arena teaching." I bit out each word through tight jaws.

"It sounds like," Lindsay said lazily, pushing herself up from the hay bale and tugging up her breeches, "you need some help around here. *Paid* help, not whatever kids you can rope into doing chores for you."

She ambled off down the aisle, hopefully to get a wheelbarrow as I'd asked, but I wasn't holding my breath.

I looked up and down the aisle, but for once, no one else was around. I could hear arguing coming from the boarder's tack room, and some squeals and laughter from the picnic table under the oak tree outside, but mercifully, no one had caught Lindsay speaking to me like that. Disrespectfully, and implying that I was using the kids for free labor.

Not that using barn kids as unpaid help wasn't an acceptable approach to equine staffing problems, but I hadn't *planned* on leading a little army of under-age laborers. They'd done it on their own.

Most of the kids had started pitching in with barn work from the moment their horses had arrived. A few of the older ones, Lindsay included, had hung back at first. They were used to horses being someone else's responsibility, mucking stalls and throwing down hay and turn-out being the kind of work one left to the help. Even they came around fairly quickly, because who wants to see a bunch of kids younger than you making an entire barn hum with efficiency? The older teens finally took charge of the younger kids, with Lindsay reigning as a sort of supreme overlord by the end of the first month.

I supposed it was inevitable that we'd reached this point, then, with Lindsay so assured of her own powers that she was questioning my decisions about how to run the barn.

I liked that girl, but she had the potential to make things

messy for me. If Lindsay were to decide to lead a mutiny against me, my little army of helpers could disappear, and I'd just gotten used to having small hands everywhere I turned, eager to grab the hose or take a pair of reins or pick a hoof. Pete wasn't afraid to rely on them, either. They swarmed to our aid without prejudice, apparently not as keenly aware as I was that Pete was distancing himself from them.

Fine, I could admit I might have gotten overly-dependent on the barn kids and underestimated how much help I needed to run the barn. But we'd been here for weeks now—how was I supposed to bring this up to the board now?

There was one person I could ask. While Lindsay enlisted the help of Jordan, Ricky, and Maisey to start doling out hay, I went out to the plastic chairs we'd put under the big oak tree, which shaded both the house and the barn with its widespread arms. I plopped down in one, tipped it back against the tree trunk, and pulled out my phone.

"Hi, Grace? You have a minute?"

CHAPTER FIVE

Grace's brisk tone was a comfort to me. Our friendship was another one of those improbable situations, one I never could have foreseen when we were first flung together.

"Ah, Jules," she said wryly. "The working student I can never replace, because after you I am too terrified to ever welcome another working student into my barn."

"I wasn't *that* bad," I protested, laughing, even though I knew for most of my time at Grace's barn I had, in fact, been that bad. Worse, even. "It's more like you'll never get anyone as competent as me."

"That's a fact," Grace admitted. "Somehow, both things are true. Hard to imagine. Anyway, my girl, what is troubling you today?"

Grace knew I'd never call just to say hello. "I think I need an assistant," I said, looking up at the trembling green leaves and beyond them, at the heartlessly blue sky. "I've been running this place with free child labor."

"Wise. And what is Pete doing?"

"Riding," I said, trying to keep my tone from giving away my irritation with him. "He has a half dozen horses now. And he teaches a few lessons a week. He handles the dressage so that I don't butcher these kids' chances before they even make it to their first event."

Grace chuckled. "You're not that bad. Just impatient. Fine, so Pete is riding six horses a day and teaching, and you're riding three or four horses a day and teaching, and you're both splitting barn work, and it's too much for the two of you, is that the size of it?"

I agreed, although I was pretty sure we were being generous with Pete's share of the teaching and barn chores. Either way, we were both busy from sunrise until late evening, seven days a week. There was no use totting up the hours we spent on cleaning stalls and helping kids with their half-halts.

"Who pays for the assistant?" Grace asked. "Because you have to have one. I'd suggest a formal working student instead of just grabbing whatever kid is running by, but you're going to need professional help at events."

"The co-op board does all the money." I sighed. "That's the problem."

"You're afraid to talk to them."

I didn't say anything, because I was acutely embarrassed that she was right.

"Jules, there's no reason to be afraid to tell a group of horse show moms and dads what you need from them. You have the advantage here."

I thought and thought, but I couldn't come up with why that might be. "But they have the money."

"And *you* have the know-how. They've got nothing without you. Jules, imagine if you broke your contract and walked because you claimed they weren't giving you the support you needed to run a safe, happy barn. They'd be stuck with a barn full of horses, no idea how to care for them, and in no position to attract another quality trainer. The mere fact that you went in there without an assistant or a barn manager shows how low you value yourself. Negotiate something better for yourself, because anyone who comes after you sure will."

I didn't know what to say to that. The front legs of my chair hit the ground, and I leaned forward, my elbows on my knees. I hadn't valued myself highly enough when I'd entered into this contract? Could that be true? I'd always thought I valued myself very highly. Most people said *too* highly.

Grace sighed. In the background, I thought I heard voices, high-pitched and young. "I've got afternoon lessons arriving. I'm going to have to get going. But Jules, listen. These are busy working parents. They don't have time to play around. All you have to do is send an email. No one will insist on meeting you in person to have some long, drawn-out discussion. Just lay out in a few bullet points why you need an assistant, make sure it's focused on safety and the advancement of their children as riders, and say how much you need for a salary. You can do it. And they'll listen to you, because they have no one else to listen to. They hired you *because* you're the expert, not in spite of it."

That made sense. I nodded slowly. "Thanks, Grace. I... I think I can handle that."

"Good girl. Was this the pep talk you needed?"

I sat up straight again. The hard plastic of the chair bit into my thighs and I stood up, ready to take charge, ready to draft that email, ready to stand up for myself. "Yes, this was *exactly* what I needed."

"Go get 'em."

There was silence, then a beeping tone—Grace had hung up, gone back to her barn and her own busy life.

I drummed my fingers against the tree trunk for a moment, considering my options. I could write the email right now, while it was on my mind. But the prospect of finding the right phrases to plead my case felt daunting. No, I wasn't ready to make a move... yet. Not until I was certain I could make my case without sounding like I was begging. I'd do some thinking first, get the words right.

There was a shriek in the barn aisle, followed by a crash of metal on concrete. I raced into the barn and saw Jordan and company flailing around two burst bales of hay and a toppled wheelbarrow. Lindsay, who was supposed to be in charge, was nowhere to be seen.

"Where's the boss?" I snorted, helping to scoop up the drifting piles of hay. The bales had been put together loosely, and the flakes lost all shape the moment the strings had released. Wisps of hay were already starting to blow off down the aisle.

"Lindsay?" Jordan shrugged. "She got a text and went behind the barn to answer it."

"And why didn't you use the hay cart, instead of stacking bales in a wheelbarrow like this?" I ignored Lindsay's absence for the moment. "I know these bales are kind of crap, but it's what we've got right now and when they fall, they break apart. As you can see."

"I thought it would be easier," Jordan said plaintively. "Lindsay just said we needed to grab a wheelbarrow and throw hay."

I'd told Lindsay to use a wheelbarrow, true, but I hadn't been giving much thought to my words. I'd just wanted the aisle to be rid of that stray bale of hay. She'd somehow turned it into a bigger task, handed it off to Jordan, and wandered off without making sure it was handled properly. I felt my jaw tighten, my molars grinding. *Dammit*, Lindsay!

She was a teenager, a sensible inner voice reminded me. It wasn't her place to oversee barn chores. It was mine.

I watched Jordan, Ricky and Maisey take armfuls of hay and fling them over stall guards, pushing aside the eager horses within. Kids were good at barn chores, and they enjoyed them. My trainer Laurie taught me her barn routine, then left me alone when I was far younger than Lindsay. I did barn chores whenever she had something else more pressing: lessons at another farm, a clinic, a horse show, the simple desire for a night away from the barn.

I'd been trialing the same approach here, thinking Lindsay, as the oldest, might default as a mini-me. But anyone who blew off throwing hay to take a text behind the barn was already operating on a different set of priorities from me.

I went around back and found her, leaning against the wall, smiling at her phone. "You missed a mess," I said.

To her credit, Lindsay did look distressed. "What happened?"

"No one died, but a few bales of hay were dropped and split all over the aisle."

"Oops," Lindsay said. "Sorry, I had to answer this."

"Your mother?"

"What? No."

"A teacher?"

Lindsay looked at me like I'd lost my mind.

"Well, what else is so important you drop everything and run out back, when you're supposed to be haying the horses?"

Lindsay's jaw tightened. She looked alarmingly like her power-suit mother. "I'm not your employee, Jules. I help out as a *favor.*"

"Don't bother with your favors if you're going to do them half-ass," I snapped. "You're sensible, you have a head on your shoulders; that's why I let you boss around the others. But if you're not reliable, you're just making more work for me."

Lindsay looked at the ground. I fancied I could hear her

teeth grinding. Well, if she was mad enough to clench her molars, my work here was done. I sauntered back into the barn, leaving her behind to think about what she'd done.

Or be furious with me a bit longer, I really didn't care.

The five o'clock lesson whirled around me, a sweating carousel of shuffling horses and panting children. Saturday night's five o'clock time-slot was reserved for the back of the class, so to speak. These were the kids who had arrived from their last barn lacking some of the basics they'd need for a successful dressage test and a safe cross-country round. Some of them could pose like JCPenney mannequins over fences and get around a hunter course on their push-button horses, but weren't ready for the slightest aberration in footing or distances. The first time Melanie, aged 12, had tried to hop her Holsteiner gelding Ares over the coop between the pastures, she'd ended up toppling over his shoulder on the far side. She'd never ridden a horse over a sloping surface before, and when he'd cantered away on his forehand, drifting down the hillside, she'd simply left his back and landed on hers with an expression of stupefaction, like a lizard falling frozen from a tree after a cold front.

"Drive your heels *down*," I called to the group as they huffed and puffed through their rising trot, forty-five minutes deep into their ride and ready to call it quits. I dug into my old *Centered Riding* memories, hoping some imagery would help the visual learners in the group. "Imagine your heels are trailing in the dirt, leaving tracks beside your horse's hooves."

Melanie's heels sank and her toes turned outward at ninety-degree angles in response. Ares felt her heels push into his barrel and lengthened his stride, nearly running over the hindquarters of Martini, who had been trotting absentmindedly ahead of them with his head down and his ears at half-mast. When Martini felt Ares running him down, his head came up and his ears swept back, threatening certain doom upon the hapless Holsteiner behind him. Spotting the domino effect of mayhem that was about to unfold before my eyes, I shouted, "Toes *in,* Melanie, *toes in, rein back sit down!*"

Melanie obliged with two out of three; she turned her toes in, stood up in the stirrups, and hauled back on Ares' face. He gaped his mouth open in protest and backed off to a shuffling walk. Luckily, the rider behind her was a little more prepared for quick changes and made a big circle before Ares could cut off her horse.

"Well, you avoided a crash," I told her drily. "But you better keep your heels down next time."

Melanie, face red with heat or embarrassment, obligingly laughed it off. She was a tough kid, determined to get it right, and she was thriving under the pressure I put on her after feeling lost and confused at her old barn. That was how most of the kids had ended up here—their parents had seen them taught to pose prettily on a horse, but developing no real skills, and they'd gotten concerned, then angry, then mutinous... and their mutiny had brought us here, to this hilltop, where I was charged with developing their children into athletes with grit and morals and everything else that made its way onto the back cover of a sports biography. Ironically, it was also the parents' mutinous spirit and sense of collective power that made me afraid of them.

"Let's drop contact, work on loose reins and walk out for a few minutes," I called. "Drop your stirrups and let your ankles loosen up. I think everyone's cooked through, yeah?"

There were some lethargic nods, but most of the kids just reserved their waning energy for sliding their boots free of their stirrup irons and letting their horses slip the reins, drooping their heads towards the hot, white sand of the arena. The sun went on blazing merrily above the pine forests to our west, baking hot and bleaching the blue from the evening sky. I thought longingly of clouds and cool wet breezes lifting from nearby storms. June, and the rainy season, could not get here soon enough.

I left them to cool out as best they could and trudged over the fence, white dust swirling around my black paddock boots and clinging to the sweat on my bare calves. I'd abandoned the professional trainer attire a few weeks ago, on the first day the temperature spiked ninety degrees, and went back to the Florida summer standby of riding boots and shorts. It was not a great look, but we all have to adapt to the climate as best we can. The breeches came out for riding and were peeled off the second I'd untacked the last horse of the day.

"Parents," I greeted the little cluster of adults standing

just outside the ring. "How goes it?"

Melanie's mother, Leah, pushed a damp lock of hair from her cherry-tinted cheeks. "It goes sweatily, Jules. Looks like you feel the same."

I pressed a bottle of water to my forehead for a moment, savoring the icy chill and the drips of condensation which pattered down my clavicle, pooling inside of my sports bra. "This is my natural state," I sighed. "I had y'all fooled because you met me in the cooler months, when I looked like a respectable human."

There was a ripple of laughter.

Leah nodded emphatically. "I don't know how any of you get through the summer! I stay inside and under an air conditioning vent!"

"Well, if you need me this summer and can't find me, just look for the icicles forming on the office window," I joked. "I'll be the one hugging that window unit."

"I love a window air conditioner," Mike, father of Maisey and Ricky, sighed nostalgically. "They remind me of the first apartment Sarah and I had together, up in Atlanta."

I decided to save my "a window air conditioner unit almost killed us" story for another time. "Well, I have to head in and start feeding," I said. "The kids will know when it's okay to come in and start untacking. They're all getting to be little experts on checking their horses' breathing and temps."

"You haven't fed yet?" Leah asked, looking surprised. "I mean—it's late, isn't it? Past six?"

"I like to feed at five-thirty, but when we have a lesson at five, it doesn't work out that way. If I feed them before the lesson, I have to skip the horses they're riding, and then there will be attitudes and pouting from those horses," I explained. "There's no point in pissing a horse off and then demanding they behave in the ring. It's much easier to make progress with a happy horse. And five is what works for most of you for a lesson, so..."

"Of course," Leah said, nodding. But a few other faces in the bunch looked doubtful. They'd all been fed lines about how important routine was for horses, and here I was telling them that on Saturdays, their horses ate when I could fit it into my schedule.

Look at these lovely sheep, I thought cheerfully, *making my argument for me.* I took a long pull of water while I considered my plan of attack. I could make my request for an assistant a plea for their help, or I could make it their idea. Nothing in my make-up was attracted to begging, so that made my decision easy. I thought about Grace's words: *they hired you because you're the expert.* Okay, I thought. Be the expert.

I took a breath and went for it. "The truth is, in a perfect world we'd have an assistant trainer or a barn manager who handles all the daily chores for me, so things like feeding wouldn't have to be put off until I can get back into the barn. The kids love helping, but they need to be supervised, so I don't let them feed until I'm there to keep an eye on things. You know, we have horses on special diets, we have expensive supplements and medications we need to be

feeding correctly, and there's really no room for error there."
I paused to gather my thoughts for the killing stroke, noting
the widened eyes and intent expressions on my audience's
faces. This was going well. "But we don't have that at the
moment. I understand we're small and just getting off the
ground, but I think it's something we'll want to consider
budgeting for in the future. Especially as the kids level up
and start eventing really seriously. Everyone's workload is
going to double then, and there *really* won't be room for
errors."

There were nods and thoughtful glances. Leah looked
especially impressed. I knew she was hopeful Melanie would
really take to eventing, and she'd made it clear to me in
previous conversations that she was ready to do whatever it
would take to help her daughter climb through the levels.

Plus, she sat on the board of directors.

As we walked up to the barn, the horses looking out of
their windows and nickering throaty requests for dinner at
our approach, Leah fell into step alongside me. She stepped
carefully, her pretty ballet flats twisting a little with each
step on the crushed shells and sand that made up the path
from the arena to the barn entrance. "Do you have an idea
of a salary for an assistant?" she asked softly, her eyes on the
ground ahead of her, seeking out the safest path for her
unsuitable barn shoes.

I gave her a number I'd plucked from my memory,
remembering job offers I'd seen in the past. "Housing would
be considered a plus with that salary," I added, "but not

necessary." There was nowhere else on the property for a person to live right now, and our little second bedroom was not up for discussion. "I think we could find a good, experienced person for that."

"There'd be steps involved," Leah said, more to herself than me. "A background check, for starters." We reached the barn and stood in the aisle entry, looking down the rows of stalls. Kids fluttered from stall doors, the tack room, wash-racks.

"Time for dinner!" I shouted, and there was a flurry of pounding feet as half a dozen kids headed for the feed room in the center of the barn, each determined to be the first to reach the rolling feed cart and start dumping in grain. I turned back to Leah. "Look, you don't have to bring this up if you don't think the board is ready for it."

"We need to do this right, Jules," Leah said, her voice taking on an intensity which I saw daily in her daughter's riding. "You don't get to the top by taking shortcuts. That's how we all got duped at our old barns."

She watched the group of kids clustered around the feed room door, egging on whoever had gotten to dump in the grain. "Plus," she said with a wry grin, "if the horses were fed earlier, I could go *home* earlier."

Lindsay was the last to leave that night. At seventeen, she was the only barn kid who could come and go as she pleased. She hung around helping me clean stalls, a duty I saved for the evening in the hottest months, when the horses went out overnight. The job wasn't too taxing, since the stalls were given a quick skipping-out at noon, and sometimes again in late afternoon, but Lindsay was quieter than normal, concentrating on her manure fork and her broom, sweeping back the clean shavings from the doorway with laser precision.

I finished the last stall on my side and unwound the hose, dragging it down to the far end to start filling water buckets. I paused at the stall Lindsay was sweeping with an obsessive-compulsive fanaticism and watched her dig the bristles into the cracks between the rubber mats.

"Is everything okay?" I asked after a moment.

"It's fine," she said.

"Why are you torturing that nice corn-straw broom?"

Lindsay stopped sweeping and looked at the broom. The bristles looked damp at the end and were curving hard to one side. "Oh," she said.

"If you find a lot of wet shavings in between the mats, grab one of the cheap plastic brooms to get it out. The nice ones get beat up by all that pee."

"Right," she agreed. "Sorry."

"It's fine."

We looked at the broom for a few more moments.

"He said horse girls are all crazy," Lindsay said suddenly, her voice filled with hurt. "He thought I was cool until he found out about William."

"That was the text?"

She nodded, her eyes still on the battered broom. "We

were going to hang out tonight. His brother told him to stay away from horse girls. I guess he used to date one, I don't know." She shrugged. "It's dumb."

Something deep inside told me Lindsay needed a hug, but that neither of us would stand for one, and not just because we were dripping with sweat and covered with sawdust. Instead, I just tried to speak from the heart— something that didn't come easily to me, either, but at least wasn't as complicated as physical contact. "Lindsay, nothing is as scary to an immature guy as a horsewoman who has goals and responsibilities. They can't stand when we put our horses first, because they think they should come first. But that's ridiculous. Who would ever put a human, who can take care of himself, before a horse, who relies on us for everything? Plus, who would expect that of you? Not anyone worth your time or attention."

She nodded, slowly, and lifted her eyes from the broom. "Did you find it hard to accept yourself?"

"What?" This was getting into deeper water than I had expected.

"Like—yourself—all of this. Giving up horses for everything else, because that's just how you identify yourself. Was that hard? Didn't you want to just, I don't know, be normal?" Lindsay's voice was almost pleading by the end of her question.

I wished I could give her a different answer, because I wanted to help her, I wanted her to feel all that confusion was normal. I was sure it *was* normal, for most girls. But for me? "No," I said honestly. "This is all I ever wanted."

Lindsay tossed the broom and manure fork on top of the wheelbarrow and pushed it into the aisle. "I'd like to be that confident," she admitted. "I thought I was done with horses, Jules. You—this—it's messed everything up for me. I always want to be here. I always want to be around the horses, just taking care of them, not even riding!"

"I'm sorry," I said, because I wasn't sure what else to say.

Suddenly Lindsay burst into laughter, her shoulders shaking. "God, it's fine, Jules. Don't apologize. I just have to get over myself." She started wheeling the load of manure down the aisle. "And my mom might need some help getting over it, too," she added.

"Wait," I said, chasing after her. "I thought your mom wanted you to keep riding. That was part of how this whole thing got started." I swung my arms to take in the barn, the farm at large, the lesson program I was running.

"She wanted me to keep riding while I still had William," Lindsay said, "so all of that money hadn't been wasted. But she definitely won't appreciate it when I tell her I want to be a pro."

I stopped short and watched Lindsay head down the barn aisle alone, pushing her load to the manure pile out back. A professional? When had this happened?

Had *I* done this?

"Well, look at you," I said to myself. "Jules Thornton, role model."

I just didn't say it very loud, in case anyone heard me, and laughed to death.

CHAPTER SIX

Leah moved fast with the board, and within a couple of days I'd been given the go-ahead to find an assistant manager for the barn. "We trust your judgment on this, obviously," she said, shading her eyes against the sun as she watched Melanie trot around the arena, working earnestly at keeping her heels down and her toes in. "But there will definitely be a background check and someone from the board will have to sit on the second interview."

"The second interview?" I grinned at Leah. "We're really going corporate on this, aren't we?"

Leah laughed and gave me a sidelong look. "What do you mean?"

"Barn interviews are generally composed of a couple of questions, watching a person halter a horse to see if they actually know how to work with horses or if they lied, and then calling their references to see how badly their old boss hates them. And their old bosses *always* hate them, Leah.

There's no such thing as a pleasant parting in this business. Just so you know... I don't want you to be shocked."

"We called *your* references and didn't have any trouble," Leah pointed out. She raised her eyebrows in a clear challenge.

"I'm special," I deflected, still grinning. Hah! They'd called Grace, but we'd kissed and made up before I left her employment. Imagine if I'd given up my apprenticeship while Grace and I were still on the outs. That would have been a reference check to remember. I probably wouldn't be standing here today.

Well, I *was* kind of special, I reflected later, slipping into the saddle to take Dynamo for an evening hack. He was still fluid and loose from our early morning dressage school, and he arched his neck, pushing at the bit, as I let him move into a walk and guided him towards the driveway. Long walks with a little bit of trot mixed in were part of our daily routine on flatwork days now, designed to really move his fitness to the next level. With Advanced competition on the horizon, I wanted him conditioned to his absolute peak. He was beginning to look more like a racehorse than he had, I suspected, when he'd *been* a racehorse.

Mockingbirds on their evening business fluttered through the scrubby white oaks lining the white-shell driveway, cawing at us with their hoarse accusations. Dynamo was a Florida horse through and through, so he was long past spooking at the threats of small gray birds flashing their tail feathers at him. Ignoring them, he dipped his head and tried to grab some of the long blades of grass swaying at the roadside, their seed heads already popping despite the dry days. I let him take a mouthful, too preoccupied with my own thoughts to make much fuss over a few stolen bites of grass. I kept thinking back to what I'd told Leah about old bosses in the horse business. Was it true? Was looking for a good reference in this game a fool's errand most of the time?

I'd been a working student when I'd gotten Dynamo, and when I'd left her barn, Laurie had been sorry to see me go, so what I'd told Leah about no pleasant partings wasn't one hundred percent true. My only other real boss had been Grace, and if our time together had been turbulent, I'd still managed to leave her employ on good terms. My record was shorter than most, because I'd managed to launch out on my own so young—*for better or for worse*, I thought now, smiling to myself. If I'd had to keep working for other trainers, my résumé would be a lot longer, and colorfully illustrated with smoldering bridges. I didn't play well with others, especially when those others told me what to do. So I'd definitely made the right decision in branching out on my own, even if things had been difficult... to say the least.

When it came to my own working students, my results were mixed. Lacey had worked for me and left on the best of terms. In fact, she'd left despite my tears, because she wanted more from her future than she thought I could promise her, not because of any smoldering feuds between us. Becky and I had parted ways in a more typically ugly equestrian fashion, but we'd made up in the end, and now

I'd recommend her to anyone. I knew Pete felt the same way about her, although she'd left his employ, like Lacey, in search of bigger things.

Of course, those weren't the stories that were gossiped over at the feed store, or shared on viral social media posts, or whispered over cocktails in the hospitality tent. What we heard about, on the regular, were tales of slave-driving trainers, abusive grooms, staff selling drugs to teenage students. The self-proclaimed survivors all had the same stories, about escaping their hellacious jobs in the middle of the night, leaving behind withheld wages and crying children and abused horses and endless, endless, endless lies. Lies about horses, lies about experience, lies about training, lies about hours worked. To hear our favorite stories, told again and again just to savor the gasps, you'd think we were a vast army of Pinocchios on horseback, galloping towards Gomorrah with our forked tongues spilling over with falsehoods.

And it happened, all of it, there was no doubt about that. But something told me there were plenty of happy endings that were never told. No one repeats the feel-good stories to an audience hanging on your every word. We wanted the gossip, to be shocked, to feel superior. No one wanted to have a juicy conversation about our competitors who were doing just fine, enjoying healthy relationships with their staff. Where was the fun in that? I grinned, thinking of all the happy hours I'd wasted in my life, going over other people's misfortunes. If I was a terrible person for it, I was in good company.

Dynamo reached for a low-hanging branch, yanking at the leaves with his teeth, and a squirrel scolded him from higher up, barking out rodent-sized expletives which the horse cavalierly ignored.

I gave him a lazy nudge with one heel: *keep on walking, son.* "You know better than to eat with your bridle on," I chided, but neither of us really cared. This was a hack. A hack was for relaxing. Nothing more relaxing than eating, if you were a horse.

At the end of the driveway, the gravel spilled onto the twin lanes of asphalt that stretched due east and due west. Ramrod straight, lifting up gentle hills in either direction, the pitted pavement of the country highway was trafficked mainly by rattling pick-ups and roaring timber trucks. Tires crunched on the gravel as vehicles went whizzing by, a few heading towards more rural destinations to the west, more towards Gainesville and civilization to the east.

It was a lonesome road in a lonesome place. Tall, slim longleaf pines crowned the hills in both directions, their trunks arranged in martially straight lines. There were virtually no landmarks to distinguish the two directions from each other; if you were lost, only the sun angle could tell you which way to turn. Our sign swayed gently in the slipstream of a timber truck. It was a plain wooden plank hanging from an L-shaped post and beam, with the words "Alachua Eventing Co-op" painted in coolly elegant Roman letters. Co-op dad Mike had done it in his home woodworking shop, where he was now working on repairing, jump by jump, the tumbledown course that had been left here by the previous farm owners. I had found this was one of the key joys of the co-op concept: the barn parents contributed not just to their own child's goals, but to the barn's greater purpose. It was so different from a typical show barn, just as my entire career so far had been so different from a typical equestrian career.

Dynamo touched his nose to the sign. It swayed, and the brass hooks squeaked with the motion, causing him to take a step back, ears pricked and neck flexed and nostrils flared, studying this new threat as seriously as if a snake had risen up from the dry grass at his hooves.

I burst into laughter and he flicked his ears back to me, then sighed, nostrils flapping and relaxing. He knew that when I laughed at him, there was no point in spooking.

"You lost your street cred with me a long time ago, buddy," I said, reining him back a few steps further from the sign. I was in no hurry to head back up the driveway. I loved my barn and my barn kids, but in my own way, which meant I needed plenty of breaks from them. I let Dynamo stretch down to crop at the grass along the front fence, where it was growing long and green in the shade of the rails.

My phone buzzed after a few minutes, and I dug it out of the pocket of my breeches. I wouldn't take a phone call on every horse in the barn, but I was confident enough in Dynamo's commitment to his snacking to answer this one, especially when I saw the caller was Pete. "What's up?" I answered, wedging the phone under the harness of my helmet.

"Hey—where are you? I can see a horse by the roadway."

I laughed. "That's just me and Dynamo. Took him out for a hack to loosen him up."

"Okay," he said. "Good."

There was a pause. I waited a few beats, but he didn't say anything else. "Is there something else?" I finally prompted.

He cleared his throat. "I'd just walked out to the truck and looked down the drive, so I was worried a horse might have gotten loose. I'm heading out and—"

"You're heading out?" I couldn't keep the edge from my voice. Leaving the farm and driving into town, whether it was High Springs or on into Gainesville, was not an idle pursuit. We usually discussed it with one another, at length, beforehand: *oh god, I have to go to town. I'm out of commission for three hours tomorrow, I have to go to town. Is there gas in the blue truck? I have to go to town on Tuesday. Kill me now, I have to go to Gainesville next week.*

"I'm riding at Penny Lane tonight," Pete explained, sounding exasperated, as if this was something he'd told me repeatedly—an assertion he promptly contradicted when he followed up by saying, "Ruthann just called me and asked if I could come prep some of their junior jumpers for a show this weekend."

"Oh," I said blankly. "Okay then." I'd thought the Penny Lane relationship had come to an end along with the Winter Equestrian Festival. The A-circuit shows that the barn's riders competed in kept moving north with the warm weather until they wound up in New England at high summer. But I guessed it made sense that they'd keep some horses here year-round. Not everyone could follow the circuit, with its thousand-dollar show weekends. Amateurs, normal people with jobs or school, would have to stay in Florida and make do with our sweaty summer circuit. "Will you be back late?"

"There's three to ride. Probably eight? Will you just stick a plate in the fridge for me? I don't want you to put off dinner for me."

"Sure," I agreed, thinking of the various bags of prepped meals in the freezer. I wasn't exactly a homemaker. "I'll just be going through the job posting replies."

"Oh man." Pete chuckled. "Please save the good ones for me."

Dynamo tugged at the reins, demanding to be allowed to nibble at the grass growing along the front pasture fence. I wasn't in much position to stop him, with one hand cupping my phone to my ear. "I promise. Listen, I better go, I want to keep Dynamo walking for another twenty minutes."

"All right," Pete said. "Sorry for the late notice."

"It's no problem," I told him. "Go ride those horses. Make sure they win their girls some ribbons this weekend."

Once he'd signed off, I focused my attention back on

Dynamo, tugging his nose up from where he'd buried it in the grass, and giving him a bump in the ribs with both heels for emphasis. "Let's go, you turkey. Just another ten days until May Days. You need to be fighting fit to take on those hills."

He ambled down the wide, grassy verge with his ears pricked and his neck swinging, taking in his surroundings. My gaze drifted with his. I loved this farm's setting, even if it was lonely out here in the outskirts of civilization. To our left, the pasture sloped upwards towards the hilltop barn and house, swathed in shadow from the protective arms of the live oaks. The field was empty, with all of the horses kept inside the barn all day—both to keep them out of the bleaching Florida sun and to keep them within easy reach for riding, grooming and the various therapy sessions that punctuated their daytime hours.

I wondered why Pete would have thought a horse could have gotten loose and run down to the road without him knowing. With everyone in the barn and plenty of boarders hanging out in the aisle and tack rooms, there would have been such a hue and cry from horses and humans alike, he would have heard the racket even if he'd been in the shower with the radio turned up. I suddenly thought of the way he'd hesitated before he'd told me he was going out, and the way he'd said he was going to Penny Lane with such aggression in his tone.

Something was not right.

We reached the end of the fence, where the longleaf

pines started up again, and I pulled up Dynamo, turning him around. His ears pricked at the driveway in the distance and his pace quickened. With horses, inbound was always faster than outbound.

"So, he didn't want to tell me," I said aloud, watching Dynamo's red ears flick back and forth, his attention torn between my voice and the allure of heading home. "Why not? Did he think I'd be against it? I'm hardly in a position to tell him to stop earning money."

Pete's truck appeared just as we reached the driveway, and he rolled down the window and leaned out. With some serious urging, I managed to convince Dynamo, protesting and swishing his tail, to wiggle close enough to the truck for me to lean over for a kiss. Pete leaned into the kiss eagerly, and I thought I must be imagining any deceit. With his bright smile and lingering gaze, he looked like an open book, not a man with a secret. "Hurry back," I told him fondly. "And be careful on those crazy jumpers."

"I will." He smiled at me, his blue eyes sparkling. "Easy money."

He was off down the highway, the tires crunching on the spilled shells in the road.

Back in the barn, Lindsay had mustered a phalanx of barn kids and was shepherding them through a thorough clean-up: sweeping out the tack rooms, knocking down cobwebs, and knotting up vast armfuls of orange hay-string. She'd been unusually conscientious after our talk behind the barn a few days before, but I'd learned my lesson about trusting her completely. Lindsay might be practically an adult on paper, but she had some time and tough lessons to get through before she would have the single-minded devotion and total reliability necessary to run a barn. Horses didn't let you off the hook for a second.

I put Dynamo in the cross-ties and took off my sweat-soaked helmet, while Lindsay stepped over and began unbuckling straps unasked, acting as if she was my personal groom. I watched her warily, wondering if she'd slipped up again while I was out, and all this hard work was just her trying to cover it up.

"Is everything okay?" I asked, tipping my head against the wall of the wash-rack and pushing my damp hair back from my face. "Is it time for camp inspection or something?"

Lindsay flipped the girth over the saddle and pulled the saddle and pad off of Dynamo's back. "Why?" she asked, huffing a little as she set the pile of tack on a nearby saddle rack. "We can't clean the barn?"

"And untack my horse without being asked? Of course you can. Be my guest. I just wonder why now, and not, say, yesterday, or any day of the past month. You're usually pretty quick to untack for Pete, but you let me manage on my own."

Lindsay turned on the hose and started spraying Dynamo's legs. "Pete was out here for a minute," she said shortly. "I was talking to him. And he said you were hiring an assistant."

"And?"

"And we don't think you should," Lindsay said tersely, her hackles up. "We can help you keep the barn running. We don't need anyone else here."

My eyebrows went up. This was unexpected. "Why would you feel that way? More help is good for everyone."

Lindsay shrugged, her face falling into that teenager mask I knew so well. So, after her confessions behind the barn, we were back to sullen silence. Lindsay did this back-and-forth a lot, I'd noticed. She was a funny one. The co-op and everything that came with it, including the fact that Mickey was standing in the co-op barn at all, had originated from her agile brain. She'd changed my life, but she'd made me work for it. When we'd first been thrown together, she'd had a caustic mean-girl veneer which gave me the same fluttery first-day-of-school feeling in my stomach that used to accompany me to the cafeteria every year of my brief academic career.

When it became clear she wasn't going to say anything else, I left her to finish up Dynamo's shower and settled down in the office with a Diet Coke. I flipped open my battered laptop. The house wi-fi just reached this part of the barn, and I wanted to take a look at the replies to my help wanted ad.

Yard and Groom was generally a good source for quality candidates, although there were some wacky responses in my messages inbox which quickly got weeded out. Michelle in Wisconsin who loved horses and hoped to learn to care for them? Best of luck to you, my dear, but when I requested experienced applicants, I meant *experienced*. Tyler in Ontario who would need a sponsor for a work visa? I barely knew the legality of hiring an American citizen; I could hardly be expected to figure out the bizarre world of immigration law.

Too inexperienced to be trusted alone, far too experienced to work for me: I flicked through the messages quickly, a little astonished at the number of applicants and yet the utter miss of what I was looking for. A woman who had been running her own upmarket dressage barn in suburban New York was certainly qualified, but downright terrifying to contemplate. I could sympathize with her desire to move someplace warm as soon as possible, but there was no way I could have someone older, with more experience running a barn than me, mucking my stalls and dumping my grain. It would give us both a complex and end in tears.

Ten messages, ten polite *no thank you's*. I closed the laptop and listened to the shouts and laughter of the clean-up crew in the barn aisle. Lindsay led Dynamo past the open door, his chestnut body glistening from his shower. I tried to catch Lindsay's eye as she passed, hoping to say thanks, but she ignored me.

Pete acting strangely about outside work, Lindsay taking over the barn duties with a decidedly hostile flair. I leaned back in my creaking desk chair and closed my eyes. It would be nice if everyone could just be normal once in a while, I thought. It would be nice if people could just be honest and say how they really felt.

But who was I kidding? How would that be like a normal barn?

CHAPTER SEVEN

The morning dew was still heavy on the grass when I brought Mickey in, his hooves leaving damp half-moons of moisture on the concrete barn aisle.

He'd been out with a few other geldings in the front pasture, and they whinnied with frustration from outside, assuming Mickey was getting breakfast and they were not. They were partially right; I gave Mickey a handful of grain from the feed room and he ate it, dribbling drool and oat spittle, from my cupped hands as he stood in the cross-ties. In the tack room, Pete rummaged through our tack trunks, pulling out galloping boots and non-slip pads. He came into the aisle, arms full of gear, while I was still knocking dirt off Mickey with a soft-bristled brush.

"Maybe we should have fed first," he said doubtfully, listening to the racket outside. More whinnies, the calls spreading into the other paddocks as everyone else got in on the shouting, were followed by a rumbling of hooves and the sharp crack of a hoof connecting with a fence board.

"That would take forever, and we need to get them out there before it's too hot," I argued. We'd discussed this last night. The entire point of doing a conditioning gallop at sunrise was to beat the May heat. By nine a.m., it would be sizzling already. If we got out now, before seven-thirty, we had time to work the horses and cool them out before nine, and only start morning chores a little late. It was a school day, so no one would arrive early and be annoyed that their horse hadn't come in for breakfast yet. "We can try feeding first next week if you want, but we'll have to feed at like five a.m."

Pete made a face which I agreed with wholeheartedly. Five o'clock in the morning was an unholy hour which we'd been glad to see the back of when we quit exercising racehorses.

"*Or,*" I went on, "we can get through this week and next week, and then by the week after that, we'll either have an employee, or the summer camp kids to handle feeding for us." I didn't mention that just bringing up summer camp caused a wave of terror to wash over me. I had no idea what I was going to do with all of those kids, five days a week, climbing all over the barn during every waking hour.

"Fair enough," Pete agreed, apparently not giving a second thought to the prospect of summer camp kids being anything but a means of getting barn chores done, and went to retrieve Barsuk from his paddock.

I was tacked up first, so I leaned against the wall,

Mickey's reins tucked over my arm, while I waited for Pete. With time to kill, I pulled out my phone and scanned my email. I gasped with delight. *"Pete!"* I squealed, causing Mickey to jump. "Pete, you won't believe it!"

Pete looked up at me from where he was squatting next to Barsuk, who was watching me with pricked ears and wide eyes. "What? Good news?"

"Lacey!" I announced, hardly believing my own eyes. "Lacey is coming back!"

And I started dancing around the aisle, at least as far as I could get with Mickey's reins still in my grasp.

Though I was bursting with excitement, there was galloping to be done, and we didn't talk much while we were galloping. Mainly because the pathways we'd carved out in the pine forest behind the farm were narrow, and we had to ride single-file. Technically, we probably weren't supposed to be out here; it wasn't public land, but there was no telling who owned these pine plantations. It could be some cowboy who lived nearby or it could be Coca-Cola or some hedge fund. The important thing was that it wasn't hunting season and outside of those few months in fall when men in camouflage seemed to swarm the forests of north Florida in search of deer to shoot, these man-made forests were typically abandoned to grow and ripen in their own due time, which made them the perfect places to ride without permission.

For the first gallop set, Pete led on Barsuk, so I held back a little after he broke into a gallop, then let Mickey go so that he could chase after him. Mickey loved the competition, and I thought that keeping his ears and eyes glued to Barsuk's dapple-gray hindquarters helped him focus on his running. Like a lot of horses, Mickey's desire to work and his desire to play were at constant war as he grew racing fit, and he was more likely now to spook at a fallen branch or a chattering squirrel than he had been when he'd been a novice horse not long off the racetrack.

As if reading my thoughts, Barsuk cocked an ear and swerved at something spooky in the brush. Pete corrected him and reached back with his stick, giving him a quick tap to remind him that he was here to work. Barsuk immediately lengthened his stride, digging his hooves deep into the churned-up sand. Mickey followed suit. The move was tactical: a working horse was a concentrating horse. A slacking horse was a spooking horse.

At the end of the forest trail, the trees stopped their march abruptly at the edge of a vast hay field, which seemed to stretch to the horizon in either direction. Here we always brought the horses down to a brisk jog, and then a walk, letting them catch their breath before we did another gallop back to the farm. When we had slowed to a walk this morning, Mickey ambling alongside Barsuk and nibbling at his mane affectionately, I cast about in my head for something to talk about.

The only thing I could think about was Lacey.

"I'm so excited," I burst out.

Pete glanced at me, a half-smile playing on his lips. "Lacey?"

"Mmhmm," I nodded. "Nothing's been the same since she left. I have missed her so much. I just feel like everything will be better with her here."

Pete's smile slipped. "I didn't know you felt that way," he said, his voice a little curt.

"What way?" Was he serious right now? "That I missed Lacey? Pete, she was my best friend! We were together nonstop until she went back up north. Obviously, I miss her."

Pete looked straight ahead, between Barsuk's pricked ears, as if he didn't want to meet my eyes. Oh, what the fuck, I thought. Was he really going to do this now? Could he not just be *normal,* could he not just be *happy* for me? When had Pete gone from this amazing, supportive boyfriend to this jealous, passive-aggressive *tool?*

Was this just what guys turned into after a while? Surely not, or women wouldn't want them around all the time. There had to be something else going on. If I had to guess who was wrecking Pete's good nature, it was that ultimate tool, Rick Delannoy, one obnoxious phone call at a time.

Mentally, I added a new goal to my year's to-do list: shut down Rick.

Idly, as if trying to distract Mom and Dad from bickering, Mickey reached over and bit Barsuk on the neck, leaving behind a gob of white foam, and I had to kick him in the ribs and yell while Pete comforted the shocked and dismayed Barsuk. There was a moment of shying and head-tossing, and then everything was quiet again. With the horses sorted out, I decided to extend an olive branch, if only because Pete's silence was pulsing against my eardrums like the pressure of deep water.

"Pete, having Lacey here is going to make everything easier for both of us. She knows what we need, so there's no wasted time breaking her in. She'll handle the barn and we'll be able to concentrate, one hundred percent, on our programs. She's going to help both of us, not just me."

He glanced at me, then flicked his eyes back to the trail. We had looped our usual path around the hay field and were almost back to the trail through the woods. In a few minutes, the time for talk would be over. "You and Lacey are a gang of two," he said finally. "I just wonder what it's going to be like when I'm the third wheel, instead of your partner."

Frustration welled up in me and spilled over. "You're acting like we can't all be friends, but that's not fair. We were before. At Briar Hill. It was the three of us and it was awesome." It was, wasn't it? I hadn't just been remembering it as some sort of golden period in my life?

Pete sighed. "You're right. Things were good. And it will be nice to have someone we don't have to train. Are you ready to gallop back?" He was picking up his reins, adjusting his feet in his stirrups.

He hadn't agreed with me, not really. A disagreeable thought came to me: what if all of that time we'd been a threesome at Briar Hill, he been waiting for Lacey to leave, so that it would just be the two of us? I knew Pete had played the long game with me, for reasons I could never quite reconcile with what I knew of myself and my utter lack of charm. I knew he'd decided, after we first met at the ACE auditions and I'd brushed off his overtures, that he'd wear me down and get past my walls and build a relationship with me. I'd never considered that he'd seen Lacey as a rival for my time and attention.

I wanted Lacey here. But I also wanted Pete. An assistant was supposed to make our lives run more smoothly, so that we could stop with the exhausted sniping at one another and get back to being partners who worked together towards our goals. I wanted Pete's smiling jokes and quirking eyebrow to come back, and I wanted to be the girl who teased him until he laughed at me again. Was Lacey going to be the one who saved us, or the wedge that drove us further apart?

Well, I'd already emailed her back and told her she was coming to Florida, then forwarded her information to Leah for the board's approval, so it was too late to fret about it now.

I gathered up my reins as Mickey picked up his head and hopped into an excited jig. "Let's get to it," I told Pete, and I led the way into the forest.

After a morning of riding, Pete came into the house around noon and started poking around the kitchen, looking for lunch. I had been sneaking a nap on the couch and was forced to pretend I had been working on my laptop, which was challenging because Marcus had stretched himself alongside my stomach and was not in a hurry to get up. By the time Pete had appeared in the living room doorway, sandwich in hand, I was still struggling to shove the beagle out of his comfortable spot.

"Oh," I said sheepishly. "Hi there."

"Sleep while you can," Pete said with a grin, settling down next to me. Marcus, a slave to crumbs, immediately departed my side and wiggled up to Pete, his eyeballs trained on the sandwich. "Summer is coming."

"Summer used to be easier," I sighed. "Now I'm dreading all the work."

"Well, you'll have Lacey," he reminded me. "Did she email you back?" Pete took a bite of his sandwich and flipped through his phone, seemingly at ease with the world. Did that mean he *wasn't* upset about Lacey, or...? I couldn't keep up with him. I didn't even know why I tried.

"She did email me... let me see what she says." I skimmed the email, then read it again more slowly, feeling deflated. "She just wants to come for the summer to start," I said slowly. "She hasn't decided if she's going to go back to school in September or not."

Pete put down his sandwich on a magazine, pushing it out of Marcus's reach before he turned to me. His face was genuinely sympathetic. "Oh," he said. "I'm so sorry."

I bit my lip, trying not to let my disappointment get the

best of me. Somehow, I realized, I'd been thinking that Lacey's desire to come back had been an endorsement of *me*, that I wasn't the trainer who had driven two different grooms to give up their dreams of riding professionally. Both Becky and Lacey had started with me hoping to be top riders someday. Both had finally looked at my life, decided it was too chaotic for them to contemplate, and gone back to school. That had been a special kind of rejection.

"Maybe," Pete said gently, rubbing my back, "you should turn her down, tell her it's an annual contract or nothing."

I looked at him with alarm. "Are you crazy? Tell her no? I *need* her here."

Pete quirked an eyebrow at me. "Three hours ago she wasn't even on your radar. You don't need Lacey. You just need someone reliable. Someone who isn't going to ditch you after a summer vacation in Florida."

I had to laugh at that. "Some summer vacation, Pete, working her ass off in the heat."

He smiled. "Okay, maybe that was unfair. But come on... is that what you want? You'll be back at square one in September."

I shrugged. "Maybe she'll want to stay."

Maybe I could do the opposite of what I'd done the last time Lacey had worked for me. Maybe, instead of driving her away from the sport, I could convince her that it was worth the sacrifices and general insanity.

I looked back over her email as Pete, judging me sufficiently comforted, turned back to his sandwich. "She says she can get a summer rental in High Springs, there are some places there that go month to month. And she's already leased out her horse for the year. I guess she couldn't afford board up there."

Pete made a noise suspiciously like *mmhmm.*

I ignored him. We all ran out of board money from time to time. If Lacey had hit hard times in student life and needed a summer gig, she had one. Right here with me.

CHAPTER EIGHT

With only a few days until May Days Horse Trials, everything normal about barn life seemed to go into free-fall. Hysteria reigned as bridles were anxiously taken apart and scrubbed, dressage tests were memorized and immediately forgotten, prized jumping boots and saddle pads in "my eventing colors!" were lost and friends were accused of theft, only for the missing items to be found in their owner's bedroom, or in the back of their parents' SUV.

When Tomeka's new halter which she'd bought for Merci's eventing debut, a rainbow-striped confection that frankly should not have been allowed in a serious show barn at all, disappeared for twenty-four hours, we were all completely mystified. No one else had a horse with a head as small as Merci's itty-bitty half-Arabian noggin. But a day later the halter had reappeared on the hook in front of her stall door when I came out to feed, having returned as mysteriously as it had disappeared.

Still, twenty-four hours before our Friday morning departure for the north Florida event, an easy hour's drive away, I felt like things were ready, and also like I would never feel rested again. I collapsed on the tack room couch after feeding breakfast, listening to the horses rumbling through their buckets, and cursed the day I'd become a riding coach.

Pete settled into the desk chair and flipped through my planner, reading out loud all of the events and shows I had committed myself to through the end of the summer until I took off one of my clogs and threw it at him.

He caught the shoe and held it in the air. "Now you are my captive," he announced, laughing. "I have won the day."

"You can't win the day by taunting me with the evidence of my hard work and dedication," I pronounced. "I have already won the day by planning out my entire summer down to the minute. Although," I considered the implications of this statement and felt rather less than fresh, "that somehow feels like a hollow victory."

Pete chuckled and put down my shoe. "You've never been short on ambition. And now that you have to extend it to a barn full of kids—that's a lot, but I think you have enough to spare."

"What about *your* summer? You're going everywhere I am. Plus, I meant to ask you, are you showing for Penny Lane?" Pete had gone to Penny Lane three more times in the past week, staying out for longer and longer each time, and I was starting to suspect this was about more than just tune-ups for amateur jumpers.

Did Pete's cheeks redden? It was hard to tell through his deep tan, but I certainly got the impression his expression grew guilty, then secretive, as he stammered, "Oh, maybe, maybe, nothing is concrete yet but it's a possibility. And they pay well so it's not something I could turn down, you know..." His voice faded off but now I was watching his right leg, which was bouncing up and down as if he was trying to calm a particularly fussy baby. That was a *nervous* leg-bounce. Pete was hiding something from me.

I got up from the couch, not mentally prepared to get into whatever *this* was. I had real things to do. Important riding coach and trainer things to do. Pete was not going to distract me. When he was done being weird, *great*. "I'm going to start packing the trailer," I announced, already halfway out the door. "Talk to you later."

With school now out for the summer, hilariously early in true Florida fashion, the kids were able to help with show prep. Lindsay arrived around ten with her arms full of clean leg wraps and her eyes big with repressed excitement. It must be killing her to remain cool and detached when she was hours away from grooming at an event for the first time. The plight of the teenager with a reputation she felt honor-bound to uphold. So sad.

She'd also brought me coffee, which was a welcome offering. I took the coffee and withheld the snide comments about how boring she must find show prep when she could be doing exciting teenager things like scoring weed outside of the gas station or playing computer games. "You're my current favorite," I told her instead, bestowing a queenly smile. "It's going to take a lot to knock you off this pedestal."

Lindsay, evidently still working to convince me that I didn't need to hire a full-time replacement for her, just nodded her head and got down to business.

We were packing tack trunks when Tomeka showed up, also bearing coffee, and then Jordan, who produced a box of donuts. Julia strolled in soon thereafter, tan arms laden with jugs of sweet tea and bags of potato chips to get us through the day. Things were looking up in riding coach country. I dubbed each of them favorites, let them scowl at each other for bringing gifts to teacher, and then sat on an unused trunk with a chocolate-glazed and instructed them on the finer points of brush-box organization. "You want three bristle types," I said around bites of sugary breakfast cake. "Hard plastic for mud, medium fibers for regular knocking off dirt and hair, and horsehair, for finishing and shine."

"Why is the finishing brush made of horsehair?" Jordan asked, holding one up and running her hands along the soft bristles.

"Magnetic charge," I replied, because I had no idea why.

Jordan nodded seriously, regarding the brush with new respect.

Lindsay looked at me skeptically. I shrugged and rolled my eyes at her. It *could* be a magnetic charge. What was she, the brush scientist?

"Let's talk about the event itself for a minute," I said, to change the subject before Lindsay really started pushing me on the fake science I was bringing to the table. "So we've got Tomeka and Julia in Beginner Novice together. I like you in the same class because I can warm you up together. But I'm also aware that we are going to have hurt feelings after the dressage, so can we just go over that right now?"

Jordan's face became worried, a habitual expression that her eyes and mouth and nose seemed to fall into with ease. She would be a worrier her whole life, poor girl. She wasn't even competing this weekend, and she was already fussing about her first dressage test. "What do you mean?" she asked.

"I mean dressage scores. It's the first feedback you'll get on how your first event is going. This isn't like a horse show class where you all walk-trot-canter in front of the judge and then you get to speculate about why someone pinned higher or lower than you. You're going to have concrete numbers with some notes alongside. And I'm going to make a prediction: you're all going to score lower than you expect, and you're all going to take it the wrong way."

I sat back and fished another donut from the box at my side. How many donuts were too many? This was only my second. I was still good. "We've talked about schooling a level above where you're showing before, right?"

Nods all around. Serious eyes focused on me. I put down the donut, to better project a solemn image of dressage profundity. "You're schooling Novice at home. It's Training

Level dressage. That is, unfortunately, the same level you'll be showing at. The dressage test is still Novice Test 1. So you're losing the buffer zone of school-one-level-up that you're going to have later, when you're schooling First Level dressage. Make sense?"

Julia nodded. "So you're saying we're not going to perform at a *Training* Level, um, level of riding? We're going to be measurably worse than what we should be doing at Training Level."

"Yes," I agreed, "because of all the outside factors that make a dressage test at a show a completely different animal from a dressage test at home. Your stress level, your horse's stress level. The different footing. The judge's stand. The loudspeaker going off constantly. Other horses freaking out. Your horses are going to hollow out, stick their noses in the air, prick their ears at everything except you, spook at flower pots, and counter-bend through every corner. And guys? That's okay."

"But isn't everyone's horse going to be like that?" Tomeka asked. "If it's Beginner Novice, shouldn't we all be in the same boat? I mean, we should still have a chance at pinning."

"That's a reasonable question, but some people are career Beginner Novice riders." I leaned over and pulled open a fat canvas bag where I had stowed all of our show paperwork. "Here's the entries," I said, opening up a small paperbound booklet. "And here's your class. You guys, a dozen others who must be just starting out, because I don't know their names, and then these three." I tapped the names. "Katie Bergen, Lara Silverstein, and Carol Potter. I don't know any of these ladies, but I can tell you they have been winning every Beginner Novice event for the past three years because that's *all they do*. They are professional BN riders. They've mastered the test, they've mastered the local courses, and they have no desire to move up."

"Well, that's frustrating," Tomeka said, and I knew she'd been planning on winning the blue ribbon at her very first event and lording it over everyone else at the barn for eternity. After all, with Lindsay out of the running, Tomeka and Julia had the unusual opportunity to be the leaders of the pack—the first to brave an actual event! How much better would it be to bring home a ribbon?

"If they *like* it," ventured Julia, a peacemaker, "I guess it makes sense to stick to that level."

Tomeka snorted. "The point of showing is to *get better.*"

"It is for you guys," I said. I picked up my donut and took another bite. "You're here to get your feet wet, not to bring home ribbons. That comes later," I assured them around a mouthful of donut. "I promise."

"Okay, Pete, can you help me with braiding this evening?" I asked as I came into the kitchen. "It turns out none of those privileged little monsters have ever done it—oh."

Pete emerged from the bedroom wearing breeches and boots with a neat black polo, his brass-buckled show belt around his hips. "Sorry," he said, looking genuinely embarrassed. "I just got called down to pick up some rides at Newberry, they have the evening mini prix show tonight and tomorrow..."

"Pete, we have an event tomorrow." I couldn't believe this was happening. If I spoke slowly and precisely enough, Pete would snap out of whatever psychotic event he was having and return to the realm of reality. "It's four o'clock in the afternoon. I have two more horses to braid. And you're going to a show to ride someone else's horses?"

"I can manage my horses and this," Pete said briskly, picking up his keys from the hook by the door. "I'm sorry I don't have time to help you with the kids' horses... but I'll be home by ten. I'll bring back supper, you should be done by then and—"

"You'll bring back *supper?*" I shouted, slamming my hand on the kitchen counter so hard that my palm smarted. "You'll be back by *ten?* Is this some kind of fucking *joke* to you? We have an event to get to tomorrow and we have kids and their horses to get ready. Those kids are the reason we have this place, Pete! They're our *job*—"

"They're your job," Pete said gently, his jaw set firmly despite his soft tone. "This show tonight—that's my job."

He didn't dare give me a kiss, which was lucky for his face—I was itching to give him a good slap—but when he closed the door behind him I felt bereft, betrayed by the moment he'd decided I was too dangerous for a simple goodbye ritual. I went to the door, my hand on the latch, close to running after him, but then his truck came roaring to life and I let my fingers drop to my side. Let him go, I thought, and get on with your day. Get on with your life, if it comes to that. Don't let him make you feel guilty for everything you've gained.

They were fine, brave words that didn't do much to fill the hollow emptiness in my stomach when I slipped my clogs back on and went back to the barn, Marcus at my heels.

CHAPTER NINE

"Where's Pete?" a parent asked, and I clenched my fists behind my back.

If I heard one more person ask that question, I was going to scream.

Friday afternoon was hot and sunny, and I wanted to climb back inside my truck and turn the air conditioning to eleven, but everyone had finally arrived at the show-grounds to hack out their horses and walk the cross-country course. Hauling five horses to the show-grounds and getting them stabled without Pete's assistance had been less of an ordeal than I'd expected, thanks to Lindsay's continued dedication to the job of unofficial working student. We'd gotten them bedded, watered, and tackling their hay-nets with dedication inside of an hour, which gave the two of us some valuable sprawl-in-the-camp-chairs-and-hydrate time.

Meanwhile, Pete had brought over Barsuk and Rogue in his own truck and trailer, then hustled out to walk the course before Lindsay and I had finished bedding down our horses. He was already gone, heading back to Newberry to ride in the evening jumper classes.

"Pete had another show tonight," I explained for the fourth time.

"Wow," Tomeka's mother said, looking impressed. "That's true dedication."

I cocked my head at her and smiled, biting back the reply straining at the tip of my tongue: that it was the opposite of dedication, that she was *looking* at true dedication, at me, standing here present and accounted for, ready to take her child out to walk the cross-country course and explain to her, jump by jump, how to ride her particular horse with his particular quirks over it.

But Tomeka's mother didn't see my rage; that's how good I had gotten at hiding my temper. Instead, she smiled back and then started fussing over Tomeka's hair, which was escaping its tight pigtails. *"Mom,"* Tomeka wailed, squirming. "Not *now*, Mom."

I turned to Lindsay, who was lounging against a hay bale, smirking at the scene. "Quit acting superior and let's get these guys out to the course," I snapped, taking my nerves and suppressed anger out on Lindsay, and knowing it was wrong even as I did it.

Lindsay gave me a doleful look. "You wanna try that again?"

"Abusing my groom is a right reserved for all trainers," I sighed. "Can't you just play along?"

107

She pushed herself up, brushing hay from her breeches. "I've never played along with anything in my life, Jules. Tomeka! Julia! Let's go get some course-walking on. Then we're having hot dogs. Then you're hacking out your horses. Look at those poor animals locked in their stalls, they need a walk! Let's move, let's keep a schedule!"

Lindsay herded the younger girls away, casting me a glance over her shoulder as she went, an expression which clearly said, *you're welcome.*

Saturday morning, event weekend. Dressage and donuts were the only things I had to look forward to in the next few hours, and one of these things was not like the other. I'd spilled coffee down my front while I was walking to the event stabling, a perfect portent for the sort of day I was expecting. I sighed and brushed at the brown drops, which had managed to land on the exposed collar of my white show shirt despite the polo shirt I'd pulled over it. Well, the stock tie would cover the mark in the dressage ring. But it did seem a bit much to already be stained and out of sorts at seven o'clock in the morning.

Maybe if I'd gotten more than four hours of sleep, I would be in better shape this morning, ready to attack the massively long day ahead of me. But Pete had gotten home at ten-thirty last night, with a few boxes of Chinese food which had probably been hot back in Newberry before he'd driven the half an hour home, and I'd been up another hour before going to bed, my skin salty with stir-fry and anxiety, tossing and turning through an all-too-short night. When my phone lit up with the alarm at four o'clock this morning, I'd nearly flung it across the room.

"Lacey can't get here soon enough," I'd muttered, pulling on jeans to hustle out and get the horses fed before driving to the show-grounds to feed *those* horses. "What were we thinking? Why did we think we could do this on our own?"

Pete just grunted. He was tired and dehydrated, too. *Good*, I'd thought peevishly. Shared misery was the only way I'd be able to avoid fighting with him today.

Lindsay had tumbled out of the truck behind me but was now tracking ahead, long legs in tight jeans covering the beaten-down grass in double-time. By the time I reached our stalls, she was already digging into the hay stacked in front of them, tossing everyone a flake on the ground before she retrieved their empty hay-nets to fill up for the morning. There were grumbles of welcome from all around us, although most of the horses in the rented stalls were already working through their breakfasts.

It was easier when you could just stay at the show-grounds, instead of dealing with a commute. Next time, I thought. Next time we'd do this better.

Then the day was all over me, and there was no time to sit and ponder what I was doing right or wrong. There was just doing. The girls arrived, white-faced and trembling, and were set to wiping down my tack by the taskmistress Lindsay. I knocked the dirt off of Jim Dear, Dynamo, and

Mickey, sprayed them with ample amounts of hair polish, and worked the shavings and hay from their tails. Their braids, protected overnight by stretchy neck wraps, were deemed good enough by everyone in the barn aisle. I looked around for Pete as I smoothed the crown of the bridle over Dynamo's ears. He was nowhere to be seen.

Dynamo did his best work after a long warm-up, but that wasn't in the cards today; I had to ride three dressage tests in quick succession, followed by coaching the girls—and get it all in before lunch.

May Days was one of those huge, sprawling events where tractors tugged flatbed trailers of spectators and leg-sore competitors around; there would be no dashing back to the barn between dressage rounds today. Once I headed out to the big flat fields where the rings were set up, I was living there for the foreseeable future. Lindsay was enlisted to tack up Mickey and bring him over to the warm-up thirty minutes before his test time; she would be due only five minutes after Dynamo and I would be giving the judge our final salute.

I swung into the saddle outside the stabling and waited as Julia ran a towel over my boots and Lindsay double-checked Dynamo's number, clipped to his bridle just below his ear. The disc wobbled a little and she pushed it home. "That's not coming loose now," she said emphatically. "Although I might have scratched up your bridle."

I shrugged; if the scratch was always covered by a number, we never had a problem, now did we? "I'll see you in about—fifty minutes?" I guessed.

Lindsay saluted. "Captain, my captain!" she declared, and then grinned wickedly at me to make sure the reference to *Dead Poets Society* didn't go to my head. "I'll be there. Go get 'em." She gave Dynamo a farewell clap on the neck before she stood back to let us ride away.

The dressage rings and the nearby warm-up were mercifully quiet this early in the morning; the only ones out here were the Advanced and Intermediate riders, and we had been around the block enough times to keep out of one another's way. That's not to say the horses were being model citizens, of course. I had to rein back Dynamo before we even entered the broad grassy area that had been roped off for warm-up, as a noted Olympian went by, cursing a blue streak, on a horse evidently intent on evolving into a pegasus as soon as possible, preferably before the bell rang for his test. I allowed the championship couple, who were putting on some pretty impressive airs above the ground displays, plenty of room before I let Dynamo enter the ring; you never knew when a horse on two legs might suddenly become a horse on four legs, all of them rushing in reverse.

"Let's just ignore the crazies," I told him while he watched the Olympic horse launch through the air in what a cowboy would call a crow-hop and a master of the Spanish Riding School would call a promising first effort. "Let's put our head down and work like a good boy."

And that's precisely what Dynamo did, because he was a good boy.

***

It felt like just a few moments had gone by before I was riding Mickey out of the ring, the second test of the day complete, and just one more to ride—but two Beginner Novice riders to warm up. I still didn't get how the organizers thought it was fine to put Training Horse on at the same time as Beginner Novice... but maybe the other trainers with a retinue of students had assistants and working students to warm up their lower classes. I didn't know how they did it. I'd never paid them much attention before, because I was too busy trying to climb the ranks, and ignoring all the work that went into coaching.

Of all my mistakes, that one never ceased to make me chuckle at myself and my own hubris. Jules Thornton, the girl who didn't think the rules applied to her. What I had learned over the past year was that maybe they *shouldn't...* but dammit, they really did.

"Julia, Tomeka, have you done walk-trot-canter yet?"

The girls were trying to keep their horses standing still a short distance from the dressage arena where I'd been riding my test—trying, but mostly failing, because the horses were keyed up with all the action, which was now reaching the typical warm-up ring fever pitch, and they kept having to circle in an effort to keep them from going bananas with excitement.

"We did," Tomeka volunteered, reining back Merci as the half-Arabian tried a dirty little plunge-and-spin trick that nearly pulled the girl onto his neck, "but it wasn't pretty."

"Oh no?" I let Mickey stretch his neck and dropped my stirrups. "Hollow and flat, like I said?"

"Yeah," Julia confirmed glumly. "Not the best."

"That's okay," I told them. "You're going to go in there and smile no matter what, and live through this, because this is just your first event. When it's your tenth, that's another story." I looked around for Lindsay, who should have been bringing over Jim Dear, but instead, my eyes landed on Pete, who was riding by on Barsuk. The dark, dapple gray Thoroughbred was looking particularly cat-like today, his strides long and his muscles sinuous, and I felt a quick rush of envy. I'd ridden Barsuk all last winter, while Pete had been riding Dynamo, and it had been a wrench to give the talented horse up. We'd definitely had a connection.

Pete looked over and saw me watching. He raised a hand. "That was a good test!" he called. "Really nice job with that last canter transition."

His compliment left me utterly deflated. So he'd seen my entire test, but he hadn't come over to help me warm up. I'd watched for him while I'd been warming up Mickey, and had been disappointed when he hadn't shown up. I'd expected him. His behavior in the past had given me every reason to do so.

Pete had appointed himself my dressage trainer, and after initially pushing him away, I'd given in and let him do it, because his passion for dressage was exactly what my cross-country-loving ass had needed. I wasn't sure why today was so different, but if my score had suffered because I hadn't been under instruction, I would just have one more thing to be mad at him about.

Great. I gave my head a little shake to try and knock the thought away. I didn't want to be angry at Pete all of the time. It was exhausting and upsetting. Pete was supposed to be the one person in the world who didn't make me crazy. Someday, in between horses and lessons and events, I had to find the time to figure out what was going wrong between us... and *fix* it.

Pete was cantering Barsuk around the warm-up when Lindsay appeared from the wooded path leading back to stabling, leading a very giraffe-like Jim Dear. He was tugging at the lead shank and looking every which way, and Lindsay had a look on her face which suggested she was going to need many, many more donuts in order for me to fix this.

"Yikes," Tomeka said helpfully, turning Merci in another tight circle as the little horse pawed at the torn-up turf. "Looks like you've got a live one there."

I could have used a third pair of hands for the horse trade-off, but somehow I managed to keep Mickey at arm's length, just out of reach of buffeting blows from Jim Dear's jerking neck, while switching sets of reins with Lindsay. She gave Mickey, who was cool as a cucumber now that he'd had his test and was anticipating some leisure time with his hay-net and a deep bed of shavings, a look of profound appreciation.

"He wasn't always this good at shows," I assured her,

yanking back on Jim Dear's reins. "Here, take this fool's halter and lead back with you. I can't use it out here."

Lindsay slid the halter over Mickey's bridled head, for lack of anything better to do with it. "How are you going to mount him?" she asked doubtfully.

Jim Dear was now walking in a fast-paced circle around me, his head and neck jerking, looking like some sort of deranged chicken. "I do not know," I sighed. "The grace of willing strangers?"

"I've got you," Pete said from behind us.

I managed to spin around, giving Jim a tug on the noseband to slow his twirling for a moment. "Aren't you supposed to be warming up?"

"Barsuk does better fresh," Pete said, hopping down. He handed the reins to Lindsay, who looked deeply annoyed to have two horses in her charge. Mickey, however, looked pleased to have his friend nearby and reached out to give Barsuk a big smacking nip on the nose. Barsuk squealed in response. Lindsay gave me a glowering look.

"When I'm ripped in two, you'll feel bad," she warned me. "You'll realize what you put me through."

"Lindsay, when you graduate high school I'm going to make you work for me full-time and I'm going to underpay you, so just be ready." I smiled at her, then turned to Pete, who was waiting for me with his hands cupped, ready to take my knee and help me into the saddle. "Thank you," I said softly, unreasonably happy that he'd come back to help me. I supposed that was the problem with being in love with someone: even if they abandoned all of their other responsibilities to you, one nice gesture and you found yourself welcoming them straight back into your good graces. I would have to work on this fault. I was supposed to be very angry with Pete, and instead, I could feel myself gazing at him like one of his lovelorn fans on stadium jumping day.

"But I'm still mad at you," I added. I put my knee into his palms.

"One—two—" he pushed my knee up as I jumped, my hands pressing into the saddle, and as Jim tried to bounce forward he caught the horse's reins just below the bit and held Jim steady while I tucked my boots into the stirrups. This was my old dressage saddle, not my fabulous Rockwell Bros. semi-custom, but the one I'd been riding in for years, and the worn seat closed around me like a very handsy glove. At least I'd be secure up here on Spooky McSpookerson. "I've got him," I said to Pete, so that he knew he could step away.

But Pete didn't let go right away. Instead, he looked up at me, ignoring his precarious position at the shoulder of a very pushy Thoroughbred. "I'm sorry I couldn't help you warm up today," he said softly. "But from what I saw, you didn't need me. For whatever that's worth."

"Where *were* you?" I asked urgently. "I haven't seen you since breakfast this morning. What's going on?"

Pete opened his mouth and I thought I'd get an answer, but the loudspeaker nearby squawked with sudden nervous energy, calling a late rider to the ring, and Jim bounced forward, forcing Pete to jump out of the way. I swallowed my frustration and focussed on getting Jim Dear to the warm-up ring to canter his foolishness out, gesturing as I did so for the girls to follow me on their horses. As I circled the bay gelding around the warm-up, avoiding the ducking juniors and amateurs prepping in nervous fear for their Beginner Novice tests, I glanced back just in time to see Lindsay helping Pete back into the saddle with the same practiced leg-up he'd given to me, and wondered where she'd learned it. Was she still helping Pete when I wasn't around?

He turned Barsuk towards the ring, and I realized he was on deck, but I couldn't afford the time to watch him. I had two nervous ducklings to warm up, and one silly horse to quiet down. "All right, girls," I called, "circle here in the center near me, don't crash anyone, and let's just try inside leg to outside rein until we get some softening, okay?"

CHAPTER TEN

Somehow we got through the dressage without anyone going crazy (anyone being me) or anyone getting hurt (anyone being the kids). Neither Merci nor Rumors liked the idea of the dressage ring, especially not the very scary horse trailer being used as a judge's stand at the far end, but they got around their walk-trot tests without anything more dramatic than a sizable spook—although Merci did fart extremely loudly when he wrung his tail Arab-fashion and leaped sideways to avoid being attacked by the cone marked with the letter M.

There was a smattering of smothered laughter at that one, but for the most part, the small collection of spectators were able to politely overlook the shenanigans in the arena, mainly because most of them were parents and their own children were about to put on similar displays.

About two seconds after Julia and Rumors finished their test, I was being called on-deck to the other arena and had to trot Jim Dear over to do our warm-up loop around the exterior of the arena. He took an immediate liking to the footing, a springy combination of shredded rubber and fine sand, which gave an extra few inches of suspension to every stride. I felt like I was riding a warmblood, which wasn't such a bad thing when heading into a dressage arena on a rather lanky Thoroughbred. The only problem with his newfound suspension was that he really enjoyed it and downward transitions were pretty much off the table for the first few movements of our test, so that the "enter at working trot—halt at X—salute the judge—continue working trot" sequence was a little more like "enter at extended trot—slide through X above the bit and with mouth gaping—come to unsteady and probably short-lived halt—salute the judge as quickly as possible—bolt forward."

Not exactly what I'd been hoping for with Jim Dear at Training Level... this was really more of a Novice performance, I thought on the way out of the arena, bitterly regretting that botched canter transition at the last corner. Ugh, maybe *Beginner* Novice.

Pete was at the edge of the warm-up area, sitting on a more subdued Barsuk, with his feet out of the stirrups.

"Shouldn't you be getting Rogue over here?" I asked, too irritated with my ride to issue anything like a "thanks for sticking around and watching me" sentiment.

"I wanted to catch your test," he said. "That was okay."

"That was a *mess.*"

"It started out a mess," Pete conceded. "It had a few

messy parts in it. But all in all, it was an okay test. It might even have been a pretty good test. Remember, you're in Training Horse. There are going to be a bunch of green horses in this division."

"Did you notice any? I was too busy with the beginners to even see another ride."

"I saw a few." Pete urged Barsuk into a walk and we headed back towards the stabling together. "Rich Bachman was on a green bean a couple of horses before you. He spooked at a flower pot and jumped out of the ring."

"No! Rich Bachman?" Rich was an elder statesman of eventing, with decades of experience all over the planet under his belt before Pete and I had even been born. He'd ridden with Pete's grandfather back in the day.

"It happens to everyone."

It did happen to everyone; Rich's blunder was a good reminder. I wiggled my feet, clear of the stirrups at last, and revelled in Pete's company. Maybe it hadn't been such a bad test, after all.

Cross-country was supposedly why everyone was here—so why did everyone look so pale? They needed a pep talk.

"Buck up, guys, you've got this."

Two round-eyed girls blinked down at me from atop their horses, looking like a pair of terrified owls.

I was having a hard time feeling sympathetic, although I was trying. Come on, the Beginner Novice course was a bunch of tiny logs and a few tires strung on two-by-fours! A granny who had never jumped before could handle it. Saying as much did not win me any popularity with the troubled children, though.

"What if Merci runs away again?" Tomeka asked, clutching the reins as if Merci, who was currently trying to graze on the thick grass at the edge of the field May Days designated for cross-country warm-up, was about to bolt wildly. Both horses had toned down their behavior considerably since all they'd done yesterday was a dressage test, but today their concept of the second day of an event was about to change forever. This was the last time these two riders could enjoy a quiet horse before their cross-country round. Naturally, I was not sharing this information with them.

"Merci ran off with you *one time*," I pointed out impatiently. "And that was because Sammy tripped and Jordan only managed to stay on his back by putting her hand out and catching Merci on the rump. And you stopped after, like, five strides! Why are we having this discussion? Merci has never run off with you, now that I think about it."

"He ran off once when I was younger, too," Tomeka muttered, glowering.

"Wasn't that the time we all went on a trail ride and the horse in front of you stepped on a beehive?" Julia asked helpfully. Tomeka favored her friend with the glare she'd had focused on me.

"No one is running off with anyone," I said, cutting them off before there was another argument. "And what do I always tell you about horses who are running away?"

"They'll stop eventually," Tomeka and Julia intoned together. "All we have to do is ride it out."

"That's right." I nodded emphatically. "You know how to ride a galloping horse. A galloping horse is, at his heart, the same lazy horse you couldn't get to canter five minutes before. Ride it out and make it difficult for him so that he remembers how lazy he really is and stops."

There were nods; I had given this advice before.

"Now," I went on. "Let's get you ready to tackle this course."

I had the benefit of having already galloped across the turf this morning, and my horses had gone really nicely. Plus, and what was even better, Pete had actually shown up and behaved like his old self. We'd driven in together since he didn't have to turn right around and get to a horse show after his rides today. He came out to the warm-up and helped me with Dynamo, who went on to put in a clear, if slightly labored, performance on course. He'd listened to me talk about my worries all the way back to the barn, holding Dynamo's reins and offering me water at strategically calculated intervals, breaking up my breathless list of reasons I thought Dynamo wasn't performing his best out there and forcing me to swallow my fear and just hydrate for a moment. He'd been such a model boyfriend that I'd finally released the swell of worry about *him* that had been lodged in my chest for weeks now, and as I felt it float away, I inhaled a deeper breath than I'd taken in days. I even had a moment of dizziness, like a runner's high, as all that oxygen flowed to my brain and lapped around the corners of my consciousness.

I'd felt so much *better*.

By the time Mickey's Preliminary round had come up, he was already out on Barsuk, giving the hyper gray a long, steady warm-up, and I'd had to rely on Lindsay's help to get Jim Dear out the door a scant half an hour later, but the good, calming work was done and both horses went through their paces on the cross-country field without turning a hair. Mickey was strong but determined, moving with glorious confidence across the course, and Jim Dear was his usual adorable self, eyeballing fences we both knew he was going to jump and putting his feet every which way in the water complex, while I sat chilly an inch above the saddle and waited for him to figure out which hoof went where. He was a talented horse; he just needed extra mileage—maybe a few more miles than the average green horse. I often thought the trauma of the hurricane had affected him more than the others; he was the only one to come out of the storm with a jagged scar, after all.

Pete had met us after the course with a cheer and a bottle of water. "Now you just have to get your ducklings over those jumps," he'd said.

"And the stadium jumping in a few hours," I'd snorted, dismounting while Jim Dear kept walking, his breath coming hard. The sun was brutal, with only a few fluffy clouds floating through the harsh blue sky. "Think it will cloud over this afternoon?"

"We can only hope."

My only misgiving with Pete came when I saw how he'd bridled up Rogue. I was walking out of the barn with Julia and Tomeka in tow and peered into his stall to say goodbye and good luck. Pete was pulling on the padded cross-country bridle he'd gotten from Rockwell Bros., with that hateful gag bit attached. I knew he'd been schooling in it at home, but I'd managed to keep from saying anything there. Since he rode during the day and the kids weren't out of school yet, no one was around to see him contradicting the lessons I'd been drilling into their heads, about solving problems with training, not tack.

Today, they were going to see Pete go out there with what they'd instantly recognize as a *contraption* (my word for anything that wasn't a bread-and-butter snaffle bit and cavesson). Monday, they would have questions. And I would find their queries difficult to answer without sharing my true feelings about Pete's training of Rogue. I didn't want to undermine Pete like that; he was one of the two responsible grown-ups in the barn, and their dressage instructor. He couldn't be seen as less than me because of something I said.

So it was a conundrum, and not one I appreciated having to ponder as I took my very first pair of junior eventers out to prepare for their very first judged cross-country course. A tiny finger of resentment crept back from exile and pressed against my chest. It wasn't the whole fist that had squeezed my heart for the past few weeks, but it was enough to remind me that some things were not easily solved.

I guessed this was why the couples on TV shows were always saying: "relationships are hard work." Sometimes, your partner did things that simply could not be explained, and yet had to be defended... or at least, accepted. With grace, if at all possible.

I wasn't sure I had it in me.

A flash of white out in the warm-up ring distracted me from the girls, who had begun trotting in a circle around me. I looked past them to the hubbub in the distant ring, where a dozen horses were plunging around in various states of "oh my god we are about to go cross-country" exhilaration. Rogue was one of them, and he was definitely not taking things as easy as Merci and Rumors were. The big white horse was hauling Pete towards the vertical practice fence set up in the center of the ring, and I could see Pete leaning back, his hands above Rogue's withers, trying to coax him back with his body language before he started to use his hands—and that awful bit—to get the point across.

I understood his chagrin; the vertical was no more than two-foot-six, and Rogue had been regularly jumping twice that high in the show jumping arena. He should have been content to step over this fence, maybe even knock it down to show his total disdain for such a guppy-level obstacle. Instead, he was hauling towards it like a freight train. When his jump came, too close and too high, he nearly popped Pete out of the tack. I was too far away to see it properly, but in my mind's eye, I could picture Pete's jaw tightening, the tension that would come into his forearms, the way his heels would jam down, ready to teach a life lesson. He couldn't give Rogue a good ol'-fashioned Come to Jesus here in front of everyone; it wasn't appropriate to school a horse in a horse show setting. But he sure could get his point across with a couple quick twitches of his reins.

"Don't do it, Pete," I muttered. "Don't get in his face in front of all of these people." *And these kids, and their parents,* I added silently, not willing to say it out loud, even to myself. But I knew it was true: I was more worried about the ice-water effect a rough ride would have on my idealist co-op family, than what it would do to Pete's relationship with the horse he had wanted so badly.

On the next pass at the jump, Rogue bolted three strides out from the fence. Pete's hands came back and up, and Rogue's face followed suit—straight up, straight back. He hit the brakes so hard I thought he might flip over backward. I wanted to cover my eyes. Julia, still trotting in a circle, saw my face and turned in the saddle. "Is that Pete?" she asked, just as Pete popped Rogue with his spurs and sent him over the fence from a near stand-still.

"No," Tomeka answered her. "Pete's a better rider than that."

"Yeah," Julia agreed. "Good point. Pete rides like Jules."

That's when I dragged my eyes away and made myself focus on my students. I didn't know what was going to happen with Pete and Rogue and Rick Delannoy, but right now, I didn't have time to speculate. I didn't have time for anyone but these girls—my students. "That's gorgeous, Tomeka," I told her warmly. "I love where your hands are right now. Julia, just a little more inside leg—that's it! Feel him softening? Yeah, that's what you're going for!"

They trotted around me, my carousel of hope and courage, and once the white blur of Rogue had disappeared from the warm-up ring, I took them over to hop over the vertical and oxer there. The Novice horses had all gone out by now, and it was just the Beginner Novices, mostly children with a few adults, including the prim and confident-looking serial Beginners, who competed in and won this level at every competition in the region. I watched Julia fold herself neatly over Rumors' neck over each fence she took, and Tomeka's confident grin return to her face as she piloted Merci expertly to the base of the jump each and every time. They had been arena riders for a long time; they knew everything they needed to know right now about strides and distances. If they could get over their nerves out there, and apply that knowledge to the cross-country course, there'd be no stopping these girls.

Maybe we'd even beat the serial Beginners.

Tomeka's mother brought us a feast from the Publix deli, and we sat around a picnic table in the stabling area for a late lunch. The mood was celebratory, and I felt a warmth in my cold old heart when I looked around at my little crew. They'd done themselves proud today, no matter what happened later in the stadium jumping.

"I'd like to make a toast," I announced, holding up a Dixie cup of syrupy sweet tea. "To Tomeka and Julia, the queens of cross-country!"

"Here, here," Lindsay joined in, thumping the table with her fist. "Braver than me and twice as talented!"

Tomeka and Julia both blushed with pleasure.

"Come on Lindsay," Julia laughed. "You know that's not true."

Compliments flew fast and free around the table as my little barn family assured one another how talented they were, and I picked at my macaroni salad, fully aware I still had three stadium jumping rounds to ride this afternoon and not too interested in taking a food baby with me. Lindsay was assuring Julia that she'd been brave on the course, and Julia was denying it, but Julia *had* been incredibly brave today. When Rumors had spotted that first fence, just a few strides away from the start box, the bold mare had focused onto it like a laser-guided missile. Ears pricked, her canter rolling into a thundering gallop, she picked a long spot, ignored Julia's restraining hands, and leaped out of an extraordinary stride, twice as far away as she should have been.

The fence, a simple little construction of stacked sod, would have jumped beautifully out of an easy cantering stride. Instead, Rumors decided, mid-leap, to touch her hind legs down and push off from it again, as if she'd thought for a moment it was a bank.

Banking the fence would have been that surprising from a novice horse, but I hadn't expected an experienced jumper like Rumors to do it. *Julia* certainly didn't expect it, but her beautiful position served her well. Just as if she was cantering genteelly around the hunter ring, Julia stayed in the center of her horse, her hands still resting on Rumors' crest, her heels down. Her greatest asset, though, even more important than her model equitation, was that she just kept riding. She didn't react. She didn't panic. She didn't move at all. She just kept riding forward as if nothing had happened. And when Rumors landed safely on the other side and went rollicking along the well-worn path in the grass, I saw one hand briefly leave her neck, give the mare a big pat, and then return to its safety position.

I'd smiled.

I smiled now, remembering the elation of that moment when I'd known she was going to be just fine out there.

Tomeka's ride had been a little bumpier; Merci had been keyed up and decided to channel his Arabian ancestry with a shimmying little flat-backed canter I thought we'd schooled out of him, and with his head carried high in the air, like some sort of desert warhorse, Tomeka had found rating him to be a bit challenging. They actually came in too fast and had time penalties. But they had no refusals, and *that*, I told Tomeka, was what counted. "There's no reason to worry about slowing down to BN speed unless you're planning on staying at BN," I reasoned. "And you went clear, so once you're comfortable getting your canter transitions in the dressage test, we'll just put you at Novice level instead."

Tomeka, a little shaky from the hard work Merci had required of her, had just nodded.

A phone's alarm went off, bringing me back to the present abruptly. Lindsay pulled out her phone and frowned at it, disabling the alarm with a tap. "Time to tack up, Jules," she announced. "You ready?"

I put down my fork, sliding the tub of macaroni salad across the table. "Girls, I will see you in about two hours for stadium jumping. Full show-ring ensemble. You good?"

Julia and Tomeka nodded, their mouths full of fried chicken. Tomeka's mother made eye contact with me and smiled, a horse show mom in control of the situation. "They'll be there," she promised.

I went into Dynamo's stall first and stripped the dripping ice boots from his legs. He regarded me without taking his teeth away from his hay-net, one brown eye quietly assessing the situation. "You know we have stadium jumping today," I reminded him. "We talked about this already."

Lindsay came under the stall chain with an armful of tack pressed against her hip. "Where's Pete?" she asked, settling a saddle pad on Dynamo's back.

"Lunch with Rick," I said, rolling my eyes. I took the girth from her and waited while she settled my jumping saddle into place. "So he can give the jerk a play-by-play of every cross-country jump, and Rick can tell him everything he did wrong."

"Didn't they go clear?"

"Two stops," I sighed, handing her the girth as she gestured impatiently for it. "Not what Pete was expecting." It was the only flaw in the day—Rogue's enthusiasm for cross-country, which had been the reason Pete had transitioned him from his jumper career, seemed to be faltering under the strain of his training regimen and competition.

"Ouch." Lindsay stepped back to survey the saddle. She gave me a head-to-toe glance. "Go get dressed while I finish him," she commanded.

I paused on the way out of the stall. "Do you think Dynamo looks fit?" I asked, surveying his sleek lines and bulging muscles. Dynamo was a thick-bodied, rather heavy-set sort of Thoroughbred. He was bred for sprinting, and it had always been challenging to get him into proper shape for the lengthy courses at the upper levels. This morning, I just hadn't felt like he was one hundred percent strong enough for the course. May Days had more hills than most of the Florida courses, with a few truly miserable climbs.

"Of course he looks fit," Lindsay snorted. "He's like a monster."

I went off to find my show shirt and jacket, still mulling over the way he'd gone this morning. He'd definitely labored up the last couple of hills on course, and his pulse had stayed high for longer than I liked. The day was hot, that was for sure, but still, Dynamo was used to hot weather. This had been something else.

Age, maybe?

I shook myself, as if I could physically shake away that nagging fear, and pulled my shirt off its hanger. Dynamo wasn't too old for top-level competition. Not already, not when we'd just gotten here.

I was just looking for trouble, that was all.

The thing I remember most from the afternoon of stadium jumping wasn't my rounds, which went without fuss, or the children's, which were every bit as practiced and professional as I would have expected given their solid horse show backgrounds, landing one a green ribbon and the other a brown one. It wasn't even Pete and Rogue, who seemed to have left their differences on the cross-country course that morning, and put in a perfectly fine, clear round which meant nothing score-wise, since they'd had two refusals already that day. It wasn't the victory gallops, which I joined with Dynamo and Mickey carrying second and third-place ribbons, although notably not with Jim Dear, whose silly mistakes in dressage gave him a twelfth-place finish, hardly worth mentioning.

The thing I remember most was a slim bay horse with a build like a greyhound who was grazing alongside the ring as I thundered past on Mickey, midway through our clear stadium round. It was almost a four-fault round, because my eyes weren't on the fence ahead of us; they were locked onto that racing-fit Thoroughbred just outside the arena.

After our round I circled Mickey, brought him down to a

trot, and then a walk, filing out of the arena decorously—
then bounced him straight back to a trot and went pounding
past Lindsay, who was waiting with a halter and a newly
startled expression, in search of the bay horse. His groom
had picked up his lead and was walking him away from the
ring, back towards stabling, and my pulse quickened as we
got closer, imagining how close I'd been to missing him
completely.

It was only one we'd caught up to the woman and horse
that I realized I had no opening line. She looked at me, and
I said the only thing an equestrian can say at a moment like
this.

"Your horse is cute."

The woman laughed, then said the magic words.
"Thanks! He's for sale." She looked at him ruefully. "As of
an hour ago," she added.

Uh-oh. "What happened an hour ago?"

"I realized he was too much horse for me, chickened out,
and didn't go to my cross-country round." The woman
pushed hair from her face and blinked up at me. She wasn't
much older than me, but she had pale winter skin. An
amateur with an office job, I figured. Poor girl. "I've only
had him two months, but it just wasn't the right fit. Even my
coach could see it. I should've known better. But I'll send
him back to the dealer, and you can check him out there if
you want. She's happy to take him back. My coach already
called her about it."

I looked over the horse again; after all, before I'd only

seen him as I went by at a canter, a few stolen glances when I should have been concentrating on the jumps in front of me. He was plain bay with two white socks behind, and a star and stripe on his face—nothing flashy in terms of color, but gleaming with good health. I thought his fitness level was odd. His body was still the firm, sleek, streamlined body of a racehorse, not what one would expect from a Novice horse. He looked as if he was galloped a mile each morning. "Does he gallop in the field a lot?" I asked. "Like, nonstop?"

"Every morning, up and down the fence-line for hours. I have to bring him in and feed breakfast at five o'clock just to make him stop." The woman shook the lead shank and grimaced at the bay horse. "Can you tell?"

"He's fit," I said. "He looks like he could run a race today."

"That's part of my problem," she said. "Look for him next week. Amanda Wakefield's place."

That was the part I remembered most from May Days. When I found out this gorgeous horse was going to be for sale in a week, with Amanda the Hunter Princess.

CHAPTER ELEVEN

I woke up on Monday morning five minutes before my alarm, and looked at my ceiling fan, spinning in the dim gray light of pre-dawn. There was a feeling of dread resting on my chest. I watched the fan blades go by until I remembered what was troubling me, the thing that had kept me awake until past midnight, and wakened me again at three o'clock for an indecently lengthy tossing-and-turning session.

I kicked off the sheet and put my feet on the chilly terrazzo floor. Marcus huffed a sorrowful sigh and stood up, shaking his ears and rattling his collar and tags with a jingling like a sleigh plunging down a mountainside. Pete sat up, as he did most mornings when Marcus startled him out of a deep sleep, and then fell back on his pillow.

"God," he muttered. "Is it Monday already?"

"Sadly," I replied. I sniffed the air. "At least the coffee is ready."

Pete's reply was muffled by his pillow, so Marcus and I went into the kitchen alone. I poured him a scoop of kibble and myself a cup of dark coffee from the steaming pot. Whoever invented coffeemakers with timers was a national hero. Listening to Marcus crunch his way through breakfast, I carried my coffee over to the couch and settled down amongst the cushions. Trading one comfy spot for another, I thought, pulling my phone out of my pajamas pocket. I would distract myself with Instagram for a few minutes while I enjoyed my coffee, and not think about the problem waiting for me in the barn.

Except, everyone I followed on Instagram had been at an event over the weekend, too. A sizable number of them had been at May Days. I sighed and closed the app.

Pete shuffled into the living room with his own mug of coffee. He sat down at the other end of the sofa. We looked at each other, a long, measuring look that was far too serious for quarter past six in the morning.

"We just have to trot him up and see," Pete said finally.

I buried my face in my coffee, breathing in its reassuring aroma. Some people said coffee smelled better than it tasted, and those people were insane. Coffee smelled *and* tasted better than anything else. Especially at quarter past six in the morning.

"I'm scared it's something serious," I said into my mug, muffling my own words so that I wouldn't have to acknowledge them, so that they hadn't gone out in the atmosphere, to work their dark magic as only spoken words

136

can do.

"It won't be," Pete said.

"How do you—"

"It *won't* be."

I put down my mug. "Fine. Let's go out there."

"I just sat down. Can I have a minute."

I stalked back into the bedroom, intent on finding the jeans I'd abandoned on the floor the night before. "I'm going now."

Dynamo wasn't lame.

He was stiff, sure, but as I first watched him trot alongside Pete, and then trotted him for Pete's knowing eye, I knew he wasn't lame. That stomach-turning moment last night, when I'd been leading him out of his stall to the pasture, and my eyes had registered a head-bob on his left front: that must have been my imagination. A one-off. A bad step. A sleeping hoof, if horses could get such a thing (I supposed that was unlikely). I'd led him right back into his stall, checked for heat in his legs, found none, and did his legs up with poultice and standing wraps anyway. Now the flakes of drying clay drifted from his legs as he trotted, evenly, on the firm ground in front of the barn.

I let out a breath and stroked his crooked blaze as Pete brought him to a halt in front of me. Dynamo puffed his nostrils at my hand, his dark eyes quietly confused. Why were we out here jogging him up and down in the parking lot before sunrise, and moreover, why had he stayed in all night when everyone else was turned out, and furthermore, where was his breakfast?

"Satisfied?" Pete asked.

"I am," I said, then paused. I knelt down, and ran my hands along Dynamo's lower legs, brushing away at the cracking poultice. They were cool to the touch after soaking in all that mud, and yet not quite bowstring-tight. My fingers paused at the hollow between the tendons and suspensory ligaments, pushing white clay aside. The hollow was not as deep as it should be.

"There's some filling there," Pete acknowledged. "But that's to be expected. He was in all night after a busy weekend."

Dynamo's legs didn't stock up after an event, even after he'd been in all night, certainly not if they'd been wrapped. This was a change. I didn't like it. "I just don't know," I said, straightening up again. "He just didn't feel like himself this weekend."

"It was hot," Pete said, but his resolve was weakening.

"It's always hot. When was the last time we were at an event and not sweating our faces off? Even in January. Seriously, Pete."

He subsided, possibly sensing that I was about to rip into him with everything I had if he poo-pooed my bad feelings one more time.

So Dynamo wasn't lame, but he wasn't right, either. After the horses had eaten breakfast, I turned him out in the shady little paddock behind the barn, where he wouldn't stand out in the hot sun and get himself overheated. There was nothing on the schedule today, with all of our horses on a day of rest after the event. The kids had been told their horses and their coaches needed a day off. I had plenty of time to clean stalls and sweep the aisle and lean on the kitchen counter and worry. Once the barn chores were done for the morning, I nestled into one corner of the couch to brood, but even then, I couldn't sit still for long.

I got up, again and again, to look out the kitchen window, which overlooked the paddock where Dynamo was grazing, utterly content with his day out.

"Stop it," Pete said wearily. "You've been looking at him every ten minutes. Take a break."

"I *can't* stop," I said finally, frustrated with him. "This was supposed to be our year. He doesn't have forever to compete. And he's my only horse running Advanced. What if I don't get him to a three-star by next spring, and have to retire him instead, then what? It sets me back years." I put my face in my hands. "It sets me back *years,*" I repeated, my muffled voice echoing in my ears.

Mickey was still competing at Preliminary level; he needed another season to make the big step up to Intermediate. Jim Dear was at Training; he would be Prelim at the end of the year *if* he got his shit together, but he wasn't turning out to be a scopey jumper and I had little hope of taking him much further. He'd make a nice amateur horse for somebody once he had the mileage and steadied up. Those were all of my horses now. If I had to take Dynamo out of the running, it would be another two years before I'd have a horse to point at a three-star event... let alone a four-star, like Kentucky. I never said it out loud, not wanting to tempt fate, but I'd wanted to run Dynamo at Kentucky Three Day Event since the day I'd brought him back from the auction. Getting to four-star was the whole *point*. It was the top of the line, the pinnacle of the sport, and the only route to the Olympics.

If you weren't trying to get onto an Olympic team, what were you even doing in this game?

"What exactly was wrong with him this weekend? Can you tell me again?" Pete asked. At last, he sounded genuinely concerned; maybe he'd finally internalized just how serious I thought this was.

"He was laboring," I said, rubbing my face wearily. "You know we had time penalties. Dynamo never had trouble making the time before. The spark just wasn't there. Then he took too long to cool out. And yes, I know it's hot, but we condition in the heat every single day. That's not it." I had told Pete these things after the cross-country run, as we'd walked back to the stabling, but maybe he hadn't been listening. Maybe he'd been nodding and saying everything would be fine while in his head he was busy prepping for his next ride. Well, I couldn't blame him for that. A person had to be looking out for number one on competition weekends.

"He looked sharp in the stadium jumping," Pete pointed out. "As good as he's ever looked."

"That's true," I admitted. It *had* been a really nice stadium round. "Doesn't change what happened in cross-country, though."

"Fair." Pete leaned back, put his feet on the coffee table. He was wearing argyle boot socks with a red and black pattern. My eyes traced the angles of the crimson diamonds. "You know, there's an alternative we've never talked about."

"Straight show jumping?" I lifted my eyes from his socks and met his eyes, shaking my head. "No, Pete, that's not an option. I've got absolutely no interest in jumpers."

"Not quite," Pete said. "Although if you really hate being in an arena, it's not going to work out."

I stared at him.

"Arena eventing, Jules." Pete grinned. "You've heard of it, right?"

I got up from the couch and stalked into the kitchen for another peek at Dynamo. "We are *not* going to do arena eventing," I called over my shoulder. "Out of the question."

"It's just an idea," Pete said. "Why not think about it? Why dismiss it without even a moment to consider it? You don't have to tear up your long-format fan club membership card this very second."

His sarcasm set my teeth on edge. I looked out at Dynamo, who was cheerfully cropping the short grass under the shade of an oak tree. I didn't want to consider arena eventing for a myriad of reasons, not least that I considered it just one more effort by a generation of riders with no respect for the traditions of three-day eventing to dumb down our sport and make it into something ring-bound, sponsor-ready, a neat little package to be sold as a marketing opportunity to luxury brands with customer bases in West Palm Beach. I wanted nothing to do with it.

Pete came into the kitchen behind me and wrapped an arm around my waist. We hadn't been touching much lately, either too tired or too frustrated with one another most of the time, and I leaned back against him. "You're stubborn," he whispered, his lips against my throat. "Did I ever tell you that?"

"Arena eventing is the devil and you know it," I told him, but I couldn't hold back a laugh. Me, the stubborn one! Hello, Mr. Pot.

"There's money in it, Jules. And I've never known you to turn your back on a devil with a full wallet."

I twisted my neck and gave him a soft kiss. "You make me sound dirty," I murmured.

"I know what you like," Pete chuckled. "You have expensive taste."

"It's true. Guilty."

"I'm about to change the subject... but in case I forget, here's the grand prize for winning the arena eventing showcase at the Central Park Horse Show."

Pete produced his phone and showed me the page on the screen.

My jaw dropped.

"Uh-huh," Pete said. "I know."

"That's for *eventing?*"

"Ah, ah," he chided. "*Arena* eventing. Not the same thing." He put the phone away and began to turn his attention back to my neck. "But Dynamo would be good at it," he said. "Think about it."

"Maybe I will." My head was spinning, both from the sensation of his mouth on my skin and the number of zeroes in that grand prize purse. I remembered the bay Thoroughbred I'd seen outside of stadium jumping, the one who was going to be at Amanda's next week. I would need another horse to bring along soon; Jim Dear wouldn't be in my barn forever and if Dynamo's career was going to wind down, even in the next two years, I'd have a definite gap in my stable. Imagine if I could walk into a barn like Amanda's and simply buy the horse I wanted, rather than haunting all the websites where unwanted racehorses were posted for sale, looking for a prospect who was that magical balance of sane, sound, and not snatched up immediately by a horse flipper with deeper pockets than mine! "When is that show?" I murmured, holding out against Pete's insistent kisses for as long as I could manage.

"Think about it *later*," Pete groaned, his hands slipping below my waist. He grabbed my hips and turned me around to face him, his mouth dipping towards mine.

I turned my head slightly. "When?" I asked again.

"September. Now, will you leave it alone for now?"

I closed my eyes and turned up my face in answer, but in my mind, I couldn't help but roll through the weeks ahead, June and July and August, wondering what it would take to win an entirely new type of competition at the end of summer.

CHAPTER TWELVE

Lacey drove up to the barn while I was out in the ring with students, trying to illustrate where I wanted their upper bodies in the run-up to a cross-country fence.

"You want to be back *here*," I was announcing, bending my knees and dropping my pelvis so that it looked like I was about to pantomime something highly unsuitable for children, and I had just lifted my hands to about elbow-height when I heard a truck door slam and a peal of familiar laughter ring out.

"Lacey!" I shrieked, abandoning my semi-erotic stance. "You *nag!*"

"You *mule!*" Lacey shouted back, waving her arms above her head. "What are you *teaching* these children? I'm going to call the police!"

Julia and Maisey looked at Lacey and then back at me with astonishment. "Who—who is that?" Maisey ventured finally.

"She seems kind of... weird," Julia said wonderingly.

"Oh good god," I sighed, wondering if I'd made a huge mistake. "This is our barn manager."

Of course, I hadn't made a mistake. Lacey had always been able to conduct herself in public; I'd been the problem child in our coupledom. With the exception of that one memorable time with her and Becky at the event... but I could write that public shouting match off. We'd all been younger then, and tensions had been running high. Things were calmer now. We were adults.

With her chestnut hair bound in a messy braid and her glowing white skin revealed by a sleeveless riding top and a pair of khaki shorts, Lacey looked ready to head out on the town and hit all the local tack shops, with a stop for drinks between each one. I remembered her in ragged cut-offs and battered thrift store t-shirts. The change was impressive. After a year away and a little bit of higher ed, Lacey looked much more put-together than I had pictured her.

She had already started rummaging through the feed room when I came in from Maisey and Julia's lesson, moving things around on shelves to find an order that suited her best.

"What's this?" I demanded, swinging through the open door. "You can't just move my Vitamin E without saying something to me first. This tack room is in apple-pie order."

Lacey spun around, a value-sized shaker of garlic powder in her hands, and waved it in my face. "What is *this*?"

I snatched it from her, laughing. "To make a boarder happy. She swears it keeps the bugs off."

"We both know that isn't true. You're *coddling* them. Jules Thornton, I never would have believed it of you! Pick up the phone and tell her off, right now!"

"I make a salary now, I can't just *yell* at people anymore."

"Oh, what the hell have I done? I've made a terrible mistake coming here." Lacey grabbed the garlic back from me and put it on the top-most shelf. "Jules has gone over to the enemy. And she probably can afford actual food, too. This is an outrage."

"I swear I can't afford actual food," I snorted. "Last night I made a box of penne pasta and topped it with leftover taco meat I found in the back of the fridge."

Lacey adjusted her face into sober lines. "My god, Jules," she deadpanned. "It appears I arrived a moment too late. You're definitely going to die from that." Her grin broke through her serious mask, and we were giggling again.

There we were, Lacey and Jules together again, goofing off in the feed room, laughing at each other's idiotic attempts at jokes. I felt a startling wave of nostalgia, as if this wasn't really happening, as if I was imagining it all.

"But seriously," Lacey said eventually, when we'd begun to recover ourselves, "who organized this place? You are living in mayhem, Jules Thornton. You've got electrolytes on the same shelf as powdered bute. Daily things at eye-level, you know the rule! Please tell me you're not using so much bute that you have to keep it at eye-level."

"I'm not using *any* bute," I defended myself. "Last week one of the horses got stung by a bee on his eyelid and needed some to take the swelling down, that's all."

"That was last month," Lindsay said, walking by in the aisle. "You can't even keep your dates straight anymore."

"Oh, who was that?" Lacey asked, peering after her. "I like her."

"You would," I jeered. "Seventeen and borderline goth."

"I gave all that up for you!" Lindsay shouted, her voice echoing down the barn aisle.

"What the hell is going on in here?" It was Pete, appearing in the doorway with Rogue's halter over his arm. "Lacey! Who said you could come onto our property?"

Lacey went in for a hug while I considered the use of "our" in this context. It was "your" boarders and "your" students and "your" business an awful lot of the time, but it was "our" barn. Sure, I thought. Fine.

By the end of the first day with Lacey in charge, I was starting to wonder if everyone with a barn manager had this much free time. It wasn't like I was leaning back in my desk chair with my feet up all day, but at the same time, walking into the barn after the last lesson and realizing that while we'd been in the ring, all of the horses had been fed, most had been turned out for the night, and stalls had been skipped out was an awfully luxurious moment in my life. The girls started untacking their horses while I sought out Lacey. I found her in the feed room again, setting up the grain cart for the morning.

"You know, next week there'll be kids here twenty-four-seven and they can handle things like this for you," I told her, settling down on a stack of sweet feed bags.

"Yeah, you didn't mention my staff of a dozen children when you offered me the job," Lacey said, only half-joking. She met my eyes. "But they seem great," she said more seriously. "Everyone here loves you, which is awesome."

"Everyone?" I considered her statement with a cocked head. "I'm sure some people here have a problem with me they're just not ready to bring up yet. That's the nature of barns. They're always stewing with gossip and dark secrets."

Lacey covered up the grain cart with several empty feed bags and planted a few supplement tubs on top for good measure. "Do you have mice?" she asked.

"Not if Barn Kitty has anything to say about it. Don't worry about locking her in here, though, there's a cat door." On cue, Barn Kitty poked her head through the little flap of her door and rubbed her pink nose on the metal frame sensuously. Her single ginger-patched ear caught a cobweb and she flicked at it with a paw. "Barn Kitty, do you remember Lacey?"

Lacey gave the cat's ears an affectionate swipe with her knuckles. "Not as well as Marcus does. I wouldn't be surprised if he's waiting for me in my truck."

"He's in the house, asleep already. Marcus turns in early these days."

"I think I will be doing the same." Lacey straightened

and brushed her hands off on her neat khaki shorts. I wondered if she was going to come dressed so tidily every day. If she did, I would have to as well. Couldn't have the manager dressed better than the trainer. "My place doesn't have any food in it, so I have to stop somewhere and pick up dinner."

It was on the tip of my tongue to tell her that of course she had to stay and have dinner with us. But I was afraid that if I brought Lacey in, I'd never want her to leave. We were past the years when we'd lived as roommates, content with our ramen and our squalor... but the memories were alluring, filled with laughter and late nights. I wondered if I'd been happier with Lacey than I was now, with Pete.

"I'll see you in the morning," I said instead, pushing all that nostalgia back. It was just that: nostalgia, flickering memories that were probably very different from reality. Had we had a good time together? Yes. Had it been all sunshine and rainbows? Probably not, or I wouldn't have ended up moving in with Pete at all. If it had been so great, wouldn't I have tried to make it last forever? "I'm really glad you're here," I added.

"Of course you are," Lacey said cheerfully. "It's six-thirty and the barn is done for the night." She leaned over and gave me a light peck on the cheek. Her eyes were bright when she straightened, fastened on mine with an affectionate glow. And yet I thought I detected something else in her manner towards me, a certain amusement, as if

Lacey had grown up somehow in her year away, and I had not.

CHAPTER THIRTEEN

"Why are you going to look at a horse? You don't have any money."

"Lacey, I'm so glad you're back." I threw my good purse across the truck seat and clambered in. Lacey settled into the passenger seat, placing the purse on her lap and angling it so she could admire the embossed jumper on the side.

"This is too fancy for you," she observed. "Or you've gotten fancier since I left."

"Both answers are correct." I turned the truck on and switched the air conditioning to blizzard mode. "Is Pete coming?" I didn't particularly want him to come to Amanda's barn with me, but at the same time, it would be nice to have his opinion on the horse.

"I saw him in the tack room a minute ago," Lacey sighed, putting the purse down on the floor. "Is this a Rockwell Brothers bag?"

"Of course it is." I was texting Pete furiously. "I never buy anything. They just send me things and I take pictures of them for Instagram. Life is good."

Pete texted back immediately. *Can't come-dealing with Rick. Send me video.*

I stifled a scream and threw the phone into the cupholder.

"So, Pete's not coming?" Lacey asked idly, typing into her own phone. I craned my neck to see—she was googling the price of my purse.

"You're the worst," I said, throwing the truck into reverse. "The absolute worst."

"I missed you, too," Lacey said happily.

When I turned into the gate and Lacey spotted the sign, she stifled her own scream. "We're at *Amanda's?*" She shook her head at me. "I really was gone a long time, wasn't I?"

"Nothing has changed with Amanda," I said. "We're still not friends. But I saw this horse at May Days and it turns out she has him up for sale. So here we are."

Amanda's barn was just as elegant as I remembered, with soaring ceilings, brass halter hooks on every stall, and curving steel stall-fronts that made it look more like a magazine spread for a luxury magazine than a place where actual horses ate and slept and pooped. The chandelier hanging in the atrium, where the barn's twin wings met around the tack room and two rubber-paved grooming stalls, twinkled over our heads as Amanda came out to greet us. She was just as elegant as her barn, her whip-slim figure highlighted in plum-colored breeches with a swirling design of flowers lining the inner seams, and a spotless white riding shirt, the deep v of her collar unbuttoned. Her golden pony-tail fell over one shoulder as if it had just been blow-dried into place. I supposed it was possible. I'd been in the bathroom of Amanda's barn before; it would have worked well in a high-end hotel.

"Jules!" Amanda shrieked, as if we were best friends separated since high school and not rivals who had parted rather bitterly the autumn before, after she'd been trying to snatch Pete from me. "It's been forever!"

She held out her arms and I stepped into them stiffly, surrendering to the inevitable. With Amanda, we were all just members of her sorority, to be feted and dropped at will. Today I was her favorite; tomorrow she might post a rumor about me using a fake Facebook profile. Maybe even tonight, if I wasn't careful on this horse-shopping visit.

"And you remember Lacey?" I stepped back and let Amanda embrace Lacey, who gave in gracefully. Lacey had always been better about human contact than me.

"Lacey!" Amanda sighed. "I can't believe you came back to Florida, you crazy girl. It's a million degrees here." She brushed away at mock sweat on her forehead, because of course Amanda did not sweat visibly like the rest of us mere humans.

"I can't believe I'm really here," Lacey said meaningfully, glancing my way.

The bay horse was in the cross-ties already, watching us

with pricked ears and wide, alert eyes. He fluttered his nostrils as we paused a few feet away, and lifted one fore-hoof in a delicate, begging gesture before rethinking his decision and placing it back on the cushioned pavers. I admired his broad chest and solid knees while Amanda explained his background. "And I had him for maybe two months before Elaine bought him, and I knew it was going to be dicey so I told her that if she had any problems, to bring him right back to me. Elaine and I go way back. Obviously I wouldn't do that for just anybody! I even made sure she had the perfect coach to help her out. He schooled her at May Days, but it just wasn't enough.

"So here he is. Just needs a more confident rider. And a serious work schedule. Because if you don't exercise him, this horse will exercise himself. Apparently, he gained all this muscle running up and down Elaine's fence because she didn't keep him good and tired." She laughed and the horse picked up his hoof again, letting it hover above the floor a moment. "In a minute, Darcy," she told him. "Just wait."

"His name is Darcy?" Lacey laughed, while I waited for an explanation of why this was funny.

"I call him Mr. Darcy," Amanda explained. "His registered name is Confident Liar."

"I like *that*," I said.

"Do you?" Amanda's laugh was tinkly. "Well, it's not bad, I guess. A little weird for me, but some people *really* like to keep those Jockey Club names, even when they make no sense. Hang on while I get my helmet. Oscar? Can you finish tacking up Darcy?"

A groom materialized and began saddling the Thoroughbred while Amanda disappeared into her tack room.

I turned to Lacey.

"Mr. Darcy is from *Pride and Prejudice,*" she said.

"Which one was he?" I asked, as if I had read it.

"The one who takes his shirt off in the pond."

"Oh, that sounds familiar actually."

Lacey nodded, comfortable with her one year of college education and the advanced knowledge she could now hold over my head. "So this is weird," she said, lowering her voice to a stealthy whisper. "Are you and Amanda really acting like nothing ever happened?"

I shrugged. "My gut reaction to this horse was big enough to overlook the trainer." My gut had been right before. Mickey, and Dynamo—those two had given me the same *stop right there* reaction, and I'd been right about both of them. "Plus, I know Amanda's horses are sound and clean. Whatever else I think about her... the horses are good."

Amanda emerged from the tack room, an elegant helmet trimmed with tiny crystals perched on her head. Her ponytail had vanished into a neat hairnet, and she was fastening the Velcro on a gleaming pair of riding gloves. On my tidiest day at an event, I could not look as put-together as Amanda did on a regular Wednesday afternoon at the farm, and this was after I was fitted out by one of the top tack shops in the country. The woman would have given me a complex even if she hadn't spent most of last year trying to lure Pete away.

"All ready, 'Manda," Oscar said, holding out the reins. He'd tacked up the horse with the kind of speed usually reserved for timed events. "You want a leg-up?"

"I'll use the mounting block, thank you, Oscar." She took the reins and smiled at us. "Pete's been after me to start using the mounting block more. They were all way too used to my getting a leg-up. I forget not everyone has a groom to help them!"

Pete. The world stopped. I blinked, hoping it would start up again. I no longer felt the ground beneath my feet; I was floating away, untethered and uncertain what to do about it.

"Pete?" Lacey asked innocently, evidently not feeling our sudden loss of gravity. "You mean our Pete?"

"Yes," Amanda said, walking Darcy past us. "I just got in all of these Thoroughbreds from a client whose father passed. Really leggy, gangly racehorses. None of them are going to be hunters. So, I called Pete. I mean, I had to! He's the best for this kind of thing, getting these eventing prospects a solid dressage foundation. I just don't have the interest or the background! But he says the little things like this, like using mounting blocks, can add up with all of my horses, and he's really right. Pete's always right, don't you think?"

Lacey grabbed my arm above the elbow. "Breathe," she instructed, her voice low. "You're turning red. She'll notice."

I took a deep breath, choked on it, and started coughing. Oscar peered at us from the grooming stall, where he was wielding a broom, sweeping up the scraps of hay and manure left behind from grooming Darcy. Barn clean-up couldn't be allowed to wait until after turn-out, not here, not at Amanda's Perfect Farm. I glared at the blameless Oscar while I hacked until Lacey pushed on my arm, guiding us out of the barn while I tried to recover myself. "Better," she said, as I took a normal breath. "Now you just look red from coughing. We'll say it's allergies. Or you swallowed a fly. I'll bet Amanda doesn't allow flies here; it will distract her."

But there was no need to explain myself. Amanda was already occupied in positioning Darcy at the mounting block outside the arena, somehow managing to make the everyday act look like a major production. Darcy flicked an ear back as she finally clambered up the two plastic steps. "Good boy!" she announced as she swung into the saddle. "Nice job!" It was a lot of praise for a very basic operation. I wondered just how naughty he'd been about this before.

Darcy swished his tail and tossed his head as she held him still a minute longer, leaning down to fidget with the girth. I could see by the look in his eyes that he was preparing for battle. Just as he started to pick up his hind legs and arch his spine, she released her hold on his mouth and let his energy spill forward. He stalked into the arena like an angry panther.

"Whoa," Lacey said. "That horse has a lot of aggression in him."

"He's just strong and fit," I said, but there was something more than that. Lacey was probably right. He was aggressive. He was confident. He was convinced of his own importance. I could see how easily he would have tormented his amateur owner, why she only lasted two months with him. I suspected that this Confident Liar was a horse of many talents, and he knew each and every one of them.

If watching his expressive movement was enlightening, riding him was a revelation. Despite the suspension of his gaits, he still felt very green; I wasn't sure he should have been at an event already. He ran through half-halts and pulled hard through downward transitions, dragging his head towards the ground. He tugged me towards jumps and picked whatever take-off stride he liked, whether it was short or long. This was a horse who had never gotten into trouble over fences, and didn't even know such a thing was possible. A Confident Liar, indeed. He was out there faking it because he was convinced he was a grand prix horse. He really needed some remedial lessons, but I could feel his talent bursting through all those bad spots—it wouldn't take long to level up with this horse. He was crying out for big fences and a real challenge.

"I want him," I told Amanda, pulling up to an unsteady halt. He ducked his head against the reins and I clapped my heels to his sides to bring it up again. "I'm not going to play coy. What are your plans? Are you in a hurry?"

I didn't have anything in savings. I shouldn't even have spent the gas money to drive down here and try him.

Amanda shrugged. "I'm in no rush. You can see he went plenty backwards with the last owner. She shouldn't have bought him... honestly, I shouldn't have sold him to her. I thought if she had a good trainer, they might figure each other out, but clearly that didn't happen. It wasn't the trainer's fault," she added hastily. "They only worked together a couple of times. He needs a professional's touch."

"You were nice to take him back." I dropped my stirrups and jumped down, handing the reins to the waiting Oscar, who led the horse back to the barn.

"Sometimes I'm just too nice for this game," Amanda laughed. She tossed back her pony-tail and looked generally ravishing. I gazed at her with undisguised wonder. How did a regular person become an Amanda, all glamour and confidence? Was it really just having money, all the time?

"Has Pete been on him?"

Amanda looked at me with a measuring glance. "You didn't know Pete was riding here before this, did you?" she asked after a moment. "Or you would have talked to him about the horse already. He would have said something to me, too. I was so surprised when I got your call, so out of the blue."

I bit the inside of my cheek, tamping down my emotions. "I did not," I finally admitted. "I think that's a conversation for he and I, though."

"Nothing's going on," Amanda said, her voice serious. "Nothing ever did before, and it's not now. He rides my horses. I pay him in cash. I recommend him to people—like Elaine. But that's the end of it."

It was far from the end of it, I thought. But the rest of

this conversation was for Pete and me. "What does Pete think of him?" I asked, changing the subject back to the horse.

"He really likes him," Amanda said. "He was the one coaching Elaine with him. You should talk to him about it."

When Elaine had said that even her coach could see they were a bad fit, she'd been talking about Pete. When Pete had been missing in action at May Days, he'd been helping her—and he'd kept it from me, hiding every connection he had to Amanda.

"Did he show horses for you last weekend?" I asked suddenly.

"Just a couple," Amanda said. "At Newberry." She looked at the ground suddenly, as if realizing she'd given away another of Pete's deceptions. "It's a job, Jules, nothing more," she repeated.

I couldn't discuss it with her. "I'll ask him about the horse, then, I guess." I made to walk across the ring, to start heading home, but Amanda put out her hand and touched my shoulder. I stopped and looked back.

Her face was open, her eyes worried. "I'm really sorry, Jules," she said softly. "I didn't know he was going to keep it a secret. I—I guess I should have thought about it from your point of view. It wasn't fair of me to ask him back here."

"It wasn't," I said coldly. "Not to any of us." Deep down, some rational part of my brain knew Pete had come back to ride for Amanda because he was worried about the future, about money and about his place in what had evidently become, in his mind, *my* barn. I'd examine those problems later, I told myself. Right now, there was just one problem to be solved. "Don't sell him that horse," I said. "Even if he begs."

Amanda smiled despite herself. "That's what you want? Will that make this better?"

I shrugged. I wasn't ready to make any commitments yet. "If you can swear there's nothing going on, now or in the future, between you and Pete—"

"I swear," Amanda interrupted solemnly.

"Then that will make you and me okay."

"Alright." Amanda held out a manicured hand, and I took it with my sweaty, calloused one. "I won't sell Pete the horse. And I'll give you some time—I won't put him on the market for a few months. He needs his head put back on straight, anyway."

I winced to think of Pete and Amanda being the ones to sort out Confident Liar. "I'll figure something out," I said. "Thanks."

Lacey was waiting for me at the rail, her face a carefully held mask. I swung her braid as I passed. "Let's head home, kid," I said brightly, as if nothing had happened, and she fell into step behind me.

"Are we going to talk about this?" Lacey asked as soon as her door was closed. Amanda was already back in her barn, tossing us a final wave as she disappeared under the arching doorway.

"Definitely not," I said, putting the truck into gear. "I

don't have a single thought I can vocalize right now without crashing this truck, and I like both of us too much to kill us."

"Fair." Lacey settled back into her seat. "It's going to be a long-ass drive home, though."

CHAPTER FOURTEEN

Lacey was right. It was a long-ass drive.

I didn't want to talk about any of it, but I couldn't stop thinking about it all, either. Amanda, Pete, Confident Liar —I refused to think of him as Darcy, as some English-lit hero in a cravat, because that image would always be wrapped up with Amanda and her endless pining for Pete, her machinations and spying, and even if there was nothing going on now, even if Pete was completely blameless— although I couldn't see how that could be—I never wanted to think about Amanda's romantic yearnings ever again, even through the innocent barn name of a horse.

The drive back to High Springs was a quiet one, with the radio and iced coffees to keep us awake through the long miles of interstate and countryside. I just wanted to get home and scream at Pete, and Lacey wanted me to go home and sit quietly for a little while in the tack room and think about what I was going to say to him in a measured, calm tone. I wondered if Lacey had forgotten who she was dealing with here. Maybe during her year up north she'd remembered me as a completely different person. A better person.

"I heard from the lady leasing Margot today," Lacey said eventually. "She really likes her. She's going to take her to a hunter show next month."

I forced myself back to the present. "You know if you want her down here, we'll find room for her at the barn."

"I know." Lacey's voice was soft. I glanced at her, but she was just gazing out of the truck window, watching the passing pine forests. "I just thought it would be simpler to get down here without her at first."

I wondered if Lacey was giving me a trial run before she decided to lock herself down with me. It was harder to cut and run when you had a horse on the property.

"How long is the lease for?" I asked eventually.

"Six months. Until the end of the year, basically."

That was too bad. She'd miss the winter eventing season if Margot spent the entire year cantering around hunter courses. But maybe Lacey didn't want to compete her at all. She'd never been much of a competitor back when she'd been my student. Lacey was happiest working in the barn, keeping me well-stocked with an endless supply of tacked-up horses waiting to be worked, whisking away my hot horses to the showers. She was the perfect groom, and if that's what she wanted to do, we were both set for as long as we could avoid killing each other.

We'd done pretty great before. My confidence level on this was remarkably high. "Anytime you want her, if the lady will break the lease, send for her. We can find her a ride with someone."

"Okay," Lacey said, but she sounded tired of the subject. "What are you going to do about this horse, this Darcy horse?"

"Not call him Darcy, for starters."

"Seriously. You don't have the cash for him, do you?"

I shrugged. I didn't, but Lacey didn't have to know that. We'd been apart for a year. Let her earn her way back into my deepest, darkest confidences, like the contents of my bank account. "I might try to find someone to buy him for me."

Lacey blinked at me. "Why? Why are we doing any of this? You've told me a hundred times how overworked you are right now. And I've only been here like three days. You don't need an owner to buy you a new novice horse. If you get someone to buy you a horse, shouldn't it already be going Prelim, at least?"

I didn't answer. Lacey kept pressing. "Why does it have to be *this* horse, Jules? Seriously. There are a million horses out there."

"Why do we ever want a horse? I don't know, he just speaks to me, okay?" I hated myself for saying the words, but I couldn't think of another way to articulate the feeling that bay Thoroughbred gave me. When he pricked his ears

166

and looked at me, I felt like I was in the presence of a long-lost friend. When I'd settled onto his back in the arena, we'd fit together like two puzzle pieces. We were made for each other. I knew this feeling because I'd had it before. How many more times would I have it? How many equine soulmates does one human get? What if I was running out of my matches already?

What if he was my next big break?

I ran my equestrian life as a strictly business proposition... until I couldn't anymore. Horses came and horses went, that was my guiding philosophy, but the heart horses? I held on to with everything I had. Dynamo. Mickey. I'd cling to them through the worst of storms. I'd do anything to hang on to them. I'd already had to prove that, time and time again, over the past few years.

Horses like Jim Dear, or Virtuous, or the Twins, or even Margot, were nice enough, pleasant to have around (well, Margot was not always pleasant to me, though she always loved Lacey), responsive to training, and held enormous potential as performance horses. But nothing in my soul had ever clung to them as horses I couldn't give up. One by one, our relationship came to an end. The Twins went back to their owner, Margot went with Lacey to Pennsylvania, Virtuous was doing well in his new amateur eventing home, and Jim Dear would find his place in someone else's barn soon, too, if I was lucky. Other horses would replace them, and I would think fondly of them, if I thought of them at all, until the day I blanked while telling a training story and said,

"Wait, what was that one horse's name?"

But Dynamo, Mickey, and, goddammit, Confident Liar —they would never leave my thoughts, never be forgotten, and damn well never again go to someone else's barn without me kicking and screaming in the background. I didn't know why this horse of Amanda's was one of my heart horses... I just knew it. I wanted him, I wanted him so much I wanted to hitch up the trailer, turn right back around, and steal him from that fancy, fancy barn.

"Maybe Rick will buy him for me," I said thoughtlessly.

"Rick *Delannoy?* Pete's Rick? You don't want that," Lacey said, giving me a sideways look. "Yes, I've only been here three days, but that man is insane. Plus, it would be weird of you."

"What do you know about it?" I snapped, annoyed at having my smallest, most pointless of dreams derided. "Rockwell was Pete's sponsor, and now they're mine as well and you'd never know they didn't want me, specifically. Pete's an afterthought for them. I sell breeches and boots by the truck-load for those people."

Lacey shook her head and looked back out the window. When she spoke again, her tone was one of disappointment. "I can't believe you'd try to take an owner from Pete."

My fingernails bit into the steering wheel. *This isn't about Pete! For once! It's about me!* I wanted to scream, but I just squared my jaw and kept silent. For as long as I had known Pete, everything had seemed to be about him. The trainers loved him. The sponsors loved him. The owners loved him.

I fought for attention, I fought for visibility, I fought for everything that came to Pete easily.

Hell, I'd even fought for *Pete*, and that was after I'd clawed myself out of messes of *his* making. Getting sent down to Grace's barn in order to earn the Rockwell sponsorship—that had started with him, and yet somehow, it had become *my* job to take that apprenticeship, make it work, and win him back.

It's always about Pete, I thought tiredly. Even with Lacey. Even with the girl who I'd thought was my best friend.

The kids noticed I was in a mood the moment I stomped into the barn, and wisely kept their snide comments and arguments to a minimum when I was nearby. Lessons that night were basic jumping schools: Lacey went out and set up a line of cross-rails spaced from a few strides to just a bounce between each, and I took the intermediate class through the gymnastic a few times each until everyone was approaching the first fence and exiting the final fence more or less on the same trajectory. Then, as the shadows grew long (but the heat did not abate), Lindsay came out for a private lesson, mounted on her bay Hanoverian gelding, William.

"And how has William been going for you this week?" I asked, my normal introduction to a private lesson, while Lindsay circled the big horse around me.

Lindsay, who had learned I liked in-depth observations

of a horse's gaits and moods, launched into a stunningly detailed commentary, starting with his behavior on the ground (he had come to the stall door and nickered for her three days in a row—could this be a sign he liked his work now, or was it more to do with the granola bars she hadn't been eating at school and had taken to giving him instead?). I nodded at this, considering the ultimate conundrum: did our horses like us, or did they just like food? I was not a romantic and tended towards the food side of the debate, but at the same time, building close personal relationships with our horses was the name of the game.

"It doesn't matter if it's the food or the work," I decided finally, "as long as he's happy to see you and happy to do the work."

Lindsay nodded and began discussing his under-saddle work. I didn't hear her, though. Pete's truck had appeared in the driveway, and I could see his copper-colored hair as he stood by a group of students in front of the barn, listening to whatever earnest discussion they had roped him into. The sizzling sun was slanting towards the golden light of late evening, and the shifting rays lit him up in a metallic glow. He looked larger than life, a tall man basking in a spotlight from the heavens and surrounded by supplicants; a hero perched upon this remote hilltop, sharing his wisdom with the world.

I wondered if I was possibly going crazy from sheer jealousy.

I wondered if the kids thought more of him than they did

of me.

Then I wondered when he was going to tell me he hadn't been riding at Penny Lane at all, but actually had been lying to cover up riding at Amanda's barn and coaching Amanda's clients.

"But that left lead change is still giving him trouble," Lindsay was saying. "Any ideas?"

I turned back to her, wondering what on earth she'd been talking about. I shrugged. "More leg. Ride him forward."

Lindsay nodded, her face resigned. "I was afraid you'd say that."

"That's usually all we can say," I admitted.

By the time evening chores were done, Lacey had gone back to her apartment in High Springs, and the last of the boarders had been carted home by their parents, I should have been ready to talk to Pete about his deception... but I wasn't. The truth was, I just didn't know how to feel about it. About any of it—about Pete, about our future, about our partnership as trainers—everything had gotten confusing lately, and I just didn't know how to sort out all the snarls and knots tangling up our lives.

In the end, Pete came and found me. I was perched on the picnic table at the end of the barn, looking out at the moonlit pastures. There were mosquitoes whining around my ears, and I'd pulled on a windbreaker to keep them off my bare arms. The jacket wasn't mine; the slightest whiff of incense in the hood made me suspect it was Lindsay's. I was breathing it in when Pete sat down next to me, the table creaking when he added his weight to mine.

"Long day today," he said after a few moments of silence. "Hot."

"It will start raining next week," I said automatically. "The rainy season begins the first week of June."

"Hopefully."

I shrugged. Maybe the weather would follow its ancient patterns, maybe it wouldn't. Nothing felt predictable or easy anymore.

"Sorry I couldn't go look at the horse with you today. I didn't even realize you were shopping for one." As he finished speaking, his tone grew slightly injured. I wondered if he was really going to try and hold out for wronged-boyfriend status. I wondered why Amanda hadn't called him and told him I'd been there. It was a little delightful to think she had set him up for this fall, though—almost as if she had decided to be on my side.

"Sorry I didn't say anything until the last minute," I said tightly, feeling my fingers clench into the rough wood of the table. "I guess I didn't think it was that important."

There was a pause; Pete could sense the danger, even if he didn't know which quarter it was coming from. After a moment, he pressed ahead, feeling his way along with tentative words. "Where was the horse at?"

I swallowed. I could string him along, or I could be so

blunt, he'd know exactly why I was angry. I had never been one for making people into puppets. "Amanda's."

I turned my head to see his reaction.

Pete's eyes grew wide, soaking in the blue moonlight. He looked at me, then away, then at the ground, darting for something to focus on, but the night blurred all the edges and turned objects into smudges of darkness. Finally, he gave up, and looked back at me, his expression utterly lost. He reached out and grabbed my hand, pressing his fingers against mine, hard, and somehow, that look and that gesture made me want to forgive him.

I wouldn't, of course, not so easily as that. But for the first time in a while, I could see that Pete still put stock in what we had together.

"It was the money," he said eventually. "I was hoping..." He paused, swallowed hard. "*You're* independent now," he said, suddenly fierce. "And me, I'm not sure where I stand with anything or anyone. I just wanted to get paid, get some money in the bank, and then try to figure things out. When I don't have to grovel for money from someone, it might be easier, right?"

That's when I understood.

Pete had been a sponsored golden boy, living on his grandfather's farm and enjoying the best of everything, when I had been struggling at to make ends meet at Green Winter and failing to keep my novice owners happy, let alone get any upper-level horses into my string. Pete had to learn lessons about hardship and struggle I'd arrived in

Ocala already painfully aware of, and I'd known that for some time. What I hadn't made room for was the understanding that Pete's ways of dealing with financial struggles would be different from mine. He'd seek the big arena again, the fancy barn, the finer things, because that was what he associated with being an equestrian... not the struggle, not the dirt and the grief and the endless aches.

I understood, but I couldn't let him off the hook. He hadn't learned yet. He'd just gone back to the silver spoon, but what he needed to understand was that the silver spoon wasn't real life.

"You were my partner," I said, forcing my voice flat, without a hint of sympathy. "We had everything figured out. *You* made it difficult."

"And now?" Pete's fingers were cold. I imagined I could feel them shaking. I steeled myself. Pete needed to grow up. He couldn't just go back to the pretty face with the blank checks whenever he was feeling poor. He had to build something real for himself.

I shrugged. "I don't know. I'm here. I'm not going anywhere. You're going to have to figure out what you're doing, and let me know."

I slid down from the picnic table, letting his icy fingers go. He looked after me, stricken. I knew what he was thinking: *why is she being so mean to me? Why isn't she making things better?*

Out loud, he said: "I shouldn't have lied to you about Amanda."

I shrugged again. Didn't he know the lie didn't really matter? The problem wasn't whose arena Pete was riding in. The problem was why Pete was drawn to that arena, and why he didn't feel like he could talk to me about it. And until he figured out who he wanted to be, what sort of horseman and what sort of partner and what sort of businessman, I couldn't absolve him of all his crimes, and he had committed too many to beg my forgiveness now. He was hard on his horse. He was weak under his owner. He was lying to me about work. He was withdrawing from our —yes, *our!*—students. If Pete wanted forgiveness for all of that, I was going to need to see some changes.

"Just do better," I said finally, and I left him there in the moonlight.

CHAPTER FIFTEEN

Nine o'clock in the morning, just an hour past feeding time, and the barn was a riot of laughter, a radio was blaring, and I was hiding in the office wondering if this was going to be my entire summer, and every summer, for the rest of my life. Was this how Laurie's first summer as a riding instructor began, I wondered? Had she put her head down on the fraying laminate of her desk, as I was doing now, and wondered why she had decided to open her life to children when she could be riding some rich woman's dressage horse in the hushed silence of an indoor arena?

A simpler life, I thought rather morosely. If there was such a thing when horses and horse-people were involved.

Life around the farm had been a little strained over the past few days. Pete had placed himself in the doghouse and had no intention of coming out on his own. I wasn't in the mood to accuse him of anything *or* forgive him for anything, so as far as I was concerned, he was just going to have to mope until he got tired of it or figured his life out.

Me? I had my own problems to work out, thanks.

I picked up my phone and scrolled through a list of event dates, looking for the secret sauce that would ramp up Dynamo's fancy footwork in the arena *and* get us a place in the Central Park Horse Show's arena eventing competition.

Because, *of course,* it wasn't as straightforward as simply qualifying, or sending in your entry with a check to cover fees. The Central Park Horse Show was more of a riding exhibition at a large cocktail party for the very rich than an actual horse show, even though the competitions were recognized by the FEI. Stabling was tight and the riding arena was tighter, and so to get your horse into this show, you had to have an invitation. For a shot at that big arena eventing check, I'd have to impress the head coach of the national eventing team, and I'd never even met Henry Folkes. It was possible he'd take an instant dislike to me; I wasn't unaware of my lack of charm. But I had to take that risk; I had to get myself and Dynamo in front of him, ride like the devil in cross-country and stadium jumping, and then manage to get a face-to-face with him, whether it was in a hospitality tent or at his barn down in Ocala.

Except, it was summer, and he would be up in Virginia or New York with all the lucky upper-level riders.

I groaned and flicked through the schedule again. There had to be *something* in the southeast which lured these snowbirds down during the summer.

"Jules? Jules!"

Pete was calling from somewhere in the distance, his voice sounding strained. I put down my pen and went into the barn aisle, looking around. Lacey was passing the office door with a wheelbarrow full of manure and a small parade of followers, all with their own heaping wheelbarrows. They were mucking out a stall each before morning lessons. She gestured with her head towards the far end of the barn aisle. "He's out in the arena," she said. "With Rogue."

Walking across the arena, I had to shield my eyes against the morning sun. June had arrived without fanfare and without rain, bringing more endless days of merciless sunlight and cloudless skies that burned out their azure hue by mid-afternoon, leaving a pale gasp of sickly blue until the yellow sunset took everything down in a final blaze of hellfire. I hadn't been making up climatology when I'd told Pete it would start raining in the first week of June— generally speaking, that *was* the rule—but we were three days in and no salvation had appeared in the sky yet. I was *this* close to writing a sternly worded letter to the National Weather Service.

"What's going on?" I shouted.

Pete, walking Rogue in the far corner of the ring, pointed downwards towards the horse's shoulders. "Can you watch him trot, please? I think he's off."

I watched Rogue trot around the arena, then circle and go in the other direction. "I don't see anything wrong."

"There's *something* wrong," Pete said, bringing him to a

halt. "I can't put my finger on it."

Rogue was sweating, dark patches showing through his light gray coat. "Maybe it's heat stress," I suggested. "That's a lot of sweat for this early in the morning."

"Do you mean the horse or me?" Pete joked. He kicked his feet clear of the stirrups and dismounted. "Whatever. He can get the day off."

I thought that was a solid plan, and granted Pete a smile for coming up with it. "Give him a few days off," I suggested as we walked back into the barn. "He looks tired."

"And so do I... right?" He leaned over and kissed my cheek, his helmet brim knocking my ball-cap askew.

I straightened my cap with a sigh. "You've looked tired ever since you got this horse into the barn," I said.

"I knew you'd say that."

"When are you going to start listening, then?"

Pete stopped, reining back Rogue, and looked at me intently. I paused a few steps away, out of kissing range—he had been trying to woo me with romantic gestures when he wasn't brooding, and I was a little over the constant contact —and his expression clouded. "What do you want me to do? Seriously, Jules. I want your advice. I'm just overwhelmed right now. Everything feels wrong."

I softened a little at the plea in his voice. "It's more simple than you're allowing yourself to see. You need to take a break, and you need to give all of your horses a break, too. Maybe not Regina, since you're just taking her on walks. That's fine. But everyone else? You need to pause and check all of your priorities. Make sure your plans mesh up with their best interests." Pete started to speak; I held up a hand. "Let me finish. We both have bills. We both have goals. And we've both pushed our horses too hard before. Let's get *better* at this, Pete. We keep throwing ourselves at brick walls. Let's find the lower parts, where we can just climb over, okay? Does that make sense?"

Pete gazed at me for a moment, his expression mutinous. Then his chin and lips loosened. "Yes," he said finally. "I need to take some time to think."

"Back to the drawing board," I replied with a wry smile, hands out in a helpless gesture: *horses, what can you do?* "I'm doing it with Dynamo's schedule right now, thanks to your bright idea about the arena eventing."

We started walking back to the barn, side by side, with Rogue huffing gently beside Pete. I watched them out of the corner of my eye; the way Rogue dropped his lips to play with Pete's fingers on the reins, the way Pete slid his hand along the horse's wet neck. They were still friends, I thought, and that was the most important part. If Rogue didn't resent Pete, despite all the hard days he'd been put through recently, and if Pete still thought Rogue was the best horse that ever horsed, well, then they could still make this partnership into something beautiful.

I'd like to think the same thing about the two of us, I thought.

In the barn, Lacey was overseeing the sweeping of the aisle. Jordan made a face as Rogue dragged sand from the arena down the aisle and into the wash-stall. "We just *cleaned* that," she said resentfully.

"Welcome to my world," I told her, picking up Rogue's halter. "An endless circle of messy aisles that I *just* cleaned up."

Finally, Pete walked away from the barn without looking drained or haunted. Maybe there wasn't a spring in his step yet, but he certainly looked more chipper than usual. I watched from the office window as he paused at the side door to slip off his riding boots, and let Marcus out, who was delighted to see him. After he gave Marcus a good back-scratch, the beagle elected to stay inside with the air conditioning and followed Pete right back inside.

Well, it looked as if he was listening to me for once. He'd have to call Rick, update him on a little summer holiday for Rogue, but hopefully this time Pete would take control of the conversation and tell the owner that his horse needed a break and his schedule needed an overhaul. That would be one problem down... at least for a little while.

The Rick problem wasn't going away, though. What a jerk that guy was! I went back to my calendar, jotting down the entry and closing dates for a promising jumper show at the end of July, but I couldn't stop thinking about him. Even if Pete got that man's ego under control for a few weeks, a person like Rick didn't just cede the power he'd grabbed in the first place. Pete had been right from the beginning of this mess: if Rick decided Rogue wasn't moving along fast enough to suit him, he'd cheerfully take the horse to someone else.

I thought about the bay Thoroughbred down at Amanda's, and the promise she'd made to hang onto him for awhile. Finding a new owner to buy into him had been the subject of a few late-night fantasies, but I hadn't really been serious when I'd told Lacey I might ask Rick to do it. Not serious, just feeling desperate—the way Pete had been feeling for the past couple of months. The hollow feeling that a great equine partnership was about to pass me by because I didn't have the finances in place to get him into my barn.

I sighed, blinking my way back into the present. My training calendar was filled with criss-crosses and new dates, the horses' names written next to the spots and divisions I thought right for them. Dynamo, Mickey, and Jim Dear: my little power trio. I looked at Jim Dear's name for a minute. I would miss the little nerd when he was gone. Once he was getting ribbons at Prelim, I was going to find a sweet little amateur who would keep him in carrots for the rest of life. Amateur horses: they'd been my bread and butter for years, and I'd be crazy to think that would change anytime soon. After Jim Dear went, I'd have to find another prospect for the sales stall—but it wouldn't be Confident Liar. Or *Con*, as I was starting to think of him. It was a cool name for a horse. "Go get Con," I'd tell Lindsay. "Let's take Con to the next event."

In the aisle, the laughter and shouts of the children

echoed off the rafters and cinder-block walls. Amateurs and kids, I thought. All of this work to stroke our egos and call ourselves champions, and what we're really doing with our days is building better lives for weekend warriors and bold children who are riding as much for fun as for ambition.

This thought was so deep and inspirational and saccharine that I closed my notebook and went out into the aisle, bellowing for quiet, and tacked up Mickey before I could get any sappier.

CHAPTER SIXTEEN

I had set the kids to cleaning tack for an hour, buying myself some quiet time in the air-conditioned cave of the house. Marcus was curled up against me, and my bare feet were tucked between the seat cushions of the couch. I was *very* cozy. It was almost possible to forget that I had to go back outside shortly and find something else to occupy all of those monsters.

Summer camp was two days old and I was already worn out.

Lacey came inside, the screen door banging behind her. Marcus looked up with interest. "No food," Lacey said, holding up her hands for inspection. "See? Jules, I'm going to pick up hay. Just came in to grab the truck keys. Want anything from the convenience store?"

"A Slurpee," I said dreamily. "A cherry Slurpee."

"If you get a Slurpee, everyone will want one."

"Can't you hide it?"

"Tell you what." Lacey grinned at me. "I'll run into Winn-Dixie and get a big case of Otter Pops."

"Genius," I sighed. "Lacey, my life was a sham before I met you."

"And a Slurpee for you," she added with a wink, before heading back out the door.

With no adults left in the barn, I knew I had to go back out and be responsible. Even if I was just two walls and twenty feet away, the potential for a child-inflicted barn disaster was exponentially higher than when I was somewhere under the same roof, keeping them out of dangerous experiments with the sheer force of my presence. Lindsay was still on her reliability kick, still showing off how she could control the herd whenever she thought I might notice, but I was pretty sure that if something went wrong and I wasn't in the barn, I'd be the one in trouble.

Meanwhile, Pete was at Amanda's—yes, I'd insisted he keep the job as long as he wanted it, there would be no blaming me for a negative bank balance—riding her Thoroughbreds before their show this weekend. *Our* show. I had Dynamo entered as well, part of his new arena eventing ramp-up. I'd never spent as much time with straight show jumping as Pete had, but this summer, I was going to become a dedicated speed demon in the jumping arena.

Marcus looked up at the screen door and made a gentle *whuff* sound that was his version of a scary bark. Marcus had ninety-nine problems but scaring away intruders was not one of them.

The screen door opened an inch. "Jules?" a small voice asked.

I sighed. "Jordan? What's wrong?"

"We just wanted to ask you about something we found in the tack room."

"Is it..." my mind scrolled through a lengthy list of unpleasant possibilities. "Is it *alive?*"

"What? No. It's a bridle. We just wondered what it was for."

My eyes widened. I sat up, and Marcus scrambled to his feet, ready for action. They'd found Pete's awful gag bit.

"So here's the thing," I began, once everyone was assembled around me in the tack room. "Professionals find themselves using some pretty strange-looking equipment sometimes. For one thing, we ride horses which aren't as quiet and well-trained as the ones you're used to. And on a big course, you sometimes need to get an answer to your request really fast, or someone's going to get hurt."

Julia looked conflicted. "But why wouldn't you just train your horse more?"

This was a good question. Fortunately, I had an answer. "Sometimes fit horses just don't listen," I explained. "They get carried away because they're so in shape, they think they can do anything."

"That's true," Ricky agreed, nodding solemnly. "I've seen Mickey take some flyers with you when you're out jumping."

There was a general air of amusement in the room as everyone considered the number of times Jules had looked ridiculous on horseback. Apparently, the total was more than I'd realized. "You've *all* seen me get bad spots with Mickey?"

Nods and grins.

"Great," I said. "Super. Anyway, this bit is called a gag. There's a cord here—see that?—and when you activate the reins, it tugs the cord and lifts the bit in the mouth—like this." I made an attempt to demonstrate but ended up knocking the bridle on the floor.

"Maybe we should try it on a horse. Just gently, but so we can see how it works," Jordan suggested.

"Oh, no," I said, a little too quickly. "I mean—you get the general idea. None of you will be riding with one anytime soon." I hung the bridle back up. "What else can I tell you about bits?" I was hoping they were done with the gag, and we could move on to subjects I was more comfortable with: French links, and loose-ring snaffles, my go-to tools of the trade.

"Whose bridle is that?" Julia wanted to know.

"It's Pete's," Lindsay said when I hesitated. "He jumps Rogue in it."

"Not still," I interjected. "He only used it once or twice. He used it at the event last weekend, for safety." I remembered when Julia and Tomeka had seen him use the gag in the warm-up arena and then decided that couldn't possibly be Pete out there.

"Oh, he's using it still," Lindsay corrected me. "I saw him use it a few days ago, before he decided to give him a couple of weeks off."

This was unwelcome news. I bit the inside of my cheek, unsure where to steer the conversation next. The bridle hung next to me, its obscenely large rings glinting gently under the tack room's overhead light. I felt a rush of anger towards it. I *hated* gags. Even more, I hated seeing horses in gags and martingales combined, being wrestled around a course of fences with a series of conflicting commands. It was one reason I'd never prioritized going to jumper shows. I didn't care for the tack I knew I'd see at them. If turning quickly for the next fence was that important, I'd find some other way to amuse myself.

"Pete won't be using this bridle anymore," I said finally, and took it off the hook. I waved my hand at Julia and Tomeka, indicating for them to hop off the tack trunk they'd been sitting on, and opened the lid. I lifted up a few packages of new standing wraps and dropped the bridle in, then put the wraps back on top.

"There," I said, closing the lid with a satisfying thud. "That's the end of that."

The kids looked back at me with round eyes. Lindsay smirked. "I thought harsh bits were only harmful with harsh hands," she said mockingly. "Are you saying Pete has bad hands?"

"That's a proverb people say to feel better about

themselves," I snapped. "If you have to ride with a threat in your hands, you're missing the point."

"The point of what?" Lindsay asked.

"Of everything," I said dramatically. "Of all of this work we're doing." I gestured around at the tack room, at the barn, at the horses, at the world. I knew I was going too far, but it felt like I'd already turned the corner and there was no going back. I was Jules Thornton, Crazy Person. That was just who I was now. "I mean, if you really think about it, none of this makes any sense. What's the point in teaching horses to jump things and trot with their heads down? What's the point in perfect transitions and round circles? Why are we out here in the middle of a hot summer day when we could be in an air-conditioned room, watching television or reading a book or taking a nap? What is the *point?*"

Even Lindsay looked alarmed now.

Lacey stepped through the door, arms full of popsicle boxes. "Otter Pops," she announced. "Come and get 'em!"

Heads swiveled. Lacey read the room. Her startled eyes met mine. "Jules, your Slurpee is in the truck. Go and get it."

I hesitated.

"Go and get it and drink *all* of it," Lacey insisted. "Now."

Once I was about halfway through the jumbo-sized Slurpee, enough sugar had hit my bloodstream to make me uncomfortably aware of my recent departure from sanity. I crept back into the tack room, ready to make amends, and found the whole group sucking down Otter Pops while Lacey told them the story of how Pete and I first met.

Lacey smiled at me over their heads and kept talking as I settled down on a tack trunk. "The thing was, Pete could have been the best rider in the world and Jules would have been angry at him," she explained. "Because Jules thought she'd never had a lick of good luck in her life, and she was ready to take it out on anyone who even *looked* like they'd had a better shot at the scholarship than her. And Pete definitely looked the part."

"You weren't even there," I interrupted. "I went alone."

"Now Jules," Lacey said happily, "did you come in here to interrupt story time?"

"I can't believe you didn't like Pete," Julia guffawed. "I would have been like, in love with him at first sight."

"That's what men want," I sighed. "And you should never, ever give a man what he wants. That's your first mistake."

"Well, I guess we'll finish this story later," Lacey said getting up. "It's time to feed afternoon hay. Let's go!"

The group clambered to their feet and crowded out the door, throwing away their plastic Otter Pop wrappers on the way. I picked up the wrappers that didn't make it into the trash can. "Sorry about earlier," I said to Lacey as she lingered, waiting for me.

"It's fine." Lacey stuck her head into the aisle to check on the kids' progress down the aisle. "Next time, don't skip breakfast."

"How did you know?" I said jokingly. "I meant to get something to eat when I went back inside earlier, but I was just so overwhelmed, I couldn't even manage to open the fridge. I just curled up on the couch instead."

Lacey frowned. "That doesn't sound like you. Maybe you're getting sick."

I didn't think I was catching anything, though. I didn't feel any symptoms of a cold or the flu... just a weight on my chest when I thought about my day, and how many things I had to wedge into it, and all of the kids that were my responsibility, all day long... my breath fluttered in my lungs.

"Oh, man," I sighed. "I think it's anxiety."

"Over what? Money?"

"No." I gestured to the barn aisle, where the din was rising in proportion to how long Lacey and I were staying in the tack room. "The kids."

Lacey put a hand on my shoulder and gave it a squeeze. "They don't want anything from you but your attention," she said. "You're the trainer! Remember how much you wanted your trainer to love you?"

I thought about Laurie, always busy, always brisk, but always the person I adored more fiercely than my own mother. I sought her approval constantly; getting a compliment on my riding or the barn chores I was laboring through on her behalf was worth more to me than gold, or good grades. Laurie had a barn full of students who paid money for her attention, but I worked for it, and every smile or kind word or expression of thanks I got from her made my position as the working student feel enviable, instead of pitiable. But more than that, everyone else in the barn loved Laurie, too. The seeds of my competitive streak had been sown when I'd realized that we were all vying for Laurie's attention.

I wondered if a similar competition was playing out amongst my barn kids. Probably so—I could already see the way Julia cast sidelong glances at Lindsay, five years her senior and probably everyone's clear pick for Jules's favorite. Melanie and Maisey were constantly eyeballing one another, especially in group lessons. And then there was Jordan, shy and awkward and on the sidelines, watching me carefully and always offering to take on the dirty jobs she thought I wouldn't want.

"You're right," I said slowly. "They're not waiting for me to slip up. They're too busy trying to be my favorite."

Lacey nodded. "Bingo. Now, how you deal with that? A whole other problem. But if you're worried about what they think of you, or how they're going to judge you when you don't amuse them every hour of every day during this so-called summer camp? Not an issue. They're just happy to be here."

Lacey ducked into the aisle, clapping her hands for attention and shouting instructions. I heard the hay stall door slide open, and the rumbling wheels of the hay wagon being fetched. Up and down the aisle, the horses recognized the sounds of impending snacks and began to nicker and neigh their pleasure.

I sucked the rest of my Slurpee dry and considered the tack room, the theater where I'd put on such a show today. I was taking things too seriously, I thought, putting away the saddle soap and sponges that had been left out from the tack-cleaning session earlier. We weren't on a curriculum here, there weren't going to be any quizzes or grades or medals for a summer camp well done. We were just going to take each day as it came, learning from each other... and from our mistakes.

I looked at the tack trunk where I'd hidden Pete's bridle. Should I take it out, put it back on its peg alongside the other bridles? Interfering with Pete's training system was probably not a great look. On the other hand, I'd made a stand today, for better or worse. I'd done some pretty vehement lecturing on the topic of gag bits. If I backed down, what kind of lesson was that?

When the barn's residents had all been hayed, I told the whole group to amuse themselves for an hour while the horses ate. "Then we'll go on a trail ride," I promised. "I'll show you where Pete and I do our conditioning gallops. There's shade and everything."

There was a general cheer.

Leaving Lacey to be the resident adult, I went back into the house, past Marcus wagging his tail from the couch, and into the kitchen. I took down the bread and the peanut butter and made myself a sandwich. I couldn't do any of this while I was hungry, I thought. And then I added a generous pile of chips.

CHAPTER SEVENTEEN

Thunder rumbled outside the barn, rattling the windows in their metal panes, but I didn't look up from the saddle I was soaping. Jordan did, her thin fingers quivering above her tack. "It's getting closer," she said, her voice a little tremulous.

I knew Jordan was timid, but I'd never expected a Florida girl to be nervous about thunderstorms. The rainy season had arrived at last, a full two weeks late but determined to make up for its tardiness, and for the past week we'd been having tumultuous late-afternoon storms that sent rivers of rainwater washing through the arena, cutting streams through the white sand footing and pooling around the depressions in the take-off and landing points around jumps. Just this morning, Lacey and I had dragged jumps around, resetting the course, in hopes of convincing the sand to resettle in its old resting spots... but, of course, it was more likely we'd just end up with twice as many ponds in the jumping ring.

Rain caused nonstop problems around a horse barn. Had I really been praying and wishing for the rainy season to strike? If so, I was second-guessing myself every day around three o'clock, when the gathering clouds turned black, the wind began to whip around the oak tree outside the barn, and the thunder began to interrupt conversations. Besides the ankle-deep puddles in the arena and around the pasture gates, the stall where we kept hay had decided to leak, and we'd had to do some emergency reorganizing to keep our stock of hay from molding. Bridles which were hung up damp from sweaty rides turned green overnight, and I was running the air conditioner full blast to try and suck out the moisture in the air, without seeing much in results. Thrush was popping up in several horses' hooves, and rain rot speckled the hindquarters of more than half the horses, even though they were turned out at night after the rains had passed. The very humidity was enough to cause bacteria to get into their skin and the soft parts of their hooves, and flourish there.

Then again, the days weren't nearly as hot. With clouds growing fluffier and spreading across the sky hour by hour, the sun's brutality was filtered somewhat, and temperatures that had been spiking into the nineties in May and June slipped down a few degrees. That was the main argument in favor of the rainy season: the natural shade provided by those thick cumulus clouds were the only thing that made a

Florida summer livable.

"It's just a regular old thunderstorm," I said, hoping to make Jordan feel a little better. "Must be three o'clock. Better than an alarm clock. Lacey will be coming back to do evening feed and stalls soon." And to punctuate my words, the storm outside made another deep growl.

"Finished," Jordan said, hanging up the bridle she'd been cleaning. It was my good jumping bridle, with a flashy figure-eight noseband and a puff of white sheepskin where the leather straps crossed. Jordan had buffed the leather and polished the brass fittings with the dedication of a country house butler. "I'll finish that saddle if you have something else you need to do," she offered.

I knew she was just looking for a reason to stay snug in the tack room, so I graciously allowed her to finish polishing my jumping saddle (the Rockwell Bros. Quickstream model, with a monoflap, thank you very much) and wandered into the barn aisle. Things were quiet: with the storm coming on, most of the kids had retreated into the boarder's tack room, where I'd installed a TV and a shelf of eventing DVDs I'd bought for cheap online, and they were eating pretzels while talking through a five-year-old installment of Badminton. I congratulated myself once again on the TV. Buying a babysitter for the kids you were babysitting? Brilliant, methinks. And bonus: they were learning. Earlier this afternoon I'd spent some time going over some rides from the London Olympics with them, and they seemed to have embraced the spirit of peanut gallery commentary. I paused outside the doorway to listen and heard some real gems.

"LEG, LEG, LEG OH GOD NOT ENOUGH LEG! She's down. Nice try. Not good enough." (This was from Ricky, who was internalizing my constant refrain of "more leg, more leg, more leg" nicely.)

"I wouldn't have taken the short route. That late in the course? Her horse's strides were already shortening. He needed more room to get up to that fence. I would have gone long, swapped leads right *there* and then bounce-bounce-bounce, kick, and over." (A thoughtful appraisal from Lindsay, who was fascinated by the technical courses at the five-star level.)

"I'm never doing Badminton." (Julia, sounding nervous.)

There was a flash of lightning outside, bright enough to make me blink, and a crash of thunder a few seconds later that made a few horses neigh in surprise. I recognized Jim Dear's high-pitched whinny and turned back down the aisle to the far end where my horses and Pete's were stalled. Mickey pushed over his stall guard to see me, hay trailing from his mouth. I gave him a quick rub on the forehead before continuing to Jim Dear, who was looking out at the wind-whipped pastures from his stall door, his expression nervous.

"What's up, buddy?" I asked him. "You're not afraid of storms."

Jim Dear glanced at me and then back outside. He whickered again, gently at first, and then neighed a loud trumpeting blast, like he was trying to get someone's attention. I turned to look out the barn aisle, over the pastures, and something white caught my eye.

I looked left and realized Rogue's stall was empty, as well as his halter peg. Someone had taken him out.

"What the *hell?*" I burst out. I didn't understand. Was Pete even here? On Thursday afternoons he went to Amanda's. I'd seen him leave. I'd told him to be careful. (Of the horses, and crazy drivers on the interstate, not of Amanda, who had apparently moved on from her obsession with Pete and immediately fallen into the arms of a six-foot-five Argentinian polo player, according to the photos in *Equine Scene*.)

He must have come back, I thought, watching the white horse moving quickly along the farthest fence line. I couldn't tell if Rogue had a rider—the ground between us undulated too much, and I couldn't get a clear look at him with one hill leading into the next—but it didn't look good. I slapped the back pocket of my shorts, looking for my phone to call Lacey—but there was nothing there. I must have left it in the office.

I ran down the aisle, my barn sneakers slapping on the concrete loudly enough to get the attention of Jordan and the group watching Badminton. Heads poked out of the tack rooms on either side of the aisle. "What's going on?" someone asked, maybe Lindsay.

"Do you know if Pete's here?" I asked, skidding into the office and snatching up my phone.

"He came back an hour ago," Jordan volunteered, having

followed me from the tack room.

"Where was I?" My fingers flew over my phone, texting Lacey to come back from High Springs as quickly as she could. I didn't know if Pete was hurt out in the field, but I wasn't taking any chances. I needed every hand on deck if this was a true emergency.

"You were watching the Olympics in the boarder tack room," Jordan said. "Remember?"

That's why I hadn't heard him come in. I'd closed the door to keep the hot air out, and everyone had been shouting and laughing through my commentary. "Did he take out Rogue?"

Jordan shook her head. "I don't know. I saw him and then like five minutes later I came in and watched with you guys. Then we went in to clean your saddle and bridle. I haven't been in the aisle at all."

"He must have," I said. A gust of wind seized the barn and shook the metal roof, rattling the gutters. A whirlwind of dust and shavings went spinning through the barn aisle, throwing sand into my eyes. I winced and rubbed at them. "Goddammit," I swore. "Why is there always a *storm?*"

I wished we had a Gator tractor like the one we'd had at Briar Hill. There was no fast way out into the furthest pasture, and with no road out there and no tractor to take me, I'd have to just run. I briefly considered getting on Dynamo, who was the horse most likely to keep his head in a crisis, but another flash of nearby lightning made me run right past his stall and straight out into the eerie light of the pre-storm wildness. Maybe I'd get hit by lightning, but I sure as hell wasn't risking Dynamo.

I skipped the metal gate—I had a horror of opening gates when there was lightning nearby, certain I'd be roasted with my fingers fused to the chain for eternity—and went straight for the pasture fence, climbing over it and jumping down on the other side. That's when I realized Jordan was running at my heels, her face white with terror under the yellowish light filtering through the thick clouds all around us. "Go back to the barn," I yelled as a fresh wind gust pummeled at our backs. "It's dangerous out here."

"You can't go alone," she insisted. "Look! He's coming up the hill now."

A long stretch of field and another fence remained between us, but Jordan was right: Rogue was coming this way, and coming fast. As we bolted towards him, I could finally make out his saddle, bridle, and trailing reins—there was no rider to be seen. "Fuck you, Rogue," I muttered between panting breaths. "You left him out there, coward."

"He's going to jump!" Jordan shrieked. "What if he catches his leg in the reins?"

There was nothing we could do; we were still too far away to change his mind. Rogue was coming at the three-board pasture fence at full tilt, his legs churning, his head high, his white mane whipping in the wind. Thunder rolled, making the air shudder around us and the ground tremble beneath us, but nothing was slowing that horse down. He balanced, gathered, jumped—and landed without issue, galloping towards us with his ears pricked.

"Do you want me to catch him?" Jordan called.

"No! Stay away from him!" I didn't trust that horse; in his current state of panic, it was just as likely he'd kick out at Jordan as it was he'd let her grab his reins and calm him. "He'll go back to the barn. He made it this far on his own."

The grass bowed before the wind like rolling waves on the ocean, standing up and flattening down again in constantly flowing ripples. There was lightning flashing every few seconds, or so it seemed, and the thunder was deafening. But it didn't rain. We climbed over the second fence and went skidding down the steep hill of the far pasture, looking everywhere for Pete.

Jordan spotted him, a little heap of blue and tan near the coop built in the fence between two pastures. "Of fucking course," I groaned, doubling my pace. I wasn't a runner and the stitch in my side was killing me, but there was no pain I wouldn't outrun for Pete.

He lifted his head as we approached. The yellow light was turning his face a ghastly shade, but even in the storm's glow, I could see that his complexion was pale beneath his tan. "Where does it hurt?" I gasped, sliding onto my knees beside him.

"Everywhere," he said shakily, his voice just a breath, and then he gestured towards his left leg. "Mostly there."

I looked—then glanced away quickly, forcing a smile that felt like it would crack my face in two. "Yeah," I agreed. "I can see why."

"Caught the fence," Pete sighed, a pause for breath after every other word. "With my leg."

Jordan was on the phone. "Yes, he's breathing," she was saying patiently. "Yes, he is conscious." I recognized the familiar patter of emergency dispatcher questioning.

"Where's Rogue?" Pete asked, concern creasing his face.

"Heading for the barn," I said. "Someone will catch him."

"The bridle," he said. "I found it."

I stared at Pete. "What are you talking about?"

"The *bridle*. You hid. I got it back."

It shouldn't have been possible to feel angry at this moment. I should only be concerned—*afraid*, even—but not angry. And yet here we were. "You put him back in that bit? After we *talked* about giving him a break? And after I buried it under all my pillow wraps—you went back out in it? Pete, what the fuck?"

Pete closed his eyes and I felt a momentary flutter of terror. It went nicely with the outrage, a bitter cocktail made of spite and fear. "Thought I knew."

"It's fine, Pete, it's fine," I made myself say. "It wasn't the bit. Your hands are quiet enough to ride in a gag. That's not what happened."

Pete opened his eyes and met mine with a startlingly clear gaze. I realized suddenly that the storm was passing by: the thunder was growing further away, the wind was dropping off, and the sickly yellow cast to his face had been replaced by what could only be a blush.

"That's what happened," he sighed.

***

The waiting room was filled with people who had been taken by surprise that afternoon. A tree trimmer who had stayed too long in the oak tree he'd been sculpting, until the wind swept him right out of its branches and down to the hard earth below. A young woman in shredded Spandex who had been riding her bicycle on the rail-to-trail route and lost control of her bike while swerving around a downed tree limb, winding up with some road rash she wouldn't forget in a hurry. A shell-shocked middle-aged man wearing socks and sandals, who had been in a house struck by lightning. I didn't know what exactly had brought him to the emergency room. Maybe he just wanted the scientific reassurance that he was still alive.

Pete had gone through the swinging ER doors on a gurney and disappeared deep within the bowels of the hospital hours ago, but I still sat in the emergency room waiting room as if I thought he was in triage for a sprain and would be out again shortly, eager to be out of the wheelchair they'd forced him to ride in and ready to grab some dinner on the way home.

Pete had gotten hurt before, but things weren't going to be that simple this time. I knew it, yet still I sat there. Waiting.

Lacey had taken Jordan home, and Lindsay had taken her place; then Lacey had come back after the barn chores were done for the night. "They'd done almost everything," she'd said as she'd settled into the plastic chair next to me. "You've got a wonderful bunch of kids, Jules. They'd do anything for you."

She was asleep now; her head was resting on my shoulder, her chestnut curls tumbling down my chest and arm. I couldn't feel my right arm anymore, but I didn't move. I was too thankful someone was there with me to risk waking her, reminding her that she could be anywhere but here, in this waiting room.

"Surgery tomorrow," the doctor finally told me. She said other things, reassuring things, then medical things with too many syllables, then more reassurances. I looked up at her, a crick in my neck; Lacey was still asleep on my shoulder. "But all in all, it's a straightforward break in a good place," she said finally. "I wouldn't be surprised if he wants to walk out of the hospital."

I started to cry, my shoulders shaking, and Lacey woke up then and thought the worst, and she wailed, and the doctor took a step back as if rethinking her excursion to the land of civilians, and the other people waiting for their turn swiveled their heads and touched their faces and covered their mouths, thinking there was a death. "It's okay, he'll be okay," I sobbed, swiping at Lacey, who had stood up and was advancing on the doctor crying, "what happened, what happened, what *happened?*"

Afterward, though?

I just felt angry.

CHAPTER EIGHTEEN

Our summer's plans were broken.

I got home from the hospital at two o'clock in the morning, nearly twelve hours since we'd first spotted Rogue running free beneath that storm-tossed sky, and all I wanted to do was fall face-first into my bed and go to sleep, but of course there was no possibility of that. Marcus came wagging to the door, relieved to see me at last, and I had to give him a very thorough cuddling on the couch. He'd eaten and gone outside for breaks, thanks to the barn kids, but he didn't like spending the night alone, and there was a lot of relieved whimpering and whining and licking to get through, before I could attend to the thoughts that had been rattling wildly around in my brain during that whole long, dark drive back from Gainesville.

Who was going to ride Pete's horses, who was going to show them, how long would he be out of commission... and could I get through the summer show plans we'd made without him?

My calendar was out in the barn, and it was all I could do not to go out into the night, open the desk drawer in the office, and take it out... as if going over all of those plans and dates was going to make a difference. As if there was a single thing I could do about it tonight—or this morning, depending on how literal I wanted to be about the clock.

Now Marcus wanted me to go to bed; he settled down alongside the bedroom doorway with his head on his paws and his saddest hound dog eyes fastened upon me, but he'd woken me up with his cuddling, and now my brain was racing. He was fully capable of going in and curling up on my bed himself, but he wasn't going to be satisfied until there was a warm body to curl up against. I went to the kitchen and rummaged in the fridge, looking for comfort food that might put me on the road to snoozeville, and Marcus sighed. He knew there wasn't anything good in there, or he'd have been right between my legs, checking with me.

In the end, I settled for wine. There was a bottle, gifted by the parents at the beginning of summer camp, perched on top of the fridge, and now I pulled it down, tugging off the hand-written note still tied to it with curling ribbon ("thank you for giving us all a summer vacation from our kids!") and tugged out the cork with a camp corkscrew we took to events. I settled back onto the couch with a coffee mug's worth of wine, because I didn't trust my tired fingers with a delicate wineglass, and attempted to drink away my problems.

The problems didn't go away, but the wine did manage to put me to sleep before I was down to the bottom of the coffee mug, so I supposed it was a win for everyone but Marcus, who had to settle for sleeping on the couch with me that night.

After the events of the past few days, Rick Delannoy was the last thing my week needed, but here we were.

Pete was home and settled in the living room with heaps of pillows and painkillers, Marcus curled by his side, by the time I'd gotten around to calling the ringmaster himself. Rogue was fine; he'd suffered nothing but a few scrapes from his incident, which apparently had been an attempted run-out from the coop, an over-correction from Pete which resulted in some rearing, a little movie-worthy drama courtesy of that gag bit and Rogue's lack of appreciation for what it did to his face, and finally a twisting leap over the coop which happened to whack Pete's leg into the fence-post on the way over. Had it been a regular fence-post maybe none of this would have happened, but it was the fat, telephone-pole style post used for corners and gates, and Pete's tibia did not appreciate the blow.

Metal rods are magical, though, and Pete really had been able to hobble a few steps on his own, between the wheelchair and the car—we'd taken Lacey's coupe, as there was no contemplating asking Pete to climb up into one of our trucks—and from the living room to the bathroom. This last detail was essential, as nothing kills the romance like having to take your broken man to the toilet. There was some physical therapy in his future, and lots of hopping around on crutches, but the doctor discharging him told us he'd be riding again in no time.

"No time" didn't actually mean within the next two to three months, of course, which was the time-frame that had me fidgeting with worry. It didn't even mean he'd definitely be in the saddle by autumn. But it did mean he'd be riding again in the nearish future, and that nothing was broken irrevocably, and that was something.

Since Pete was drowsy on painkillers and couldn't be trusted to construct full sentences yet, it fell to me to call Rick and give him the news. I sat at my desk, the office door closed to the sounds of kids wiping down stall bars in the aisle, and considered the best way to tell him Pete had come off Rogue and broken his tibia in the process. If I could make it sound like Rogue's fault, and as if Rick could be found liable should we decide their business relationship was not worth salvaging but a lawsuit might be worth chasing, that would probably be my best bet. Express anything even close to an apology for an accident involving his horse, and Rick would assume it was rider incompetence and pull the horse out of the barn. Even if he accepted that falls and injuries were part of the game, he would be likely to pull Rogue and hand him to another trainer. I had to be strategic, and make Rick think he was on the hook to keep *us* happy. And wouldn't that be nice if it were true? I'd like owners a lot more in that case.

It used to be that manipulation came rather easily to me, and I wasn't ashamed to admit that. But this afternoon, staring at my phone and willing myself to get the courage to pick it up and just make the damn call already, I wasn't feeling the spirit move me at all. I remembered calling Grace that day more than a month ago, and telling her I was afraid to ask the board for money. I felt the same way right now. Like I'd been left powerless. Like everything that had happened over the past few years had bulldozed my confidence, instead of building me up. Even though I could make a list of all of the things I'd succeeded at since I'd lost my farm, including taking Dynamo Advanced level for the first time, and successfully bringing a syndicate on board to buy Mickey for me, and selling some very nice horses for very nice price tags, there was still this awful, nagging fear keeping me from acting with the outrageous confidence I'd approached life with before. Everything I'd done from the day I'd left Laurie's and struck out on my own, had been because I'd believed in myself, even when everyone else told me I was crazy.

Now, people believed in me while I told myself I was crazy.

I left my phone on my desk and went into the barn. For a break, I told myself. I'd come back and call Rick in a few minutes. I just needed to walk up and down the barn, see the horses, make sure Lacey didn't need any help, the usual barn manager sort of thing.

The aisle was a hub of activity. Lacey had everyone running back and forth with sopping wet towels, running them up and down the stall bars to pull down dust. The floor was soaked, the kids were soaked, and the horses were hanging over their stall guards, hugely entertained. Lacey was sitting on a folding chair by the wash-stall, looking at her phone.

"I take it you don't need help with anything," I said, leaning on the wall next to her.

"Nope," Lacey said cheerfully, looking up from her phone. "You can't use me to get out of whatever it is you're avoiding."

"How did you know?"

"Lucky guess. You should have denied it, I would have believed you."

I looked up at the rafters. "Cobwebs," I observed.

"That's going to be a pressure-washer job," Lacey said. "Don't even ask me to do it. What are you avoiding?"

"Calling Rick. Telling him what happened. Getting him to let me ride Rogue."

"Don't ask, just tell him."

"What?"

Lacey stood up, pocketing her phone. She took me by the arms and gave me a little shake. "Snap out of it, Jules Thornton. You don't ask. You tell. You're going to call Rick and say, 'your horse dumped Pete and I'm taking over the ride until Pete's back on his feet, and by the way, it was a broken tibia, surgery went well, and we'll keep his training calendar in place exactly as it was agreed upon.' That's it. That's the call. You've done calls like that before. I've heard you."

"Why don't I feel like that person now?" I asked meekly.

Lacey shrugged. "You've gotten beat up a little, Jules."

In the end, I made the call from Mickey's stall, with my gray horse curiously exploring every button on my polo shirt while I was at it. I did it just as Lacey said to. Because if there was a person besides Pete who knew the real me, the confident, tough Jules I'd been until lately, it was Lacey. If she told me I was purple with pink spots, I'd believe her. If she told me I was brave and tough and could push around a rich guy with no boundaries, she was right.

Rick answered on the fifth ring, when I was starting to think voicemail was inevitable. "Yes?" His voice was impersonal; he didn't get calls from me, and it was likely he didn't recognize the number.

"Hello, Rick, this is Jules from Briar Hill Eventing," I said briskly, using the business name Pete and I still showed our personal horses under. "I'm just calling to let you know we're changing riders for the summer on your horse Rogue. Unfortunately, he gave Pete a nasty fall yesterday and Pete had surgery on his leg this morning. I'll be taking over the ride until Pete is ready to ride again—should be in time for fall eventing. We have a full show schedule for this summer that won't be affected." I stopped talking and took a breath.

Mickey ran his nose over my shoulder, tugged at my shirt collar, and blew hot hay-breath on my neck. "Can I answer any questions for you?" I asked, taking care to add a note of impatience to my voice. "I have a few moments before my next horse is tacked."

When Rick spoke, his voice was slightly dazed. "Where is Pete? Can I talk to him?"

"He's on quite a few painkillers at the moment," I said. "He's sleeping. I think it will be a few days before he's up to business calls."

"Right... and, I'm sorry, you said he fell off *Rogue?* It was my horse?"

"He was riding Rogue, that's correct. I didn't see it. They were out in the field." I didn't volunteer any explanations. The less said now, the less that could be used against us later. "The horse is fine," I added, since Rick didn't ask. "I gave him the day off, but I'll add him to my schedule tomorrow."

"Fine," Rick said finally. "Fine. Can you call me and tell me how the horse goes? Pete usually—"

"I don't think I can fit that into my schedule," I said, picking up my chin and smiling, as if Rick were standing in front of me and I was turning him down in person. "I do give my owners a weekly call. I'll put you down for Fridays at three-fifteen. I'm afraid that's my only spot at the moment."

"I—right," Rick agreed. "Three-fifteen. I'll put in my calendar."

"Talk soon, then," I said cheerfully. "Bye now!"

I ended the call without waiting for Rick's sign-off.

Mickey had gotten bored with my buttons and collar and had gone back to his hay. I wrapped my arms around his warm neck and gave him a squeeze so tight he took a step backward, lifting his big head in protest. "Did you hear that?" I asked him. "I put Rick in his place. He'll know that Jules is in charge now."

Lindsay poked her head into the stall. "Are we being intimidating to the patriarchy?"

"We are," I said happily.

"Good for us," Lindsay said, giving me a casual salute before walking on down the aisle. "Good for you."

CHAPTER NINETEEN

I decided to tell Amanda about Pete's accident in person. It was a nasty fall when all was said and done, and she cared about Pete. Picking up the phone was tempting, but I thought news like this should probably be delivered in person... plus, I could get a look at the bay horse again. Just to make sure the spark was still there, and he really was worth obsessing over.

I'd been riding Regina in the field, but now the rain was coming down in sheets outside, and everyone was holed up in the tack room with Lacey, who was telling them ghost stories about my spooky past. I'd walked by with Regina, having gotten back to the barn just as the first raindrops began to fall, and heard Lacey stage-whispering: "and who was there, to start a fight with everyone in sight?"

"JULES WAS THERE!" her audience shrieked, delighted.

"I should have left you in Pennsylvania," I called, and everyone laughed even harder.

"Whatever," I told Regina, leading her into the wash-stall. "We don't need them."

Regina, Pete's queenly liver chestnut mare, very pointedly looked away from me. Evidently, she considered the use of the word *we* to be going a little far for what we had together. Even if I had helped nurse her back to health after she nearly sliced her own hoof off, I was still just another barn servant to the queen. "You know you're basically mine for the summer," I told her as I stripped her tack. "So you might as well stop being so high and mighty with me."

Regina ducked her head and rubbed her face against her own knee.

Pete's disdainful mare was the only one of his horses who hadn't welcomed me onto their backs with good cheer. Barsuk and I were already good friends, since I'd competed him last year while Pete had been riding Dynamo. Rogue was a little uncertain of me, but I just took him out for a little getting-to-know-you flatwork session, and by the end of the forty-minute ride, I thought we were getting along pretty well. He wasn't a tough horse, he'd just been spoiled by incompetent riding at his former barn, and he was the sort of horse that took that kind of thing to heart.

Adding more riding onto my daily schedule had sounded daunting at first, but with Lacey here and the "summer camp" providing so many hands eager to get dirty with barn work, the first day, at least, wasn't going so badly. I'd managed to ride everyone before it stormed, and in the summer time, that was truly the pinnacle of success.

Back in the cool house after putting Regina away, I tiptoed through the kitchen and made a snack as quietly as possible. Pete was conked out in the bedroom, his sleep probably the result of some medicinal assistance, and I didn't want to bother him; last night he'd had a hard time getting comfortable and I wasn't sure how much sleep he'd actually gotten. Every time I woke up in the night, he'd turn his head and our eyes would meet. "Go to sleep," I'd whisper, as if he was staying awake on purpose, as if he had any say in the matter at all, and he'd nod woozily and close his eyes, but his breathing never slowed or evened.

Poor guy, I thought, climbing into my truck with a peanut butter and jelly sandwich in one hand. I'd never broken anything, and here he was with two broken bones in two years. He wasn't doing it because he enjoyed the sensation, I knew that much.

The pounding rain stretched along the interstate from Georgia to Lake Okeechobee, making the drive to Ocala slow going. It was a Thursday afternoon, which made it a prime day for long weekenders to head south on I-75, their sights set on Orlando and the theme parks. By the time I'd gotten off at Highway 326, a gateway to north Ocala's horse farms, my jaw was set and my molars were sore. I stopped at a gas station and picked up some chips and Diet Coke to get things in working order again.

Amanda would have been expecting Pete to have arrived by three, and so when I strolled into her barn a little after that, she came out of the office looking expectant, as if she'd prepared a speech on tardiness. She stopped short when she saw me in the aisle, and I watched her compose herself, switching gears. "Jules," she said finally, mustering her usual, dazzling model's smile. "This is a surprise!"

"Sorry I didn't call," I said. "I had some news about Pete I wanted to give you in person."

She paled. I had to give Amanda credit, she could work a shocked white face with the best Gothic heroines. "Is he —okay?"

"He's fine," I said automatically. "I mean—he'll be fine. He had an accident yesterday, broke his tibia... he's going to be laid-up through September or so."

"Oh, my god." Amanda turned and walked back to the office, disappearing through the doorway. When she didn't return right away, I followed her and found her sitting behind her desk, looking at the calendar blotter on top of it with a blank stare.

"I swear he's okay," I said, sitting down in the chair across from the desk. It was a plush chair, with a deep foam cushion; I couldn't help but notice how different it was from the rattling metal folding chairs we had back at home. Maybe in next year's budget, I'd request an office makeover. It would be nice to entertain clients in surroundings that didn't look as if they'd been salvaged from a decommissioned military base. A lifetime ago, when

Amanda had still been the hunter trainer who sometimes came over to Briar Hill to ride a sales horse for Pete, she had told me once that the posh surroundings of her barn drove her prices up by at least twenty percent. The horses, the training programs, the lessons: all of it cost her clients more than the market rate because they enjoyed the luxury, not because it was a better product—and what was more, they were happy to pay the premium.

"Who did he come off of?" Amanda asked, still looking at the calendar. Like my daybook back in my office, the dates were filled with notes and reminders: farrier visits, vet appointments, jumping schools, massage sessions. We had so much in common when you came down to it. Take away the chandeliers and the custom stall fronts, and our lives were very similar.

"Rogue," I said. "Jumping out in the field. There was a storm—"

"I *hate* that fucking horse," Amanda said bitterly. "I knew he was going to do something like this. I told him. I told him before he bought him that the horse was a maniac."

I managed to hide my response, but inside I was screaming. *Before he bought him?* Pete had gotten Rick to buy Rogue back in April—that was two months before he'd started riding Amanda's horses. How long had he been back in touch with Amanda? I'd never asked him how this little business relationship had come to be, preferring to avoid any additional drama in my life—and, more recently, pacified by the knowledge of Amanda's very gorgeous polo-player

219

boyfriend. She didn't need to chase Pete now... and if Pete hadn't been chasing her before, there was certainly no incentive to, now. Not when we had our own place, and everything was going so well...

Except, a little voice whispered deep inside my most treacherous brain, *except that everything hasn't been going so well for Pete.*

"When?" I asked suddenly, unable to stop myself. My voice was cold, my thoughts suddenly crisp and clear. I was getting to the bottom of this *right now.* "When did you tell him not to buy Rogue?"

"Oh," Amanda waved a hand thoughtlessly; she was still looking at her calendar, but now her eyes were shifting as she ticked through dates in her mind, thinking no doubt of the wreck of her training schedule. "It was when he was riding him for Penny Lane. I sold them a few horses and I was there checking on them before the trial period was up. Must have been... March?"

"You just... ran into him there? You didn't plan to meet him there or anything?"

Amanda looked up at me. Her brow creased. "Jules. Of course I didn't."

I refused to give an inch. "Honestly, Amanda, I just find it odd that you two keep ending up in the same barns. You can say Ocala's a small town all you want, but we're not even in Ocala... and neither is Penny Lane. Forgive me for thinking it's odd that you're all the way up in Alachua County when there are ten thousand barns within five miles of you here."

"Well," Amanda said. "At least you're being honest now."

"Now?" What the hell was that supposed to mean?

"You came down here to see that horse and found out Pete was lying to you. But then you didn't raise hell over it. You just brushed it off. And I know you didn't give Pete any trouble about it, either. Trust me, he would have quit if you'd told him to. He listens to everything you say, Jules. You've got him by the balls, so tell me, why did you just lay low this time? It's not like you." Amanda's earlier shock had slid away entirely, and now a knowing smile played across her face. "This little play... it's all been about Darcy. You want to keep me sweet as long as I have that horse in my barn."

I stiffened my spine to keep from shifting under her gaze. "This is not about Dar—about that horse. I don't suspect Pete of anything. It's *you* I don't trust."

"Oh really?" Amanda stood up. "Well, why don't you get the fuck out of my barn, if you think I'm here to steal your man? Why don't you tell me what a home wrecker I am? I know why, Jules, and he's in stall six, and guess what—he's officially for sale to *whoever fucking wants him.*"

I thought of Confident Liar and my insides twisted with longing. I *loved* that horse. *I* was the one who fucking wanted him. "I'll buy him," I said, not rising from my chair. I folded my hands in my lap, pretending I wasn't bothered by the turn the conversation had taken. "I'll find the money." As if it was that simple for people like me. As if we could snap our fingers and make investors appear, the way the Amandas of the world could.

Amanda stayed standing, her eyes narrowed, a flush creeping up her porcelain cheeks. "Forget the horse for a minute. Let's be real about this. You never let Pete out of your sight, until you might get something out of it. You don't want to let him near me, but I dangle a prospect you like in front of your nose and you're ready to hand him over. What does he see in you, Jules Thornton? You're a grasping, ambitious witch. Sooner or later he'll find out the truth. And it's too late for *us*, so don't think I'm going to be there to pick up the pieces." She flashed a hand at me, and the sparkle on her slim finger gave away a diamond so large I was surprised I hadn't seen it the moment I walked into the barn—or drove onto the property. "Does *this* convince you there was never anything going on?"

It did. It convinced me. At her heart, Amanda was a small-town girl with all-American aspirations. She wanted a house with gingham curtains (albeit a very large house, with designer gingham curtains) and someone to admire her all the time. Pete, with his laser-focus on his horses and his distracted manner out of the saddle, would never have made her happy... and she'd probably figured that out long before I made the connection.

The anger seeped out of me, leaving me too deflated to shout back at her. Sure, she'd called me names, but what about them? They were all true. I stood up and met her eyes across the desk. "I'm sorry," I said, and it cost me, physically drained me, to say it.

Amanda just shook her head. "It doesn't matter if you apologize to me," she said. "You're nothing to me, and I'm nothing to you if you're not jealous of me. It matters that you're ruining Pete's life. You dragged him out to the middle of nowhere. You try to get him to teach a bunch of beginner kids. You get in his way with the horses he's training—I know you undermined him with Rogue, so don't look surprised—"

"But you *just said* you told him not to buy Rogue, that the horse was dangerous." This was too unjust not to be pointed out. If Amanda thought I was ruining Pete's life, fine. I had other opinions. But she wasn't about to contradict herself when she was busy accusing me of crimes I hadn't committed.

"I did," Amanda agreed. "I don't think that horse respects people at all, and he'll do whatever he thinks he needs to do to get his way. But Jules, at least I didn't *hide his bridle.*"

I felt winded, as if Amanda had punched me in the gut. She might as well have. She'd just let on that Pete had talked to her about me, that Pete had shared his frustrations with her... but not with me.

"It's time for you to get going," Amanda said. "Call me if you find the money for Darcy. I might turn him out for another month, so he can get his head on straight. But then he's going. Maybe I'll call Rick Delannoy, see if he wants another horse."

"Do it," I spat, turning for the door. "I'm riding Pete's horses while he's out. So I'll just make sure I keep that ride for myself."

Amanda's furious expression was deeply satisfying.

CHAPTER TWENTY

Stay busy enough, and there isn't time to worry. That was what I told myself every time I slowed down that summer.

Put my head up long enough to look around, and I might have seen that things were constantly on the edge of a precipice. I might have seen that Lacey was the only thing standing between me and a colossal loss of control, as I juggled responsibility for schooling my horses and Pete's, for riding lessons and the daily tomfoolery that was summer camp, and the horse shows we'd scheduled every other weekend throughout June and July. Pete stayed inside most of the day, engaged in something intense on his laptop—as best as I could tell, he was working on a website, something we'd never had time to put too much thought into. There was a lot of typing, anyway. I wasn't inside often enough to see what he was up to, and I knew that I couldn't stand having someone looking over my shoulder when I was typing, so I afforded the same courtesy to Pete, and stayed out of the office when I heard his fingers playing across the keyboard.

Still, I thought, he might tell me what he's doing without being so secretive about it. Then, I'd squash the thought, and put myself back on horse thoughts only. Hold Mickey for the farrier, schedule a bodywork treatment for all of the upper-level horses, get Rogue's teeth checked again to make sure there was nothing going on in there that had caused his spaz attacks. And lessons, lessons, lessons, lessons.

There were so many lessons, so many children all around me, all of them with questions about their horses, and questions about their dressage tests, and questions about their tack, and questions about what I thought seventh grade would be like, and questions about the merits of carrots and apples versus fancy equine cupcakes someone had found on Instagram, and questions about going barefoot or going bridleless or going without a flash noseband. The interrogation was nonstop. I just kept answering their questions, assuming I'd reach the bottom of their curiosity someday, and on that day, maybe I'd allow myself to think about something besides the barn and the horses and the students.

That day did not come.

It was a hot, wet summer once the rains finally started, in the middle of June. The weather gods seemed determined to make up for their tardy arrival. The pastures turned to mud first, then the arenas. Water dripped around the nails in the roof and pooled around the gravel at each end of the barn. We rode early or we rode late; it was folly to make any exceptions. The storms crashed around the farm around two o'clock nearly every day, and dumped inches and inches of rain until past four, then they moved away and the clouds slowly parted, while we hustled to ride the rest of the horses before the sun could zap us with her final, dying rays before sunset. If there was a show coming and the weather had been particularly uncooperative, we even rode after sunset, the arena lights flipped on, past nine o'clock at night. The parents leaned against their cars, slapping at mosquitoes as they sat glumly at the picnic tables outside the barn, or they stayed in their cars, listening to talk radio and typing on their laptops, waiting with grim resignation for us to finish feeding our obsessions.

Fortunately, the horse show gods paid us back for our hard labors. At the jumper shows we went to, the ribbons piled up around the trailers, and kids began to string double, then triple rows of baling twine on their horse's stall fronts, necessary to hang the dozens of ribbons they were bringing home. When Lindsay put up a fourth strand of twine, I had to put my foot down. "Your poor horse won't be able to see out of his stall," I told her. "Time to take some ribbons home."

The fathers were browbeaten into making ribbon boxes and rails for their children's bedrooms; eventually, Mike, the woodworking dad in our midst, was prevailed upon to build them in his garage workshop. Ironed free of their wrinkles and scrubbed clean of their fly spots, the ribbons were gathered up and pressed behind glass in pretty shadowboxes, although the latest rosettes were always left on the stall bars, to flutter in the afternoon breeze and trumpet their owner's success, for at least a week or two.

Dynamo's show jumping game became tighter and cleaner than ever, as did mine. Pete was prevailed upon to come outside and give me lessons, and he put us through agonizing gymnastics and pointed us at tiny arrow-shaped corners, poles leaning on top of the uppermost fence rail to force us into perfect take-off spots. I hated corners, but they were the modern course designer's darling, especially in arena eventing, so they couldn't be shirked.

That arena eventing spot in September was still my goal for Dynamo, and the big check looked closer than ever as summer ticked by—if I could find Henry Folkes and convince him to put me on the team.

By August I was dying for a proper event, even though the weather was no closer to bearable than it had been in July, and I packed the trailer full for the early season opener at Sunshine State Horse Park. It was the perfect place to bring my horses, and Pete's, back out after the two-month break since May Days. We all knew the permanent fences, and most of the temporary ones, at Sunshine State.

The students were elated—perhaps a little too elated. Lindsay, Jordan, Julia, Tomeka, Maisey, and Melanie all elected to go as well. It took me nearly two hours to sort out all of the entries. I looked at my printed confirmations with more dismay than pride. Six students, and five horses of my own to ride.

"I can't do this," I told Pete.

He looked up from his laptop. He'd been on the sofa, his injured leg propped up on an ottoman, and Marcus curled at his side like a spotted fox, when I came in from the barn office. The wind had just picked up ahead of the afternoon storm, and a few raindrops smacked the living room windows. He closed the laptop and gave me his best reassuring smile. "Of course you can do this," he said. "You can do anything. You've proven that over and over again."

This sounded rather banal, sure, but it was also pretty close to the truth. I accepted the compliment and sat down alongside Marcus, running a hand over the beagle's back as he stretched and sighed. "Six students and five horses is... five students and four horses too many for this event. I need to concentrate on Dynamo this time around. I have to get Henry Folkes to notice us."

"The best way to do that would be to win," Pete said helpfully. "Can you do that?"

"Probably. It's Sunshine State, where the course is flat as a pancake," I mused. "We have that on our side—there won't be any fitness issues out there, if the May Days hills really were the biggest problem."

"His jumping is as tight as it's ever been," Pete added. "I think you have a definite shot at winning."

"It's *Advanced*, though." I sighed, considering the competition. "Even if Dynamo's the best he's ever going to be, so are all of the other horses."

"That's the problem with being at the top of your sport," Pete said, grinning.

True, but not helpful. "Maybe a lot of folks will still be up north?" I was grasping at straws. Sunshine State's August trials was so early, it was stretching the truth to even call it part of the Florida winter season.

"Oh, definitely. That's actually a great point." Pete leaned back into the cushions, considering. "Now that I think about it, this is really the perfect spot for you to get out there and get his attention. If he comes."

Somehow, this made things both better and worse. I wanted to show this Folkes guy that I was worthy of consideration for the national eventing team programs *now*, not after the winter season when I'd be in his face for six months straight. Next year, Con would be long gone. I needed the big check now.

"You know," Pete said, "even if you don't win, if you have a good season, he'll definitely want you on the team next year."

I shook my head at Pete. "Next year? Pete. It's like you don't even know me."

Everyone at the barn was enlisted to help at the event, whether they were competing or not. With Pete and Lacey leaning over the couch and offering unsolicited suggestions, I typed up assignment cards for everyone and handed them out on Saturday morning, bright and early, before I took

Dynamo out to warm-up for dressage. A few students were assigned hay-net duty; Ricky had to check water buckets every hour, Ashlyn was assigned stall-picking duty, much to her chagrin. Within ten minutes, everyone had been assigned a job which would occupy them all weekend—and my only responsibilities would be to ride my horses and coach my students.

"That's still too much for you," Pete had admitted, looking over the ride times with me a few days before. "I'll take these three." And he pointed at Lindsay, Tomeka, and Jordan's names.

"You'll take them?" I repeated, hardly daring to believe it.

"Yes," Pete had said, as if his assistance had been an assured point I should not be questioning. "From now until Sunday night, consider them my problem. I'll give them lessons tomorrow morning."

Now I surveyed my junior crew from Dynamo's back, while Lindsay wiped my boots with a towel and Lacey straightened the bridle keepers, setting every leather strap just so.

"Are we ready?" I asked them.

There was a resounding, "*Yes!*"

The morning was hot, the sun filtered slightly by high clouds streaming in from a hurricane off the Atlantic coast. The storm had caused a lot of chatter amongst the eventing community, but I'd barely noticed its presence... I'd been so busy keeping my head down and working, working,

working. "The clouds are weird," I'd said to Pete this morning, and he'd told me about the storm, laughing as he did so.

Whatever the cause, the subtle shift in the sunlight was welcome, taking the edge off the vision-blurring extremities so typical of Floridian summer days. I had tried and failed to wear sunglasses while riding, and the ability to actually see the dressage letters above the blinding white sand of the arena was a considerable plus.

One by one, from Advanced to Novice, I put in my five dressage tests. Dynamo went first, putting in a remarkably steady round. I'd decided to go for consistency over brilliance, recognizing that the effort of getting a few breathtaking moments of impulsion and collection would be counterweighted by some less-than-thrilling moments of flatness. Dynamo wasn't exactly putting on a two-by-four impression after a very good canter pirouette, but he was still going to have to shake out of the movement before picking up the next one. I'd found that by riding him to a less exacting standard, I could get a solid, consistent test... and arguably, that was what dressage judges were really meant to want.

Mickey was a good boy, Barsuk an honest man, Jim Dear was a little bit of a dolt but ultimately got through it... and then there was Rogue.

I'd been riding Rogue for the past four weeks, after giving him a break to get his head back on straight. He was a strong horse, opinionated and aware of his own power, which I'd known from watching Pete ride him. I'd been a bit nervous about riding him, especially after Amanda had said she thought he was a problem horse, too.

But there are "lady's horses" in this world, and as competent and forgiving a rider as Pete was, I truly believed I'd found one in Rogue.

He wasn't interested in how strong I was, or what I could do with my upper body. He didn't respond to pressure on the bit, whether it was a double bridle or a French link snaffle. He was swayed entirely by leg and seat, and tiny changes in where my fingers manipulated the reins. He was a horse of extraordinary strength, moved only by extraordinary delicacy.

I don't know if men truly ride differently than women, but it seemed like there was a humility necessary to ride Rogue that many men, including Pete, might find difficult to summon.

Luckily, if there was one thing I had, it was light hands, and if there was another, it was a responsive seat. Once I'd figured out what Rogue was looking for, our relationship blossomed. So, on this scorching hot August morning, we trotted into the dressage arena together and put on what might well be considered the ride of my life. Which may not be saying a lot, since we were only competing at Novice level, but it wasn't about the complexity of the test. It was about the partnership. And we nailed it.

I rode the test alone; Pete was away at the warm-up ring with the three students he'd claimed, as well as my other little ducklings, helping them get their horses into something resembling a Novice frame. Lacey had gone back to the farm, to take care of all the horses who had stayed behind (and Marcus). The other students were kept busy at stabling with their assignments. I came out of the arena to a light patter of applause from some attentive Pony Clubbers and their friendly moms, and that was it.

It was a little anti-climactic.

But when it all came out on paper later, there'd be written evidence that Rogue and I had put in a truly memorable round. At least I'd have that.

Kaitlyn, who hadn't felt ready to bring her Thoroughbred, Martini, to his first event, was charged with collecting horses, and she appeared from the direction of stabling with a Gatorade in one hand and a halter and lead dangling from the other. I rode up to her and dismounted. "Hey girl," I said, taking the bottle of Gatorade as she slipped the halter over Rogue's head. "You missed my test."

"I had the time wrong," she said apologetically. "How was it?"

"Amazing," I said happily. "Absolutely amazing."

CHAPTER TWENTY-ONE

"You just have to hold yourself together a little while longer," I told the horse, watching his ears flick back and forth nervously. "Just a little longer, a nice easy gallop around the course, then it's back to your house for hay and a nap. Doesn't that sound nice?"

It sounded amazing to me, anyway. Rogue wobbled a little and I walked him around the starting box one more time, glancing anxiously at the starter, who was holding up his stopwatch with a dramatic air. "It's gotta be time," I said half-jokingly. He held up a finger in response—*almost.*

Then he dropped it. "Three, two—"

I gathered the reins to get Rogue ready to trot out of the box. The horse doubled up his neck in a coil, pressing his chin nearly to his chest, and I felt all of his energy sink behind me. "Oh no," I breathed. "That's not it. Easy, easy, easy." I remembered an old trick of Laurie's suddenly, something I hadn't done in years, and blew air through my closed lips, creating something akin to a raspberry, while I hummed a quick, upbeat note. The sound made Rogue's ears flip back around to me, attentive, and he let his neck uncoil a length or two, and I felt some of that volcanic energy ease out of his hindquarters. He immediately felt more like a horse, and less like a dragon, and that was all I needed as the starter said: "Go! Have a nice ride!"

What was it about that silly little raspberry noise? I pondered its efficient way of calming and centering Rogue as we trotted without incident out of the start box. A few strides out, I let him pick up a rolling canter, and focused his attention on the little flower box about ten strides away: the first fence on the Novice cross-country course.

I made the raspberry again a few strides out, then I sat gently in the saddle, half-halted to balance him, and let him find his place before the fence. Rogue was an experienced show jumper: he knew how to spot a distance, shorten and lengthen his strides, extend for a spread fence and bottle it all up for a vertical. He just got worked up too easily to *use* all that knowledge. All he needed from his rider was someone to keep him calm enough to think clearly.

Our only hiccup came in the tree-lined hollow where the water complex was nestled. A willow tree hung over the pool of water, and beside it was a small canoe-shaped log. We had to canter down into the water and jump out over the log, a little step-up of maybe two-six. Rogue continued to be astonished whenever he was presented with a water complex; the idea of getting his hooves wet *on purpose* was still confounding to an arena horse of his prowess, and we didn't have anything to practice on at the farm, relying instead on a few trips to our friend Haley Marsh's cross-country course. It had been a while since we'd schooled there, though. Maybe a little too long.

Rogue tiptoed into the water after hesitating for so long I was sure the jump judge was about to mark it as a refusal. Then he teetered over the edge of the water, staring in with his neck arched, like a duckling who wasn't quite ready to learn to swim even as his family floated away from him. Eventually, he splashed his way through the pool, but as the water grew knee-deep we were both confronted with the age-old problem everyone faces when you've entered a water complex too slowly: it's hard to build the impulsion you need to get out comfortably once you're already in the drink.

Now, *I* knew Rogue could have jumped out of the complex and over the log from a standstill. It would have been a big jump and it would have been uncomfortable, but it was possible. Rogue, however, was confronted with the idea that not only must he jump out of this impulsion-sucking water splashing around his knees, he must also jump *up* onto land *and* he must also clear this log that was *clearly* a boat as well. A boat! I could hear him thinking as we trotted slowly towards the edge of the complex. Who tells their horse to jump over a *boat?* He was utterly confounded.

I tried the lip-blowing trick, but there was no answer.

His ears never left their steady focus on that canoe, coming closer to us every second. I pushed my heels, with my nubby little Novice horse spurs, against his sides: no reaction, his stride was growing shorter and less enthused with every step. I looked rather desperately at the long racing whip I carried in my right hand. It was for last-ditch efforts, as I had yet to meet a horse who truly did better on course when given a spanking (possibly because I rode Thoroughbreds who were not wanting in the forward department). The stick was for big asks: *hey buddy, I know you're tired but I need you to jump this big, and jump it now.* It was for reminders, too, a quick wave through the air: *dude, we have talked about this and if you slow down in front of this fence I will be forced to give you a whack on the butt.*

The reminding function was one reason I carried a racing whip: the feathering of short leather tassels near the whip's head made a whizzing sound in the air. It was something to make a horse listen up and say *oh, gotcha, my bad, speeding up now boss,* without actually having to touch the horse with the whip.

The stick was the only possible way to get Rogue's attention now. The fence was only a handful of strides away, and he was looking at it like I was asking him to leap over Mount Rushmore without damaging a single hair on a single stone president's head.

I flipped the whip into standby position using the elastic I kept wrapped around my ring finger, wishing that I'd done this at least once before with Rogue.

The fence was just in front of us, he was sucking back, getting ready for refuse—

I swung the whip in a sweeping arc with my right hand, letting the leather feathers whistle past his ear and give him a little incentive to stop ignoring me and start moving forward *now*.

Thoroughbreds are used to a whip fanning alongside their neck. It's part of racing.

Warmbloods are... *less* used to this practice.

Astonished by the whistling feathers in his ear, Rogue *jumped*. Of course, the jump Rogue took was too soon, too big, and too dramatic... but on the plus side, it got us out of the water. On the negative side, I found myself thrown onto his neck, lost my right stirrup, and nearly tumbled over his shoulder when he took the opportunity to put his head down and buck. In the midst of all this I realized that we were galloping out of control up a hill, that I was half-off my horse without a realistic plan for getting back on him, that there was a crowd of people just ahead at a pretty picnic table jump set at the crest of the rise, and that everyone was going to see Jules Thornton fall off her boyfriend's horse... at *Novice* level.

When I say I died a thousand deaths in the next three strides, I am not joking. There is no metaphor extreme enough for the mortification I was facing if I didn't get back onto Rogue's saddle, feet properly home in the stirrups, reins sorted out and horse cantering at a regulation pace, before those cameras started clicking. I pushed and I pulled and I grunted and I cursed and by god it was ugly... but I got there. Once we'd finally emerged from the woods and were heading towards the hilltop fence, I was right where I was supposed to be, and so were all of my appendages, and Rogue's ears were pricked, ready for the next fence.

There were six more jumps on the course after that, all straightforward Novice questions, and by the time we cantered over the last one, a tidy little log decorated with dozens of those tiny birds florists put into floral arrangements, a sign announcing it was sponsored by Ricky's Tropical Birds of Ocala, both of us had managed to put the water complex incident behind us. I only hoped the jump judge and the handful of spectators hanging out down there hadn't been bothering to take video of me.

"We got the water complex on video!" Ricky screeched as I swung down from Rogue.

My legs were already shaky from five cross-country rides today and now they threatened to collapse under me entirely. "You got *what?*"

Kaitlyn was pulling Rogue's nosebands loose and giving him a squeeze of water from a sponge; she'd become a remarkably effective groom after catching five horses today. "Ricky topped off all the water buckets and then ran down to the water complex to take video. He said it would be the most exciting part of the course, just like Badminton." She took the reins and started to walk Rogue away. "He wasn't wrong," she said over her shoulder with a well-timed grin.

That little minx. I was going to have to watch Kaitlyn.

She was a dark horse, quiet and reserved around the others, but with all the makings of a future Lindsay.

I liked her.

I took off my helmet and accepted the Gatorade Ricky handed me. "Blue, my favorite," I joked, pouring about half of it down my throat.

"I like purple best," Ricky said thoughtfully. "But Maisey says that means I'm a monster."

"Maisey only likes lemonade flavor, you can't listen to her," I assured him. "Well, I have to get our team ready for cross-country in a few minutes, but first I'm going to sneak over to the concession tent and get a hot dog. Would you be able to head back and tell the riders to meet me at the warm-up ring in twenty minutes?"

Ricky nodded. "On it."

"Hey, Ricky?"

He turned back. "Yeah?"

"Keep the video to yourself for a little bit. We'll watch it together at home, figure out what went wrong and what could have been done differently. But I don't need anyone watching it before they go out for their round. Might make them nervous. Okay?"

Ricky nodded gravely. "Okay, no problem."

"Thank you."

I drank the rest of the Gatorade and watched Ricky head back across the field towards the stabling in the middle distance. He called out to Kaitlyn, and she circled Rogue until he caught up with her. Hopefully, he would tell her about the video embargo.

All I needed was Pete seeing footage of that... whatever that was. On my walk to the concessions, I considered a few different ways to steal Ricky's phone and delete the evidence. The only hard part would be getting past his password lock... should I just drop it in a water trough and pretend it had disappeared? How long were phones waterproof for, anyway? There had to be a time limit.

I found a picnic table shaded by the concession tent and tore into a grilled hot dog. I'd laden it with ketchup and mustard, pumped out of giant red and yellow vats alongside a fly-strewn collection of napkins and straws on a slowly collapsing folding table, and it didn't really resemble anything I should be eating while trying to stay clean and in skintight pants, but it was the first food I'd allowed myself since a pre-dawn granola bar, consumed a good eight hours ago, and the salt and sugar prickled like pop rocks on my tongue. It was all I could do not to moan with pleasure. A grilled hot dog, really! Sometimes it's better than a filet mignon. Not that I'd ever had one, at that point in my life.

"I've never seen anyone look happier about their lunch," a male voice said, deeply amused. I glanced up, startled, with a mouth full of hot dog, and saw a remarkably good-looking man looking my way. I regretted the move instantly and dropped my chin instantly, as I strongly suspected there was a splash of ketchup and mustard on my upper lip. I put down the hot dog and put a napkin to my face, realizing as I did so that my hands were smeared with dirt left behind after I peeled off my sweaty riding gloves. I was a mess.

Undeterred by my retreat into my napkin, the good-looking man grinned and sat down across from me, though at the opposite side of the picnic table, giving the impression he was just grabbing an empty seat rather than joining me for a meal. He had that weird internet familiarity I ran into so often at shows and events: a person I'd definitely seen in photos with friends but didn't actually know. He put down a paper bag from the concession stand in front of him.

"I don't eat at events until I'm done riding," I said after swallowing, a singularly heroic effort considering the size of the bite I'd taken. "I got off horse number five, and suddenly I was too hungry to bother being ladylike."

Grinning, the man reached into the bag and removed *three* hot dogs. "I eat more here than I eat anywhere else," he said. "After I'm done, that is. Is your day a wrap, then?"

"I still have six students to prep for BN," I said. "Well—three," I amended, remembering Pete was covering three of them for me. But we'd all be in the warm-up together. It was close enough to the truth, and it made me sound like a rock star. *Six* students! Hot damn! Look at Jules!

"So, Pete's helping out?" He took a chomp of hot dog that put my own monster bite to shame.

I studied him more closely: short blonde hair, tan face, blue eyes, strong nose and chin. He could have been any of two dozen different young men on the Florida circuit. "Do I know you?"

He swallowed, grinned, moved on to the next hot dog.

"You're Jules Thornton, so you're here with Pete Morrison. That was easy enough to figure out. Although I saw him earlier and he's on crutches, yeah?"

"Yeah... but I still don't know who *you* are," I said bluntly. Was this stranger danger? Maybe this guy was stalking me. It was pretty easy to stalk me since I repped Rockwell Bros. Saddlery on all of my social media channels and had to post what I was up to, what I was wearing, and where I was riding every day of the week. Plus, there was the slight media coverage that comes with being an upper-level event rider.

"No?" He shook his head and wiped his mouth with a napkin. His hands looked very strong, like Pete's. A man who rode, cleaned stalls, and stacked hay bales, all in a day's work, developed the kind of hands people want to sculpt— or, you know, do other things to. Women's hands, unfortunately, tended to respond to that kind of routine by getting stringy and ugly. I reflected once again on the intense unfairness of the human body.

"I'm Evan Folkes," he said, once he was convinced the evidence of the hot dog was gone. "I guess I'm new on the Florida circuit. But I knew Pete in the U.K."

Evan *Folkes!* Oh, shit, I thought, as the name sunk into my slow cerebellum. Oh, fuck. Oh, no. "You're Henry Folkes's son?" I asked, though in my gut I already knew it was true.

"That's right," Evan Folkes said, his grin slipping a little. "I was based in England and I didn't see any reason to come back to the sweat and the sunshine. But my dad isn't feeling so great, so I came back to look after him a little. Well, to look after the farm and the team, mostly. My dad doesn't like to be looked after."

"That's too bad—about your father," I amended. "I was hoping to meet him this weekend."

"Oh really?" Evan picked up his third hot dog and eyed it appreciatively. "Would you consider me the next best thing?" he asked mischievously.

I looked down at my empty paper plate, suddenly nervous and sweaty-palmed. Was Evan Folkes *flirting* with me? It certainly felt like it. I was probably just flattering myself, though. He'd opened with a joke about my boyfriend. I forced a smile and looked back at him. "I want a spot on the arena eventing team at the Central Park Horse Show," I said. "Can you make that happen for me?"

Evan had taken a bite of his hot dog and at this statement he actually started to choke. I watched cooly as he forced down the mouthful, coughed, and took a long pull from his soda. Once he had gotten his throat back under his control, he regarded me with what I thought was admiration. "Would you have asked my father that bluntly?"

"No," I said. "But you're not your father. You're the guy who sat down across from me without being asked, and then choked on a hot dog."

Evan's eyes sparkled. He had dimples, I noticed, which popped into his cheeks just before his grin reached full deployment. *It would be better*, I reminded myself, *if you did not see these things.*

"I like you, Jules Thornton," he said. "And it just so happens, the arena eventing team is entirely mine this year. Let's talk after this weekend is over."

CHAPTER TWENTY-TWO

Sunday was stadium jumping, and it was a very good day. Sure, I'd just spent the past six weeks taking the kids (and the horses) to evening jumper shows every other weekend, but that wasn't the only reason I felt insanely comfortable as I trotted each of my five horses into the arena for their rounds, and walked out patting them on the neck like they'd just won the Kentucky Derby.

I didn't want to admit it, even to myself, but the reason was Evan Folkes.

It started early Sunday morning, when I left the kids back at the stabling to handle our dozen or so horses under Pete's direction, and went to walk the Advanced course. Dynamo was handling like a Ferrari in the stadium phase these days, and I was walking broken lines and considering diagonal approaches to any number of fences when I felt a presence at my elbow and turned to find Evan, smiling in a way that brought his dimples very urgently to my attention.

I found myself desperately wanting to be his friend. Pete probably wouldn't love the idea, but Pete had been pretty out-of-bounds lately, anyway. "Come to offer me some advice?" I asked him, smiling back.

"Insider info." Evan winked. "I put some money on you, I want to make sure I get paid."

"I hope they gave you good odds." I didn't know a thing about betting, but this seemed like something reasonable to say.

"Very short," Evan replied mysteriously. "Almost as if they think you're a sure thing."

I blushed and turned my attention back to the jumps surrounding us. We looked at the fifth fence for a long moment. It was flower-bedecked vertical, with pink and blue poles set at max height. The fence stood alone against the far side of the arena and was approached by a left-hand turn from a wide oxer.

"You're going to cut this corner pretty hard, aren't you?" he asked, after a moment's contemplation.

"I am," I agreed. "I've been concentrating on my horse's stadium form all summer. Time to see if it's been worth my time."

"And why have you been doing that?" Evan smiled coyly.

"Didn't I already tell you I want to go to Central Park in September?" I decided against playing games. Any hint of being coy, and I would be flirting as well as trying to get his approval to go the arena eventing competition. The gossip would be awful, and word would surely get back to Pete, which would make things doubly embarrassing. And if I was dealing with a minor crush on this guy (and I was beginning to suspect this was the case), I'd better just stay out of those murky waters until I got over it. I tried to turn the conversation back to how much I loved jumping. "We've been show-jumping all summer. Tight turns and skinny fences are our new favorite things, until you mention broken lines, and then our hearts are *all* aflutter. We'll win this for fun today, based on this course."

"Such a cheap date," Evan sighed. "I'd have accepted a top-five finish, but here you are plying me with your accomplishments and promising me blue ribbons like some kind of hussy."

"A top-five finish?" I grinned. "You know we're in third right now, right? And there's no chance of a rail down unless the wind blows it right out of the cups. All we need is one mistake each from two horses—or two from one horse, I'm not picky."

As one, we both looked up at the cloudless morning sky, aware that a chance thunderstorm could blow out of nowhere and change everything. Florida was like that.

Evan leveled his gaze on mine, and I pushed my heart out of my throat with effort. He was just a man, I told myself, just a man with an influential father. His attractiveness was happenstance. He was not like Pete. *Pete* made me happy. Or... he had. Or... he would again. Things were confusing. What was Evan saying? Oh god, I was so flustered... "a top-five finish is all my father would ask for, I promise. I can get you onto the team if that's what you want, and if your stadium is as good as your dressage and cross-country have been so far."

"What?" I asked blankly. Had he really just told me I was as good as approved for the arena eventing team? That couldn't be right.

"Seriously?" He laughed. "Listen, take the broken line here. If you can get this distance, you can get anything they'll throw at you in Central Park. And over there—" he pointed at the combination of 8A and 8B, "take those *aggressively*. Because that height on 8B will really get you if you don't come in with all rockets firing. Right out of the arena corner, heading away from the in-gate? It's a total trap."

"I will," I agreed reverently, gazing at the fences, which were just a stride apart. The combination should have looked alarming to me, but after the shows we'd been competing in, and in the presence of the charismatic Evan, I felt like we could tackle anything. "Piece of cake," I felt compelled to add, and I liked this extra-confident Jules so much that I winked at Evan, just to see what he'd do.

His dimples deepened, and I felt a thrill of conquest— oh, he'd liked that, had he? I had plenty more where that came from... whatever that meant. Stop that, Jules, you're definitely going off the deep end. *Whatever that means.*

"Your horse takes a little putting-together, right?" Evan asked, warming to his subject. I nodded. "Okay, so approaching the sixth fence, try to get him all the way over to *here*—" and he planted his feet in the dirt several feet left of the fence's standards. "Approach from this angle and you'll have an extra stride to get him back on the bit so he's collected enough for that vertical's height."

"That's good," I agreed, measuring the distance with my eyes so I'd be able to hit it once I was in the saddle—a surprisingly difficult connection to make, from the ground to in the saddle—and seeing that I actually would get a full extra stride of ground before the fence. "You don't think I'll be up against the clock if I go this deep into the turn? Maybe that extra stride is too much, combined with a few others here and there."

"You can make this one up between eleven and twelve," Evan said, pointing across the arena. "Look at that. Easy six... but a *forward* five. And you'll come whizzing off twelve, sail right over that last oxer, and be through the flags half a second later. That's all you'll need. I think the time for this course is quite generous, actually."

"I'm still a little new to Advanced," I admitted, forgetting I was supposed to be impressing my vast experience upon him so that I'd be the obvious rookie addition to the arena team. "Dynamo isn't, though—he did it all last year with Pete."

"That's right," Evan said, looking interested. "You gave your ride to Pete. Handing over your big horse to your boyfriend to keep him afloat. That's very generous. Most women in this game wouldn't have done it."

I wanted to tell him it wasn't like that; we'd been hanging on for our lives, and Pete had needed an Advanced horse to keep the Rockwell Bros. sponsorship that had been supporting us with a stipend and tack—so much tack! But presenting myself as a martyr to the sport wasn't the story I wanted to campaign ahead of me, and if Evan had the power to lift me up from the *rising star* status I'd been granted forever ago, and level me up into *actual star*, then I would take that rise without sharing my baggage, thank you very much. It was easier to rise up when you weren't hoisting the disasters of the past along with you.

"It was worth it," I said instead, and left Evan to decide what part of lending my good horse to my boyfriend had been worth it.

We were leaving the arena together when I spotted Pete leaning against the fence. The crutches under his arms were sagging, not bearing his weight; I knew he found them tiresome and they hurt him after a short while, especially while crossing the rough ground here, and he had been finding places to rest every chance he got. He caught my eye, and then his gaze rested momentarily on Evan. His left eyebrow lifted, that old trick of his expression which told me I'd been found out even when I hadn't realized I'd been hiding something.

"I'd better go and see if Pete needs anything," I said hastily. Then, remembering that Evan had said they'd been friends in England, I asked if he wanted to come over and say hello. "I'm sure he has a minute."

"No, no," Evan said, waving me on. "I have to go and meet an owner for coffee first. We'll talk soon."

I hustled over to Pete, who was letting his eyes flick lazily from me to Evan, and back again. "You're over here early," I said, realizing too late that it sounded like I'd been hoping to avoid him.

"I thought you'd want me to walk the course with you," Pete said. "But I see Evan was here to fill in for me."

"I just ran into him out there. I met him yesterday," I said quickly. "At lunch. He has pull with his father; he says he can help me get on the team for Central Park if I can pull off a good finish here. And, I mean—we're sitting in third. I have a shot."

"I know you are," Pete said. "That's why I thought you might want me to walk the course with you. Because you have a shot."

Shit, I thought. Pete was jealous of Evan. I did not have time for Pete's emotions, on top of everything else. Couldn't he just tamp them down, like I did? Didn't he realize that if I spent as much time *feeling* things as he did, I'd never get anything done? Honestly, men. I fought to keep my voice patient. "I know the crutches have been a lot this weekend," I explained, "and I was trying to keep you from having to drag them through all that sand in the arena."

Pete looked down at the crutches, and I saw a crease of exasperation slide into his forehead. "Maybe that's for the best," he said finally. "Thank you for thinking of me."

I wasn't fooled for a moment into believing he was fine

with my coursewalk with Evan. He didn't mean it, he was just *that* tired of schlepping around those crutches. But anyone would be, so I softened. I put a hand on his arm and squeezed. "We just need to get you healthy again, Pete. I think that means you have to take it a little easier, though. I appreciate your helping me with the students this weekend, but I think it's been a little rough on you."

He lifted his head and gave me a piercing look. "If I take it easier, *you* have to," he said. "Because let's face it, Jules, you can't handle every single thing you take on."

I clenched my jaw. What a thing to say to me, as I stood here in boots and breeches, white shirt covered safely by my dark blue polo shirt, just an hour away from taking my big horse over the Advanced stadium course. What a thing to say to me while my students hustled around back at the stabling area, taking care of all of the horses and making sure I didn't have to worry about a thing but riding. Pete was supposed to be back there this minute, keeping an eye on things! Why didn't he do what he'd said he would? Sure, Pete had taken on the warm-ups of three students yesterday, but I knew I could have dealt with them as well, if I'd had to! I hadn't *asked* him to school those students—that had been *his* choice! "I'm completely in control," I said stiffly, dropping my hand from his arm and taking a step back. "I appreciate your help, but why don't you take the rest of the day off? You're clearly not in any condition to be out here, and it's wearing you out. We can manage without you."

Pete looked as if I'd slapped him across the face. The

color drained from his cheeks, but his pupils dilated and his eyebrows came together in one angry line. His expression was the angry confusion of storm clouds overtaking a bright blue sky. "You have a lot of fucking nerve, Jules Thornton," he said, his voice low and taut. "I always knew that about you; I admired you for it. But that was just your ambition talking before. I don't know what this is."

He turned, gathering up his crutches beneath his arms, and started to push off. I felt my stomach lurch; I'd gone too far. I put a hand on his shoulder, felt it tense beneath my grip. "I'm sorry," I said. "That was wrong of me. I'm nervous, I'm not thinking straight. I took things the wrong way and got mad." I made all of my confessions in a rush, before I could stop and think about them, tell myself that I was justified, that I was right and Pete was wrong. I knew that's what I would do if I gave myself so much as a moment. That's the joy of knowing oneself, I suppose. "And I'm worried about you," I added lamely, knowing it would sound like an excuse, even though it was true.

Pete's words, when they finally came, were tense and measured, as if he was afraid to fumble them on the way from his brain to his lips. "You don't have any idea how much I do to keep you going," he said. "Even like this, even on crutches, I do everything I can to keep you from realizing how overpromised and overextended you are. Someday, you're going to thank me for it."

He couldn't have said anything worse to me. Because if Pete *believed* that, really believed his own malarkey, after the past few months of leaving me alone to struggle with the demands of the farm and students, then his entire view of our life together was warped... maybe permanently, I didn't know.

Later, I'd wonder if this was some sort of natural reaction to the abrupt turns Pete's life had taken since we'd gotten together. One day you're daydreaming about a girl who won't give you the time of day, the next you're hauling her out of her shattered barn and moving her into your guest house. A few months later, you're running a business side by side and then the walls come crashing down, one after another, faster and faster. That can't be a healthy progression for anyone to have to take, and add to it that Pete came from a privileged background, the grandson of a world champion rider, heir apparent to one of the sport's most beautiful farms—no one would have a good reaction to losing all of that.

But where I saw promise and hope in the chaos of Alachua Eventing Co-op, Pete seemed to see only how far he had fallen, and now, I suspected, he was choosing to blame his topple from the perceived wealth and power of Briar Hill upon me, the clueless girl he'd given up everything for. An appealing narrative, and one I was sure made him feel better about himself... but unfortunately, it just wasn't true.

"I've had this horse since I was sixteen," I told the reporter from *The Chronicle of the Horse,* stroking Dynamo's hot neck.

The huge blue rosette hanging from his bridle tickled my bare arms as it fluttered in the breeze; I'd taken off my coat and flung it to the closest reaching hands as soon as I'd dismounted after our round. That those hands were Evan's didn't register with me until afterward.

"He didn't put a foot wrong," the reporter remarked. "But the two horses ahead of you each missed the mark at the second fence in the combination. 8B, I think? You were the first one to come in with enough impulsion to get over that oxer. Very impressive!"

I remembered Evan describing 8B to me: *it's a total trap.* "It just looked like a question I'd answered already this summer," I told her. "We've been doing a lot of jumper classes to tighten up our stadium phase."

"Well, it definitely shows. And so you did all of this horse's work yourself, if you've had him since you were a teenager?"

"Yes, I did all of his training. The only other person who has ridden him is Pete, when he competed him last spring while his horse was recovering from an injury."

"Pete's your boyfriend, of course," the reporter confirmed, her teeth pressing against her smiling lips. "Pete Morrison, of Briar Hill Eventing."

"That's right," I agreed, curling my fingers into Dynamo's red braids. "Pete's my boyfriend."

CHAPTER TWENTY-THREE

Once Evan had given me back my jacket and told me he'd be calling in a few days, and I'd moved on to ride my other horses in their stadium jumping rounds and collected their ribbons—a red one for Mickey, a green one for Jim Dear, who got his act together and managed to leave all the rails up in stadium at last, a white one for Barsuk and a blue, yes a *blue!* for Rogue—I went down to the warm-up to find Pete and coach our little BN students before their rounds. There was a whipping wind rattling the poles in their cups, and a billow of white clouds with dark bellies in the west, signifying an oncoming summer storm and putting an extra spring in the steps of all the keyed-up horses in the ring.

In those clouds, I spotted an opportunity, and I called the entire crew over to clue them in on it.

"You've got a shot to beat the career beginners now, girls," I told them conspiratorially. "A change in weather means a change in horse. And if our ladies liked change, they'd have moved up to another level years ago. So can you embrace your horse's extra impulsion and excitement, and make it work for you?"

Pete looked at me like I was crazy. "What are the career beginners?" he asked. "What are you talking about?"

"You weren't there for that conversation," I sighed. "Katie Bergen, Lara Silverstein, Carol Potter. They take turns winning Beginner Novice. They've been doing the same division for years. Everyone here wants to beat them."

There was a silent chorus of solemn nods from the riders circled around us.

Pete shook his head. "I had no idea."

"You've never had beginner students before," I said with a shrug. "It's a whole new world down here."

"Hey!" Lindsay interjected. "I protest the use of the word 'beginner.' And also 'down.'"

"Save your anger for the ring," I told her. "Now let's go hop these ponies over those rattling rails before the wind knocks them over and the ground jury starts rethinking our ride times."

By the time my students were lined up near the in-gate, awaiting their ride times, distant rumbles of thunder were starting to roll across the flat landscape, and people were looking nervously at the sky. Parents were sidling up to trainers and pointing out the clouds, as if we professionals were somehow numbed to the approaching weather after so many days spent out in the elements, and wouldn't have noticed the impending doom from the skies. I supposed that to a certain extent, we were.

The stadium jumping was running in reverse order of placing, so the first rider out was the lowest placed rider after cross-country. It made for a more exciting final round if the person in first place managed to hold that position all the way through the flags. I was just happy the opening round was not one of my student, but the third person on course was my Melanie, whose first event had been a little difficult so far. She had dealt with two stops on cross-country, plus time faults after she lost a stirrup after a long spot, and lost some valuable time walking her horse while she tried to get situated again. Ares had been strong in each phase so far, tugging at her with his thick neck, and Melanie was a recovering hunt-seat poser, so her core strength was not yet what it should be. Now the wind was whipping his tail through his legs and he was flinging his head up and down, as Melanie, white-faced, gathered her reins to head into the ring. I caught her by the boot and walked alongside her, half-skipping to keep up with Ares's energetic pace. Foam from his bit spattered my breeches as he tossed his head.

"He knows how to get around a little course like this," I told her. "You just point and shoot, and keep at him in the bridle to keep his mind on the game, okay? Don't let him look around. When he puts up his head to stare, you give him a kick in the ribs, bend him to get his feet under control, and *make* him focus. Going fast won't hurt you, so don't be upset if he speeds up. You really do have this, Mel."

She was still stone-faced, but she glanced down at me and nodded, and I saw her chin set determinedly. Her fingers tightened on the reins. I let go of her boot and stepped back.

Oh, it was a fast round, all right. It was a watch-through-your-fingers kind of round at times. Every time Ares picked up his head to looky-loo at a plastic bag flying through the air on the storm's stiff winds or flicked his pricked ears at a group of people standing too close to the arena fence, Melanie gave him a kick, just as I'd told her. The inelegant solution kept him moving forward, and as long as he was moving forward, she could point him at any jump she chose and let him find his own way over it.

Despite similar reactions to the incoming weather and the overall strangeness of the weekend compared to their usual horse show experiences, Jordan, Julia, Tomeka and Maisey all followed similar strategies as their horses went in with their heads and tails high, and their capacity for tomfoolery even higher.

Then, as the first flicks of cool rain spattered against my cheeks, Lindsay went in on her old campaigner, William. He wasn't bothered by rain or wind, William. He wasn't fussed by thunder or crowds, William. And neither was Lindsay. As my oldest student, Lindsay was a double-edged sword to me. She was accomplished and responsible and capable of advancing far more quickly than my younger students. But unless I made a move to keep her, she would be gone far too soon, almost certainly swept away to college by ambitious parents with deep pockets who wouldn't want to hear the words, "working student" or "professional trainer" uttered anywhere near her.

But when I watched her now, putting in a picture-perfect stadium jumping course with a horse who had no notion of spooking or playing the weather for kicks, I thought that come next spring, I might have to risk her parents' wrath and say those magic words. Maybe sooner than that.

"She's good," Pete said softly.

"She's a star," I said. And then: "Pete, your cast is going to get wet."

"It's not really raining yet."

I looked up at the sky as William made his final canter circle and Lindsay tossed a polite nod to the judge's stand, her face glowing with a smile after their clear round. The ruffled front edge of the storm cloud was rippling and splitting overhead, light fighting dark, as an Atlantic sea breeze pushed back against its eastern march. The sea breeze would buy us a little time, but also fuel a storm even stronger in the end, one that lasted for hours. That was the risk of August horse shows; the storms this time of year could turn into epic four or five-hour events, as the ultra-warm land and the humid sea breeze clashed in pitched battles over the center of the peninsula, precisely where we were all just trying to ride our horses without dying.

"When it does rain, it's really going to turn to mud out here," I said. "Let me go find you a golf cart ride back, just to be on deck, okay?"

Lindsay was walking William out of the ring, her face triumphant. I put a hand out and touched her foot as she rode past, and she gave me an exhilarated smile. *She's hooked,* I thought, remembering the burned-out show rider I'd met last winter. The Alachua Eventing Co-op had been formed by parents who had seen relentless horse showing suck the joy out of riding for their children. Now, despite the impending storm, I could see the same thrilled happiness on all of their faces.

Then thunder rumbled, louder and stronger now, and I came back to reality with a thump. Lindsay was definitely in first place now, with just the career beginners still to go, but I didn't have time to stay and watch them—I had to go and find Pete a golf cart before the heavens opened up.

The ring steward was gesturing for Carol Potter into the arena on her bay pinto gelding, but his eyes were flicking back and forth between the clouds overhead and the crush of horses still crowded around the arena. There was a lot of nervous movement amongst the spectators, riders, and ground crew alike. With only three riders to go, the ground jury wasn't about to abandon the stadium jumping phase because of weather—but the thunder was growing louder and the lightning more brilliant, and pretty soon insurance rules alone would dictate that everyone would be told to seek shelter. And when that happened, golf cart rides would be impossible to come by.

I pushed through the little crowd by the in-gate and

found Evan leaning against, of all that was holy, an empty golf cart. He grinned at me. "You looking for a ride outta here?"

"I'm praying for a victory gallop first," I said.

There was a *thunk* from the arena and a sigh from the crowd.

"You just got one pole closer to it," Evan smiled. "Fingers crossed."

"I do want a ride for Pete, though. Could you get him back to the stabling area? I'm afraid if it rains he'll get his cast soaked through."

"Or just sink into the mud," Evan said. "Of course! Anything for Pete. I'd been hoping we would catch up this weekend, but he's been elusive. Every time I think I've caught his eye, he disappears again."

"Crazy," I hedged. "Thank you. I really appreciate it. He's at the in-gate."

Thunk. Sigh.

"Another pole closer." Evan stood to one side. "You can see from right here," he said, gesturing to the open spot he'd made in front of his golf cart. "No one in front of me here."

I hesitated, looked back towards the in-gate; but Pete was invisible below the backs of so many horses clustered in the pathway. "Thanks," I said, pushing in next to Evan.

The space he'd made for me was smaller than I had realized; though there was no one in front of his golf cart, there were plenty of spectators to either side, and I found myself pushed right up against him. I wished for the jacket

I'd discarded back at the stables; I was still wearing my sleeveless show shirt, but now there was a chilly breeze rushing down from the storm, and my bare skin was pressed against the muscles of his upper arm with a suggestive prickle of arousal I hadn't had any intention of feeling. I tried to sidle away, and failing that, to hold myself so rigidly our arms would barely touch, in no mood to fall into some rabbit-hole of sexual attraction when I was trying to get, and keep, my life in order.

In the arena, a disappointed Carol Potter had ridden out with eight faults, and Lara Silverstein was cantering a highly suspicious chestnut gelding towards a panel fence which was swaying a little with every gust of wind. A mammoth blast of cold air struck the panel and set it swinging with a creak of metal jump cups, and Lara yelped. Her horse, who had been ready to jump, heard her shout and spooked down and to the left, dropping his shoulder... which made a very easy exit for Lara. She toppled down his right shoulder and collapsed in a little puff of dust at the base of the fence.

"Oh," I said, "that's a rough one. He was totally going to jump, too."

"Spooking yourself right off your own horse, that's a bad day," Evan agreed, a grin playing around the corners of his mouth. "Well, one more." He looked up at the sky; the clouds had won their battle against the sea breeze, and were pushing overhead again, blotting out what was left of the daylight. Pinpricks of cold raindrops fell in short, windblown fits and starts. "We might even have time for it."

The last rider, in first place after dressage and cross-country, was Katie Bergen. She'd been riding Beginner Novice at the Ocala events for four years. There was no greater career beginner than Katie. Her face, as she rode into the arena under those threatening skies, was as white as a hunter pony at Devon.

I'd been right when I'd said the career beginners depended on predictability to bring home their ribbons. There was nothing wrong with it—at the end of the day, they were just doing what they felt comfortable with, and their horses became so bombproof from the sameness of the event grounds and courses that every successful round made it a little tougher for them to ever consider taking a chance on moving up. But without taking chances, there was no growth... instead, there was complacency, which was the opposite of growing. Without exploring disastrous scenarios through small, measured steps up in complexity, there was no way to adequately plan for the worst case.

And in Florida, the worst case very frequently came from the heavens above.

But it wasn't the wind or the cold scent of rain or the crackling thunder which did in Katie's chances at bringing home another blue ribbon today. Or maybe it was all of those things, because once they were added up, the sum of distractions proved too much for Katie's placid bay gelding. He snorted at everything he saw, from the people lining the fences to the carnations in the first jump's flower box, and before she could so much as approach the jump, Katie's gelding put in a monster buck, spun on his heels, and raced back to the in-gate.

To her credit, Katie did hang on. She hung on for the first buck, and for the spin, and for the race to the gate. What she maybe didn't expect was that when her gelding reached the in-gate and found a pole across it, blocking his quick exit, he would get mad and spin again, launching another buck for good measure. Combined, the move was too much for Katie; it might have been too much for anybody. She ended up in the dirt, just as Lara had.

"Carol must be feeling pretty good right now," I said to Evan, who laughed, surprised.

"She's the only one who didn't get dirty, that's for sure."

I made sure to wipe the smile off my face before I ran back to Lindsay, who was sitting on William with her feet out of the stirrups, looking admirably cool. A few more raindrops smacked my face and left wide transparent spots on my thin show shirt. I realized I was about to show everyone the cut of my bra. "Is there going to be a victory gallop?" I asked the ring steward, who was looking at his radio with an irritated expression.

"No one is telling me anything," he said dramatically. "I have absolutely no idea, sweetie."

I didn't love being called *sweetie* by anyone, whether it was an eighty-year-old cattle rancher or a thirty-something gay man, but I let it go in consideration of bigger problems —the rain was actually starting to fall now. I turned my back on the ring steward. "Lindsay," I called. "If he says go in, then just go in, take your ribbon, and do a round at an easy canter. Then come right back to the barn. Pete?" Pete turned, eyebrow quirked.

"Yes, ma'am?"

"I got you a ride," I said, pointing through the thinning crowd to where Evan was still leaning against his golf cart, watching us with an unreadable expression. "Let me help you over there—the ground is really rutted from all the horses going in and out today."

Pete looked at Evan and then me. "That's the best you could do?" he asked quietly.

Thunder echoed around us, sounding like the aftermath of an explosion. There were a few frightened whinnies, and dogs barked. "Head back to the barns!" The ring steward shouted, waving horses and riders away. "We'll have ribbons for you to collect after the storm! Everyone, clear the area!" There was a mass exodus all around, people and horses suddenly making tracks for the stabling area. The more nervous riders actually let their horses break into a canter, breaking a horse show taboo. When the crowd was gone, Evan was still there, waiting.

Smirking.

"He said you were friends," I said, confused. "Did he lie to me?"

"We were friends," Pete said. "I don't know that we still are."

"Go get on the golf cart, Pete." It was raining now. Pete's khakis were growing wet around the cast. My shirt, true to the useless, thin polyester that it was, was drenched through and my bra was letting everyone know just how chilly the rain was. "This isn't about us. This is about your health."

Evan got into the driver's seat and rattled over to us. He pulled up alongside Pete and patted the seat. "Let's go, mate," he said, and I heard a trace of the accent that Pete had come home with after his summer in England.

Pete cast me a tired look, then slid into the golf cart, carefully placing his injured leg against the molded dash.

"There's room for you on the back," Evan said. "If you hang on tight."

I shrugged. "Get him back dry," I said. "I'll wait it out under the announcer stand."

"Righto," Evan said, and waved as he drove off.

I walked over to the announcer's stand and took shelter beneath its second story. A few other trainers had elected to stay put and a few glanced at me, ready to welcome me to their gossip sessions, but I found a post to lean against and kept my own counsel. The weekend, exhausting even with all of its triumphs, was ending on a particularly confusing note. For the first time, I was starting to wonder if all the fighting with Pete was actually leading towards a final showdown.

CHAPTER TWENTY-FOUR

"So, Evan, I guess *you're* in my life on the daily now," I said drily. My phone was pressed to my ear under my helmet harness. Beneath me, Mickey moved in a placid walk, cocking his head occasionally to watch a scurrying lizard run across the driveway. "This should make my life that much more difficult."

Evan Folkes laughed. "You're very brutal, Jules. They warned me about you, you know. There was a general air of *oh no, what are you doing,* when I said I was bringing you onboard."

"So heartwarming," I said. "Such a warm welcome from my compatriots."

"I know *team* and *Jules* aren't two words that typically go together, but I have high hopes for you and Dynamo. Very high hopes, if you catch my meaning."

Mickey reached out and took a bite of the nearest oak

bough hanging over the driveway. I tugged at the reins to get his face out of the poor tree. They all needed trimming. I'd have to ask Mike about it if no one on the board took it on first. I was aware I was focusing on the trees instead of attending to the phone conversation I should be having, because it was just easier. I didn't really want to face the issues that Evan was about to bring into my life: not just the practical concern of working around trailering Dynamo down to Ocala for team training sessions, but also the enmity between Evan and Pete, and the unsettling way it apparently revolved around me.

"So you're on the email list and when we get the training dates scheduled, you'll get an invite," Evan was saying. "And then we'll ship to New York a few days beforehand, probably just three days—there's not a lot of room there and they build the stabling and arena at the last possible minute. The team will handle your transfers and your hotel, and cover cabs to and from the park, but you'll be on your own for most of your meals and any extra transportation in the city. Then we do our thing, we win our prize, and the next day we load up and ship home. Think you can manage all of that?"

"I can manage," I said, my mind struggling to wrap itself around the enormity of Evan's plans. It all seemed too big to have happened so quickly. Last week I'd been stressing over the first event of the season. Now I was part of the US Arena Eventing squad. I was shipping Dynamo to Manhattan to compete in Central Park. Teenage Jules would have been very confused about all of this... but I thought she would have been thrilled, too. "It's going to be a lot, but it's worth it. This is what I asked for, right?"

"That's right, good man." Evan chuckled. "It's a lot, but we'll have a good time. I'll let you get back to your day."

I slipped the phone back into the pocket of my riding tights and picked up the reins, walking Mickey back towards the barn. The day was still young and sunny, with just a few fluffy white clouds floating overhead, drifting on calm winds. Inside the barn, the first morning's class was tacking up for a flatwork lesson. Lacey was out front, watering the impatiens she'd planted between the parking area and the barn.

"How does your garden grow?" I asked, pulling up Mickey nearby. I dropped my feet from the stirrups and looked at the ground around Lacey's feet, where she was nudging black strips of soil back into place. "Not great?"

"Between Marcus and Barn Kitty, I don't know why I bother," Lacey complained. "Plus *someone's* tiny feet," she added, shouting the *someone* in the direction of the barn aisle. I heard a groan, and Maisey yelled back: "I said I was sorry!"

"Don't harass my children, Lacey." I hopped down from Mickey's back. "Consider my income."

"Your income is all I consider," Lacey huffed. "Because if you don't get paid, I don't get paid. I've worked for you before, Jules Thornton. I know how rare a paycheck can be when you're in charge." She bent over her flowers again.

I stared down at the back of Lacey's head, not sure what

to say next. We'd never really talked about money before. We'd been young, and friends, when she'd last worked for me. I'd thought we were both cheerfully living in equestrian poverty—you know, that strange state in which the outside world thinks you're rich because you have horses, but you can barely afford to feed yourself—because we were a team. But now I was starting to question everyone I'd ever thought was my partner. Pete had drifted away. Who was to say Lacey had ever really been all-in with me?

I picked up Mickey's reins and led him into the barn.

"I was *kidding!*" Lacey called after me, but I just held up a hand: let it go. She'd only been partially kidding. Some things were obvious from the moment they left your lips.

I untacked Mickey silently, stepping aside only when Lindsay materialized from somewhere within the barn and started hosing him down. I leaned against the wall and watched her for a few minutes.

"School starts in two weeks," I said eventually.

"Yeah," Lindsay said. "My last year, though. I only have one afternoon class."

"If you're coming straight here afterwards, that means some kids won't have rides," I pointed out.

She frowned. "I hadn't thought about that."

"You're not the official barn chauffeur," I said, "but it's something to consider."

Lindsay turned off the hose and picked up a sweat scraper. "One of my friends texted me and asked if I wanted to get a job with her. Her aunt is starting a cafe in downtown High Springs. There'd be tips and stuff."

"Money's good."

"Horses are better." She squeezed the water from Mickey's coat with long, careful strokes. "I'd rather be here. My mom said I should consider the job, though. She said I should broaden my horizons. I said, through making coffee and clearing dishes? She said it was a normal teenager job. I don't know. It sounds boring. Not like riding, or taking care of horses."

"The right thing will work itself out," I told her, deliberately sidestepping the questions she was asking in as many words as possible. Was Lacey staying, did I need extra help, could she have a part-time job? "You might have to wait a little while, though."

Lindsay hung up the sweat scraper and nodded at me, her hand on Mickey's neck. "I'll wait."

I let her take Mickey out to graze while I went into the office to grab some water before the kids' lesson. The air conditioner was humming away, and I couldn't resist throwing myself into my chair and letting the cool air blow over my sweaty face. I closed my eyes and thought about the crazy dynamics of my barn. Lindsay, out there throwing herself at me for a groom job. Lacey, two weeks from the end of her summer session and not yet ready to volunteer whether she was staying through the winter or not. Pete, sitting in the house alone, typing at whatever secret project he'd been at since he'd come home from the hospital. Evan and Amanda, watching us from the sidelines, knowing we were stuck fast in their webs. Where would we all be when autumn finally rolled around, when the kids were back in school, when Pete was out of his cast, when Central Park was over?

"Sitting trot!" I called.

There were groans and a few audible sobs from the more dramatic students in the bunch.

"How are you going to get through life without a good sitting trot?" I asked them. "This is the basis of your entire riding career. Your up transitions: sitting trot. Your down transitions: sitting trot. Your best bends, your shoulders-in, everything you do that isn't walking or cantering: sitting trot. So squeeze your stomach muscles and show me what you've got!"

I went on barking commands as the lesson circled around me, their sitting trots a variety of bumps and plunks. Long-suffering horses flattened their backs and stuck out their noses to avoid the worst of the damage. I spied longe line lessons in the future for every one of these little heathens.

"That's enough," I said finally, and everyone lurched back to walk. Maisey leaned over her horse's neck and panted in the cinematic style of a thirsty man in the desert. "You guys hot?"

There was a chorus of *yes* from the sweaty children.

"Okay. After you get in, popsicle break."

I walked away from their cheers feeling rather pleased with myself, and thinking about my own popsicle—orange, if there were any left—when I nearly ran right into Pete, swinging his way out of the barn aisle and towards the arena. He looked tense, but honestly, that was just the way Pete's face was these days.

"Easy there!" I said, putting up my hands in case he needed steadying, but Pete had gotten agile on the crutches and he managed to catch himself despite the quick stop to avoid hitting me. "What's wrong? You look like you got bad news."

He shook his head. "It's nothing."

"Well, where were you going?" Nothing, my foot. If it was nothing he wouldn't look like a thundercloud had taken over his brain.

"Just... out."

"Out?" I looked over my shoulder at his truck. *Out?* In the middle of a weekday morning? I bit back an impulse to interrogate him further. Fine. If he wanted to go off driving around Alachua County, wasting gas we couldn't really afford to waste, *fine.* "Okay, then. See you later."

I slipped past him and into the barn.

"Jules!"

I turned. *"What?"*

I couldn't see his face; the glare outside turned his expression into dark shadows. But his voice was hard and angry—that couldn't be hidden. "Don't trust Evan," he said. "He's a womanizer."

"So? He's arranging the eventing team, not taking me out to slip a roofie in my drink. I'm not worried about him, and neither should you."

"He just—he's manipulative, Jules. I've *seen* him."

"Why don't you have a little trust that I'm tough enough to say no to a man I'm not interested in, Pete?" But at the back of my mind, a little voice awoke and reminded me that I'd found Evan... let's say, I'd found Evan not altogether unpleasant, and leave it at that. Well, that didn't mean I was going to run away with him, did it? I was with Pete. I loved Pete. Pete and I were in love.

I thought so, anyway.

Pete was clenching his fists on the handles of his crutches. I stepped a little closer, so that I could see his face, see his flushed cheeks and his angry, wild, scared eyes. "Pete," I said, "you should stay. You're too upset to be driving around."

"I have to go out," he said. "I need a break from... everything."

"Fine," I said again, but gently this time, my own rage simmering down and cooling. "Be careful."

I turned and went into the barn, letting him go his own way.

I figured we both needed that small bit of grace.

The kids were eating popsicles, but there were no more orange ones and I was craving something orange-flavored, so I went into the house and found something surprising: an actual orange. I mangled the peel for a little while and then managed to pull out a few sections. Marcus watched me, wagging his tail hopefully.

"Dogs don't eat oranges," I told him.

Marcus wagged his tail harder, assuring me that they did, in fact, eat oranges. *Loved* to eat oranges.

I shook my head at him and wandered through the house, my sweaty feet cold on the terrazzo floors. I stopped in the office door and looked at the desk there for a long moment. It was pushed up against the wall next to a window, and Pete's laptop was on it. Open.

My thoughts immediately plunged into epic, bloody warfare. I had two choices before me. I could back out of the room, and continue without looking. That was what most people would consider the only ethical choice. Or I could walk over to the desk, click the trackpad once to light up the screen, and perhaps get a glimpse of what occupied so much of Pete's time. That was what most people would consider the only *actual* choice. After all, ethics aside, Pete and I lived together. We were joined up emotionally. And we were stuck in a rut. If I just had a better understanding of what he was doing while I was out riding and teaching, maybe I'd be able to find the right tool to get us out of it.

I crossed the room in two strides and clicked the trackpad. The screen lit up welcomingly.

There was a document open. The cursor blinked at the end of a sentence, half-finished.

Some say the goal of dressage is to achieve total partnership with the horse, some say it is total submission. I believe dressage is more than the sum of its parts. The goal of dressage is

My eyes darted across the document. There were page numbers at the bottom. This was page three of one hundred and thirty-two. I flicked up to page one. It was headed *Introduction.*

He was writing a book. He was writing a book of dressage, or maybe eventing, and he'd gone back to work on the reason *why,* and he'd gotten stuck.

"Oh boy, I feel that," I said.

Marcus came in, his claws clicking on the terrazzo, and I jumped. "I thought you were Pete!" I exclaimed. He wagged his tail and panted at me.

I quickly scrolled the page back to three and made sure the blinking cursor sat at the end of the unfinished sentence again. Now everything made a bit more sense. Pete was writing a book, and it was driving him crazy. He started overthinking everything. He turned his frustration with his book into his dislike of Evan. He made Evan the root of all evil and decided Evan was chasing after me. Then he'd just had to get out of the house before he went crazy. It all made sense, in a roundabout kind of way.

I was aching to read the rest of what he'd written, but I put the laptop back to sleep and tiptoed out of the office, as if there was someone in the house who might find me out, and went back to my mangled half of an orange in the kitchen. I gave a wedge to Marcus, but he didn't eat it. He nudged the wedge around on the floor, and then sighed deeply at it.

"Told you," I said.

CHAPTER TWENTY-FIVE

By the end of summer, the hours of daylight were growing shorter, but my days were somehow growing longer. It was the number of horses and lessons and conversations and decisions I had to fit into every day. Whereas once chores had felt endless, now, with other people handling the basic barn work, I found myself doing grittier, tougher work that required constant finessing of tempers and calming of nerves —plus riding, riding, riding. I rather missed mucking stalls and dumping feed, actually. The mental downtime of doing barn work had been whisked away from me, and now I was always on.

My horses were feeling the change, too. My training was more focused, and so their work became more precise. I could sense a new power in the way they lifted their heads when I picked up the reins to start working, in the way they concentrated on fences and bent through the corners of the dressage ring. Though I fought to keep myself from training them with the same sharp commands I was constantly giving myself, I knew that because I was sitting up straighter and riding with more intensity, they were responding in kind.

It was a breakneck pace, but we were hurtling towards something amazing, and that was what kept me going.

The first training session for the arena eventing team took place at the Folkes farm in Reddick, close to Briar Hill. I deliberately drove the long way around to avoid driving past our old driveway. Though my professional life was now a hundred times stronger than the cobbled-together string of amateur horses I'd been riding at Briar Hill, I still didn't have any burning desire to revisit the place I still thought of as Pete's home, the place I still remembered as where we'd been happiest.

Pete hadn't wanted to come along to the training session, which had surprised me a bit. I'd thought he might want to come and guard me from the attentions of the evil Evan Folkes. And, short of that, I'd thought he'd just want to get away from the farm. He seemed to need frequent escapes from his secret book, because he'd get into his truck and drive off, disappearing for an hour or two at a time, before hitching himself back into the house and settling down at his desk again. Every time, I would creep into the office the moment his truck disappeared, and every time, I would find the same thing: the document open and the cursor blinking at a sentence left half-finished, a deep thought about some esoteric element of horsemanship which was clearly eating at him.

I didn't like to think of him driving aimlessly around the rural roads, in and out of cell service, with one leg in a cast. For a while, I was chewing over my worry while I was riding, letting Pete's disappearances distract me when I should have been schooling my horses. Eventually, though, I had to push it all aside. Pete would do what Pete would do. I'd never been able to stop him, and I had enough to think about, with the prep for New York taking the front and center spot in my mind.

Down at the Folkes farm, the team gathered for intense training sessions, focused on the technical show jumping skills we'd need for the arena eventing competition. Evan explained the unique challenges of not just the event, but the setting: Central Park Horse Show was held in a tight, oddly-shaped ring, with hills all around, and skyscrapers rising up from the park's borders. It felt like being in a bowl, Evan said, and some horses found the arena claustrophobic. It would be dark, too; even if the event began in early evening, Midtown's shadows would cast early twilight over the southern end of the park well before true sunset.

"It won't be like anything you've experienced before, and it's going to be impossible to totally prepare for it," he told us, and the six of us nodded and tried not to look too worried. But I could tell by the sidelong glances and nervous reshuffling of reins that we were all flustered. For my part, I was starting to wonder about the ludicrous position we were placing our horses in. We were event riders: our entire sport was based upon proving we could take on wide-open spaces with well-behaved horses, galloping over fields and flying over natural obstacles at speed. Why on earth were we taking them to the middle of a city to jump them over solidly-built show jumps set in tight, trappy combinations?

"The thrill," Evan suggested, when I asked him a version of that question later. "And the money," he went on, considering the question more deeply. "Right? *You're* doing it for the money. You've never made a secret about preferring long, open courses."

I was untacking Dynamo, who was hot and breathing heavily, in the shed-row of Evan's long, breezy barn. We were on the south side, alone; for some reason, the other riders had all chosen the cross-ties on the north side of the barn. The shed-row overlooked a long sloping pasture with a round pond in the center, and cross-country jumps dotting the grass all around it. I wished we'd been out there today, not holed up on the red clay of the jumping arena, practicing corners and combinations.

"I'm partially doing it for the money," I admitted, setting my saddle on the nearby saddle rack. I placed the girth, sweaty side up, on top of it, tucking the ends into my stirrups so it wouldn't fall off. "But partially for prestige, I guess. And at the time I met you, it felt like the right thing for Dynamo."

"At the time? What about now?" Evan was leaning against the wall, his hands in the pockets of his close-fitting jeans, watching me with interest, as if he'd never seen a person untack a horse before. "Having second thoughts?"

"I thought it would be easier on him," I said, realizing even as I said it that I'd been silly to believe it. I'd known Dynamo was starting to feel creaky, that his joints were starting to complain, and that his desire to gallop at Advanced speed was waning as well. Now that we were several weeks into training for this new challenge, though, I could see that I'd been focusing on the galloping problem, and ignoring the other problems that age and a tough early life visited on a horse in his late teens. Dynamo was coming out of these sessions stiff and cranky. He was taking longer and longer to warm up one, two, even three days after a training session. I could tell that his joints were feeling every twisting turn and tough combination Evan was throwing at us.

It shouldn't have been a surprise. It happened to racehorses who had campaigned hard for many years. It happened to show jumpers and dressage horses and reining horses and cutting horses. It happened to anyone, horse or human, who pounded their joints day in and day out, pushing to the extremes on a regular basis. You could only push past your optimum zone and into the extremes so many times without exacting damage on your body that would last a lifetime. Dynamo had already done that by the time he'd come into my life. He'd already lived a whole athletic history I knew almost nothing about—other than the universal facts: he'd galloped just as fast he could, over and over and over again. After that, he'd become an event horse, tackling long gallops and big jumps and exacting dressage tests. His joints were feeling every furlong he'd ever covered, and they were tired.

Dynamo still loved to go, but he didn't want to be an Advanced horse.

The realization was like a knife in my gut.

I shouldn't be doing this, I thought, forcing myself through the motions of unwrapping his legs, peeling off his bell boots. I could lease him to someone in my barn to be their Young Riders horse, but I shouldn't be pushing him any longer.

There would be no four-star in our future, much less a five-star. I had missed my shot with him. It had all come together too late.

"I'm worried about him," I blurted, still on my knees next to his forelegs, a blue rubber bell boot in one hand. "He's coming out of these sessions so stiff. I think it might be too much for him."

Evan was next to me, holding out his hand to help me up, his face arranged in concerned lines. "Stiff or lame?"

"Just stiff." He'd still never put a hoof wrong, and I wondered to this day if I'd really seen him take a bad step after May Days, or if it had all been in my mind.

"Stiff we can get through," Evan said, smiling reassuringly. "There are plenty of therapies to help him recover more quickly. I'll send you home with a few things. I have some great magnetic boots... actually, I probably have a whole sheet I can spare. Have you ever used a vibrating plate? They're fantastic for stimulating blood flow and sometimes that's all you need to get a horse going again after a tough workout. If the magnets don't do it, keep him here for a few days and let's see if the vibe-plate makes a difference."

His kindness was a balm to my raw soul. "Thank you, Evan," I said weakly. "I really appreciate it."

"Hey," Evan said softly, his eyes locked on mine. "Anything for you, Jules."

I realized he was still holding my hand. My gaze fell down to my fingers, firmly grasped in his tanned hand. He let go immediately, but he didn't step away. I kept my eyes down, afraid of what I'd see if I looked up and met his gaze. Something told me there was something very intense waiting for me there.

He's a womanizer, Pete had said bitterly, and I had been angry because I thought Pete believed I wouldn't be able to push Evan away if he started hitting on me, but what I hadn't expected was that Evan's presence would feel so comforting, or his touch so compelling. Maybe I'd never considered that being a womanizer was made possible with a strong dose of charisma, to make a seduction all the more possible.

"I better give him a shower," I said finally, stepping back and ducking under Dynamo's neck to break the spell. I busied myself picking up his lead rope, snapping it onto his leather halter, unbuckling the panic snaps on the cross-ties.

"Of course," Evan said. "I'll go find those things for you. They're up in my tack room... don't leave before I come back, okay?"

I wished I could. I didn't want to see Evan again, not today, not while the confusion of what had just happened was still resting on my shoulders and curling in my stomach. But whatever he had that could help Dynamo, well, I needed that more than I needed my own comfort. The horse always came first. Dynamo would always come first.

Especially once we got through this show together.

I'd finished hosing down Dynamo and was letting him graze on the lawn in front of the barn by the time Evan came back, empty-handed. He smiled apologetically. "It's not in my tack room. I think I stuck the extra magnetic stuff in one of the bins up at my house. Do you want to put your horse in a stall and you could run up with me and help me find them?"

I looked at him for a long moment, considering the proposal. Evan's expression was open and good-natured. There was nothing in his face which suggested he was going to proposition me. He was a nice person, whatever Pete thought of him, and it wasn't necessarily his fault that I found him attractive. He wasn't luring me into his home... he was just asking if I wanted to go and help him find a therapeutic aid for my horse. He was being a good coach. He needed his team in top condition, and this was part of the preparation.

"Sure," I said.

Evan found a flake of hay and tossed it into an empty stall for Dynamo, who was more than happy to chill out there with a snack instead of getting back on the hot, bumpy trailer right away. I followed him over to his golf cart, intensely aware that just on the other side of the barn, the other team members were grazing their horses or waiting for their turn on the wash-rack, while I was motoring off with the coach, alone. It felt very strange, and I was happy when he turned the golf cart away from the barn, following a driveway that hid us from their view.

"This is a great place," I said, watching the green fields and lush trees unfold around us. We'd spent all of our time at the jumping ring just a few hundred feet from the barn, but the farm was huge, with rolling pastures, live oak hammocks, and, of course, cross-country fences everywhere. "It reminds me of Briar Hill."

"You can actually hack there if you know the right shortcuts," Evan said. "We're only a few minutes away as the crow flies."

"I can tell by the terrain. Everything is so rolling and green, just like it is there. This is the most beautiful part of Florida."

Evan nodded and turned the golf cart up a path between two pastures. The engine whined as we rattled uphill, towards a small wood-frame house surrounded by oak trees.

"Yours?" I asked, surprised. I had expected something larger, to go with this luxurious property.

"The foreman's house," he explained. "It was empty for a little while, so I moved in last month when I came back to help my dad. It wouldn't do to live in my old bedroom up at the big house. It's still got my crayons in my desk drawer, I think." He grinned at me. "Maybe if you're nice I'll draw you a picture."

"Do you draw?" I imagined a small schoolboy Evan scribbling horse pictures. "Can you draw Dynamo?"

"Abstracts," Evan said, winking. "I'll draw him entirely in triangles, or something. I can't make anything look lifelike, so I just experiment with shapes. It's not exactly good, but it's interesting." He parked the golf cart by the front door of the house. Sparrows flew out of the thick hedge growing up against the walls, protesting our arrival. "Come in and I'll show you."

We'd come up here to find a magnetic blanket, and now we were looking at his art.

The living room was dark and small, dominated by a sagging blue sofa ("it was here when I moved in") and a large painting of red circles in a pattern which suggested... "a horse jumping?" I asked eventually, having studied it in silence for a period of time which was beginning to feel awkward.

"That's it," Evan agreed, and I thought he sounded relieved. Maybe he'd been worried I wasn't going to catch on. "Something to drink? Water, tea, something stronger?"

"Oh, no thank you." I made a show of looking around at the open doors around the living room as if searching for his office. "I can't stay, gotta get home before the kids burn the place down."

"Right," Evan said, leading the way through a door to our left. "The kids."

"You sound disapproving." I looked around the office. It was more of a storage room, with plastic bins stacked up to the ceiling on two walls. An old desk sat under a window against the farthest wall, though the light was mostly blocked by the live oak a few feet from the house. The tree's branches tapped against the window, like a disapproving chaperone telling us to hurry it up.

"I think you are extremely talented." Evan pulled down a few bins, popping open their lids before shaking his head and pushing them aside. I glimpsed heaps of carefully wrapped bridles, green New Zealand rugs, woolen coolers. There was a treasure trove of tack in this room, it seemed. Evan selected another stack of bins, seemingly arbitrarily, as if he had no idea what was really in here. "Why are you using all that talent to teach a bunch of beginners?"

"They're not beginners. Quite a few of them have A-circuit backgrounds."

"Eventing beginners," Evan clarified. He lifted a handful of splint boots from a bin, looked at what had been hidden underneath. "You're spending too much time on them, and not enough on yourself. You should be in an intensive program. You could go further, faster, if you went to ride with a top trainer. Someone like Mary Davis, in Vermont." He paused, then looked at me appraisingly. "Or with my father and me."

I was too shocked to say anything at first. Of course, other people were always telling me I should go sign on with this or that Big Name Trainer. They never thought about how riding for someone else would fit into my personality, only how it would fit into my ambition. They never considered how much I loved my independence... or being in charge. "That's very kind of you to say," I said finally. "But we have a good arrangement. I'm happy where I'm at."

Evan fished out the magnetic boots at last and held them up. "Front and back," he said triumphantly. "Now we just need the blanket." He started stacking bins up again. "I think I know where that is. So you're happy, are you? Are you sure about that? Wouldn't you rather be riding all day, getting better, learning more horses, than spending your time working on beginner novice riders? How is that going to help you achieve *your* goals? Shouldn't you put yourself first? We're talking about your life, here."

As his words washed over me, every doubt I'd ever had about taking on the riding program came rushing back. *Yes,* I thought, *what* about *me?*

My confusion must have shown on my face, because suddenly Evan was standing very close to me, his hands on my bare arms, his touch inducing the slightest of shivers—or maybe it was just the cool air of the air conditioning, switching on with a reassuring hum. He'd put down the boots on the desk behind him, and he was blocking the light from the window, and the room was so dim I could barely see anything but his face, just a few inches from mine.

"You're selling yourself short, Jules," he said softly. "But I can help you. Stick close to me, and I will make doors open for you."

Intoxicating words, to a woman like me. He couldn't have been more seductive if he'd whispered his wildest fantasies into my blushing ears. I felt my jaw slacken, my lips fall open, my breath quicken. I knew what was happening, and for just a few seconds, I didn't fight it.

Then I did.

I brought my teeth down on my lower lip, slicing against the sensitive skin until my mouth was closed tight, puckered against the pain. Evan, confused, stepped back, and as his grip on my arms loosened, I turned away from him, escaping into the forlorn living room. I stood beneath the garish painting of red circles. He followed me, but then stopped in the doorway, one hand gripping the frame.

"I'm sorry," I said, because he was the coach and I was the student.

"I'm sorry," Evan said. "That got... I didn't mean for that to happen. You're just—"

"No," I said. "I'm not."

He smiled then, a wry grin, shaking his head at me. "God, Jules, you just don't know it yet. Heaven help the world if you ever realize it. Stay right there, and let me grab the blanket—it's on the top shelf of my closet."

He disappeared into another room, and after some rattling and crashes, he came out with a dusty black sheet.

He put the boots on top and folded it all up together.

Back in the golf cart, we sat in silence as we retraced our drive between the pastures. From the hilltop, I could see the other members of the team grazing their horses next to the barn, and I thought again: *I hope they don't see me like this.*

"Everything I said was true," Evan said eventually. We were nearly back to the barn. He didn't let up on the accelerator, didn't seem to need extra time to explain himself or try and convince me of something. He just spoke naturally, easily. "And there are no strings attached. The other thing—that won't happen again. Now that we both know where we stand, we can move past it."

I thought about that last sentence. The word *we*. He knew, then, that I'd felt it too. I'd leaned towards him, I had parted my lips. I wished I hadn't. But I supposed it didn't mean anything. It was a crush, a reciprocal crush, and we both knew that's all it was.

I told him it was fine, and that I appreciated his interest in my career. Then I waved goodbye and let him walk over to the other side to hold court with the rest of the team. I put the folded blanket over top of my saddle, and added the boots to my grooming tote. I leaned against the stall door and looked in at my chestnut horse, eating his hay in placid happiness. I touched my fingers to my lips.

Nothing had happened.

It felt like something had happened.

CHAPTER TWENTY-SIX

I drove home thinking I'd left behind trouble at Evan's farm. Naturally, there was more trouble waiting for me. What else could I possibly have expected?

Driving back from Ocala had been an exercise in Too Much Alone Time for Jules. I'd had to turn on NPR and listen to a lot of very alarming news stories just to drown out my own thoughts. The end result, of course, was that I had doubled my anxiety by the time I was pulling into the farm driveway—I was carrying my own worries, and all the rest of the world's, as well.

By the time I got home, it was past feeding time and the afternoon clouds were clearing. What was left to us was a hot, yellow evening that would be ferociously sticky and miserable, and I fully expected to see the horses already out in their fields, tails swishing furiously against the happy hordes of flies, and everyone human packed into one of the air-conditioned tack rooms, waiting for parents to come and pick them up. This was the usual evening routine as mid-August descended like a sweltering blanket around the farm. There were a few nice, rain-cooled evenings in summer, but those were rare treats.

Instead, I came home to a messy barn aisle filled with tears and confusion. I caught a glimpse of crying children in the barn while I was still in the truck cab, one of them the stoic Jordan, and I felt the alarming urge to throw the whole rig back into drive and high-tail it out of there. My fantasy of retiring to a woodland cabin returned in a rush. No men, no children, no parents, just my horses and the chirping birds and maybe a few marauding bears in my trash cans—that was the life for me.

Just for a moment, though, and then the feeling was gone. I loved them all—the children, the parents, the horses, and, yes, one of the men. I had to fix their problems. I had a *few* maternal instincts, anyway.

So I put on the emergency brake, hopped out of the truck, and ran into the barn. I heard Dynamo shift and kick the trailer wall, angry at being left standing a moment longer than necessary. Brat, I thought. He'd be fine for a few minutes.

"It's nothing," Lindsay said quickly as I came racing into the aisle. She held up her hands: *nothing to see here.* "It's fine, everything's fine."

But Lacey, poking her head out of the office, just shook her head. She was holding her phone to her ear. "No," I heard her say into the speaker, "it's not his parents yet. They're on their way."

"What is *happening?*" I shouted, and every horse in the barn turned and stared at me, their chewing arrested, hay hanging from their mouths. For a heartbeat, the barn was frozen in place.

Then, a dozen voices began explaining what had happened while I'd been down in Ocala, jumping fences and looking for trouble with my coach. I picked the story up in fits and starts, through half-heard sentences and shocking phrases that cut through the buzz of competing explanations.

I learned that after the storm passed through, Maisey had dared Ricky to take his horse out and jump the coops in the pasture fences.

That Lindsay and Lacey had been inside stalls pulling manes, with the radio blaring from the shelf over the tack room door, and hadn't heard Ricky and Maisey's horses walking down the aisle, or they'd have checked to see why two kids were going riding after they'd all had lessons that morning.

That Maisey, thrilled that she was beating Ricky so soundly at this whole eventing lark, had pushed her horse into a gallop ahead of him, racing for the coop.

That while she'd made it over easily, Ricky, not as experienced, lost control of his horse, who got a bad spot to the coop and hung a leg, falling over it.

"Ricky fell clear of his horse, nothing broken, but we

think he might have a concussion," Lacey finished, coming out of the office at last. "We're waiting for his parents. They'll take him to the hospital—their request, I did offer to do it myself."

"I should have been here," I said blankly, pushing past Lacey. In the office, Ricky was laying on the sofa, a bag of frozen peas slowly melting against his forehead. For a moment, I wondered where the peas had even come from— I'd certainly never bought any. Lacey, I thought. She must have bought them with just this type of use in mind. Ricky opened his eyes as I came in. His clothes were streaked with mud, but someone had wiped his face clean. "Ricky, I'm so sorry," I said.

"You didn't do anything," he said, blinking at me in confusion. "You weren't even here."

"That's what I meant. Are you okay? Do you feel okay?"

"My head aches. Lacey said no napping, in case I have a concussion. And I banged up my elbow and shoulder... I think they're okay, though."

Lacey came back in. "It wasn't a bad fall. It just looked scary. Maisey thought she'd killed him—she was a real mess when we brought them in."

I looked up at the sound of shod hooves in the aisle, and saw Lindsay walking Dynamo through the barn. She put him in the wash-rack and started unwrapping his legs. I sighed. So I had a problem with the kids, and immediately forgot about a horse waiting in the hot trailer? That was just great. Was I really so incapable of running both this barn and my own eventing business? Evan had said the kids were wasting my valuable time. What if he was right? What if I had to choose between the kids and my own horses?

The thought was too big to even consider right now, surrounded by their worried faces, while the girl who hoped to follow in my footsteps was currently handling my best horse with an expert touch.

"Thank you, Lindsay," I called, and she waved her hand at me as she kept working: *no problem*. I realized she was probably just glad to find a way to beat Lacey to the punch for once.

There was a new sound, now that the tears had stopped: tires grinding on gravel in the driveway. A car purring in the parking lot.

"That'll be Ricky's parents," Lacey said, glancing at me, and for the first time, she looked nervous. Of course she was —Lacey didn't want to deal with frightened parents any more than I did, and right now she was probably feeling responsible for not realizing Ricky and Maisey had been sneaking out of the barn in the first place. The problem was, it was really my fault... for not having been there at all.

"They were kind," I told Pete later. "And that was the worst part of all."

"That makes no sense," Pete declared. He was on the couch, looking intently at his phone; I was a little surprised he'd responded to me at all. "How could being *kind* be the worst part?"

"Because it felt condescending. Like they had already had a conversation on the way over about what a child I was, and that of course I had shirked responsibility and let this happen to their kids. I feel like I'm going to get an email from the board with a list of requirements or something— like, hours I have to be on the property, or how many adults are present per child, I don't know. And if they start micromanaging me, I'll lose it. I can't handle that." I put my head in my hands, feeling desperate at the mere thought. My freedom was all perceived, wasn't it? I thought I was running this barn my way and doing what I wanted with my career, but they were still in charge... and they could crack down on me any time they wanted.

Pete looked up from his phone. "I don't think they're going to do anything that drastic."

"Why not? What makes you think you have *any* idea what they're going to do? You're always making it very clear to me that this is my contract, not yours, but you suddenly have insight into what they're thinking?"

He drew back, looking shocked. "I don't think you need to go on the attack with me."

I sighed. "I don't need to, but I'm sure as shit going to, because I have no one to yell at but myself, and I need to give myself a break."

He looked back down at his phone, apparently giving up on me. "Why not just go out to the barn and yell at Lacey, then?"

Lacey had gone home for the night, or maybe I would

have. "Pete, seriously, what if they have a problem with the training sessions... or with the entire New York plan? I haven't actually told them about any of it."

"Why not? I'd think you'd want to trumpet that kind of thing to the heavens."

"I was just afraid it was all a little too good to be true," I explained. Marcus crept over and put his head in my lap, and I tugged at his ears, grateful for his affection while Pete was being such a jerk when I was having a serious breakdown. Thank goodness for dogs! "I mean, it all just happened in such a rush. First it was, oh, I have to meet this guy and impress him, and how will that ever happen? It seemed impossible. Then his son decides to eat lunch with me, and he's like: 'Of course you can join the team, come on, let's go! Now you're at trainings every week! You're a star! Your horse needs extra help? I'll give it to you!' All of it happening, all at once, is so crazy I don't know how to deal with it. That's not how my breaks usually come, you know that."

"You mean, usually you have to work for them instead of just flirting for them?"

I stared at him, shocked. "Did you really just say that?"

Pete shrugged. He wouldn't meet my gaze.

"Pete, did you really just say I flirted my way onto the team?"

Pete looked at his phone.

I thought I'd been angry before. I'd led a very angry life, actually. This was on another level. This was the sort of rage that started wars.

I stood up slowly, gently pushing Marcus's head aside, walked across the living room, and stood over Pete. He put his phone in his lap and looked up at me. I took him in for a moment, this man I lived with. His hair was shaggy and unkempt, and there were new lines on his face, around his mouth and eyes, painted there by exhaustion and, I suspected, by pain. He looked inexpressibly beautiful to me. I wondered how I could have been attracted to Evan, when I had Pete. All I could think about, for a moment, was how much I loved him. Then I remembered what he'd said. *Flirting.* I hadn't had to flirt. And I wasn't on the team because Evan was crushing on me. I was there because I was *good*.

I looked at Pete, and I loved him, and I wanted to kill him.

Such a confusing swirl of emotions made it feel even better than I expected when I leaned down and gave him one, satisfying, palm-tingling slap.

He blinked at me and raised one hand to his reddening cheek. "Care to explain?" he asked, in a rather strangled tone.

"Do I *need* to? Did you really just say that to me? Who the hell do you think you are, implying I'm not good enough to get on the team on my riding?"

I turned my back on him and his suddenly wide eyes, on his hand pressed to his cheek and his slow comprehension. I went out to the kitchen and pulled a beer out of the fridge, then slumped at the kitchen table, my dry elbows pressing into the rough weave of the tablecloth. I was exhausted, and I was afraid, and I was angry, and I just wanted to close my eyes and pretend nothing was happening. But instead my eyes were wide open, and all around me I could see that *everything* was happening, and it was happening all at once: the summer camp of children that seemed to never end would, in fact, end, and the threat of Lacey's imminent return to Pennsylvania was creeping up on me, and the possibility of losing free rein over my own schedule felt very real, and the New York show was in just a few weeks' time, and Pete's lay-up would end soon but until then, Pete's horses were still my problem, and Dynamo's slow recovery from hard work might be improved by therapeutic tricks but the root causes would not go away, and Evan had nearly kissed me and I had nearly let him and when would *that* awful feeling go away, and somewhere, floating around in the midst of all this immediate drama, and jabbing me in the gut whenever I thought I'd forgotten for a little while, was the possibility that Amanda would sell that horse of hers before I had a chance to buy him.

It was too much, but it was always too much. There was always just so, so much to contend with. This life overwhelmed at every turn. Maybe that was just all I could ever expect.

I'd take it.

I heard the sofa creak, and then the slow progression of Pete making his way from room to room. He appeared in the kitchen doorway. If he wanted to kiss and make up, he was going to have to wait for it.

"Not now, Pete," I sighed. "I can't take this from you anymore."

"Take what?" he asked, looking pained. I could still see the pink on his cheek where I'd slapped him. I wondered why I didn't feel bad about it. I felt terrible about everything else.

"You. Your sadness. Your blame." I put my forehead down on the table, felt the tablecloth press its pattern into my skin. "Why won't you just get on board? Why won't you embrace what we've got? This isn't forever, living here. This isn't the last stop on the train. We have no idea where life is going to take us next."

The words were new to my consciousness, but they didn't surprise me. If nothing else, I had spent the past few years learning that life was not the unfolding pathway to greatness I had expected and planned on. Life was not a succession of well-deserved wins acquired through hard work and sacrifice. Life was hard work and sacrifice with maybe a few accidental wins along the way. Maybe the point was to wait out the hard times and then soak up the good moments for as long as they lasted. But maybe these were the good times *and* the hard times, all rolled into one. Maybe having too many horses to ride and too many students to coach and too many competitions to strive for was really the best-case scenario. Maybe I was so busy winning and failing all at once, I didn't even realize I was living the dream.

"We are doing great," I said slowly, testing my new theory. "We are doing amazingly. Yes, you broke your leg, but even *that* was a best-case scenario—you're going to be riding again in what, two months? Less? So maybe stop treating me like the person who dragged you to a fate worse than death, and stop acting like you're just waiting for the next blow to fall because honestly, Pete, I can't take it anymore."

"What will you do if I don't?"

"What?"

"What will you do if I don't change my attitude and give you what you want? Then what will you do?"

I stared at him. "Jesus, Pete, I don't know. I guess it never occurred to me that you'd *want* to live like this, so I don't have a good plan to deal with it."

Suddenly, he began to laugh. He lifted a hand to his cheek, to the place where I'd slapped him. "You *hit* me," he said, a trace of wonder in his voice. "But you always have a plan. Is that where this one ended?"

"That wasn't in the plan," I admitted. "That just felt like the right thing to do."

"Maybe it was." He watched me for a few moments, hand still pressed to his face. "I don't know what's going to happen," he said. "But I love you."

"I know," I said, feeling tired down to my very bones. "I love you. I guess that's why I thought you needed a good smack. So you'd know how I feel."

"Because if you didn't care what I'd said, you'd walk out," Pete guessed. "Or kick me out."

"A long time ago."

The next day I called up Leah and told her everything. Well, not everything. I didn't mention that Pete and I were on the outs, or that I'd almost kissed my team coach. I was already trying to put the Evan incident into the past, a strange near-miss in a world filled with almost-calamities. I'd almost sideswiped a car at a four-way stop last month. I'd almost gotten struck by lightning when I stayed out riding longer than I should have. I'd almost fallen off Julia's horse Rumors when I'd been schooling him over a gymnastic and he'd stumbled through the third fence and stopped at the fourth one. Who knew how many times I'd almost won the lottery because I'd been thinking about the numbers but didn't actually play it? For every solid, important thing that happened in life, there were a billion almost-happens that never occurred, and it wasn't worth the stress to think about them. I hadn't died. I hadn't wrecked my truck. I hadn't fallen off Rumors. I hadn't won a million dollars. And I hadn't kissed Evan.

If the memory of it haunted me, if I was worried I'd never quite forget that moment when our faces had been so close, our breathing had been in sync, and our nerves had been trembling in our skins, then that was something I had to learn to live with.

It certainly couldn't affect my eventing schedule, or the

looming prospect of New York City, the Central Park Horse Show, and the big check at the end of the rainbow.

Leah listened to my story without comment, and after I had wrapped up with the dates I'd be away from the barn, taking Lacey and Pete with me, a few moments of radio silence between us gave me a rising feeling of doom. I started to sweat. "Leah? My friend Haley is going to lend us one of her working students for the weekend, so the barn will be taken care of. Plus Lindsay will be working with her, and she's very capable, so I hope you're not—"

"I'm impressed, Jules," Leah interrupted. "Did you think I'd be mad? That you got onto a national team? You're going to make us look like geniuses for getting you under contract before your career blew up. I've already got other horse show moms asking me if there's room for them to join. Wait until they hear about this!" She chuckled. "Oh boy, Renata is going to be *pissed.*"

I had to assume Renata was another horse show mom, one of the ones who stuck with hunters when the rest of the co-op parents went rogue and hired me.

Well, that was something I had underestimated until now: the petty rivalries of powerful parents.

I enjoyed a good rivalry myself.

"Wait until I come home with a win," I said daringly. "Renata won't know what to do with herself."

"We might have to start a waiting list," Leah mused. "Or look into what you'd need in order to take in more boarders and students. There are empty stalls, after all."

I felt the conversation spinning towards deep and dangerous waters. Expansion was definitely not on my mind right now. "I'd better go," I told her. "Horses to ride."

CHAPTER TWENTY-SEVEN

We packed for New York at the last minute, everyone flying around the tack room looking for polo wraps and hair polish and spare hoof picks—why so many spare hoof picks, I'd wonder later, opening up my grooming kit to find no fewer than seven. Hoof picks with stiff new bristles and hoof picks with heavy rubber grips and hoof picks that folded closed in case you needed to stash a hoof pick in a stealth situation like the James Bond of equestrians—I had one of each and two of several.

Everyone came to the barn to see us off. Summer camp had ended with the beginning of school two weeks before, but on the Monday afternoon before the horse show weekend, the parents pulled into the driveway one by one and my boarders and board members emerged with going away presents and good luck cards, and I stood in the barn aisle and blinked away tears and wondered who on earth this eye-leaking person was.

The horse van, drawn by a growling semi-tractor, crawled up the driveway, knocking the leaves from the overgrown oak trees, then had trouble turning around thanks to the full parking lot. It was a nerve-wracking wait, but finally the ramp was down, and the groom and driver were coming up to me, ready to pick up Dynamo and drive north. There were already three horses in the truck, and they were whinnying and stomping, sending my entire farm into a commotion.

I led out Dynamo, who was kitted out in thick, plush shipping bandages, and a fluffy sheepskin-covered halter to protect his head from banging into any metal bars while he was reaching for hay or drinking water or trying to nap. He tugged at his lead when I stopped him in front of the ramp, and stretched out one foreleg to paw at the gravel, and suddenly I remembered him as a much younger horse, walking him away from the auction pen and towards Laurie's trailer. That day, he'd been a scrawny and mangey specimen, and had seemed utterly lacking in athleticism or personality, but I'd suspected the hidden depths buried within him—and now here he was, lightyears away from the shambling wreck I'd taken a chance on, pulling at his halter, in a hurry to be on his way to the Big Apple.

The groom took his lead from me and led him up the steep ramp into the trailer, and I swiped at my wetness on my cheeks again, feeling as if he was leaving me forever instead of just shipping out a day earlier than I was. Lacey leaned into me and gave me a squeeze on the shoulders. She knew what I was feeling.

If Lacey hadn't been there, I would have broken down sobbing as the trailer pulled out. As it went crashing through the remaining tree branches hanging over the driveway. As it turned in the distance, and went accelerating up the country road, and disappeared behind the pine trees that marched up to the farm's property line. I'd never sent Dynamo anywhere without me, and I felt like I'd handed my child over to strangers. In a very real way, that was exactly what I'd done. On the way out, he neighed twice, his familiar voice easy to pick out from the cacophony of neighs that was following the trailer down the driveway, and I felt like he was calling out to me, asking where I was sending him, and why he was going without me.

But Lacey had finally decided to stay on through the winter season, thank goodness, and so she was still there to hold me up and keep my brave face intact until the kids had gone into the barn to play with their own horses and the parents had climbed into their cars to go home, or were sitting around the picnic table swapping work horror stories and drinking soda from the office fridge. A few hovered nearby, longing to chat about the upcoming horse show. They'd become my allies, these parents. I remembered how I'd been afraid they'd be angry. But, like Leah, the others had responded with jubilation and a sense of self-congratulation that was far stronger than the actual praise they gave me.

"What a catch you are," one had told me. "We look like clairvoyants, locking you down right before you went all National-Team-Member on us. Every other mom at the school is furious right now." She grinned, as if there was no better feeling in the world than making everyone else jealous, and I had to admit, she had a point.

Lacey took me into the office, sat me down, and handed me a Diet Coke. "You'll see him in two days," she reminded me. "You'll be in New York on Wednesday night, and so will he."

I'd be in New York City in two days, and so would Lacey, and so would Pete. He was still coming with me, against all odds. Truthfully, we weren't speaking much these days. We had said everything that needed to be said two weeks ago, and then I had left him alone to figure out what came next. Since I'd gone on to spend every waking hour in the barn, it hadn't mattered much. We were only thrown together at dinner, and the short time afterward that I managed to stay awake before I fell asleep on the couch, and had to be convinced it was a good idea to stumble into the bedroom and go to sleep there like a grown-up. There was as little room for conversation as there was desire for any.

Still, I missed him. In quiet moments when I was hacking out Regina, who had stepped up to trot sets now, or when I was letting a horse stretch out on a loose rein after a workout, I had time to think, and that was when I considered the strange case of Pete and Jules, who had fallen for each other in the face of adversity, and couldn't seem to get it right now that things were good. Why had we been better off living in a tack room, or a horse trailer, than we were now, in a real house with a roof and walls and running water? Maybe the novelty of it all, or the *corps d'esprit*, had been enough to stave off the creeping depression which had slowly swallowed up Pete after losing the farm.

Whatever it was that had overtaken Pete, he didn't want to talk about it with me, and I wasn't bringing it up. Not again. Not when I'd already told him it was time to get over it, and I would be waiting for him on the other side. The ball was officially in his court.

He came into the bedroom as I was packing, or rather while I was flinging underwear and socks onto the unmade bed, looking for my favorite whites to go under my show breeches. "I think they're in the dryer," he said, correctly concluding what I was up to. It was an easy guess; I went through this exact ritual before ninety percent of all events. I *never* knew where my favorite white underwear were, and Pete always did—they were in the dryer, every single time.

"Thank you," I said shortly, and moved on to the matter of accessories: two collars, two stock pins, seven hairnets, and so on. I doubted there'd be a tack trailer in Central Park selling replacements should I lose or break or stain anything necessary to my ensemble. "Are you all packed, then?" I continued, because he wasn't moving from the doorway and I had no idea what he wanted. "What's up? Why are you standing there?"

"I got a call from Rick Delannoy," Pete said. "Earlier,

while you were wrapping Dynamo's legs."

I sniffed back a sob at the thought of Dynamo. "What did he want?" I asked, wishing my voice didn't sound so strangled. I was really behaving like a child over that horse right now. It was embarrassing.

"He's thinking about buying another horse this fall, and wanted to know if we had any recommendations."

I paused. "We?"

"Yeah. You included. He specifically indicated he wanted to know your opinion." Pete's expression was bland.

I floundered for a moment, trying to figure out why Rick would include me, then remembered I was riding Rogue. Riding him very well, as a matter of fact. Oh, shit, I thought. "Pete, you're going to be riding Rogue again in the fall. He... he knows that, doesn't he?"

Pete shrugged. "We'll see."

"I'm *not* keeping Rogue, Pete. He's your horse." After everything Pete had gone through to get that horse into the barn, I'd be one horrible person to try and keep the ride; not to mention that while Rogue and I were getting along just fine, I had only so much time in my day. When I handed Pete Rogue's reins, I already had a horse in mind to fill that time slot, and his name was Confident Liar. He was still for sale, and he was almost mine. All I had to do was win this weekend. Then, Con would be Dynamo's eventual replacement, and bringing him home would be the only bright spot in this mess. Yes, he'd be a long way from the four-star level, but he'd be *my* horse, in a way Rogue could never be Pete's, and Mickey could never be mine. Conversations like this one wouldn't happen. I put down my handful of hairnets and met Pete's eyes. "You know you're taking him back, right? I would never consider keeping the ride."

"Either way, he clearly considers you part of the team now." Pete shrugged again, shifting his gaze from mine. "Enjoy the fame."

I considered screaming, possibly into a pillow or maybe just out loud, facing the ceiling, but decided not even that outlet could suitably handle my frustration with Pete. "Can we press pause on the fight right now, Pete? I am really nervous."

"Of course," Pete said, sounding genuinely apologetic. "I didn't mean to make it sound like—anyway, he heard about a horse at Amanda's barn."

I sat down on the bed. "Please don't say it."

"Amanda told him you liked the horse."

"Pete, I swear to every saint above, please don't say it."

"He didn't buy him, he just wanted to know if we thought he should. If you really liked him that much or if Amanda was blowing smoke up his ass trying to make a sale. Apparently, she told him the horse was on the market, but she thought she'd have a sale next week with Jules Thornton. He thought that was pretty interesting. I didn't do this, in case you were thinking it. He went out there without me."

I put my head in my hands and moaned. Marcus came

trotting into the room and initiated emergency face-licking, his tongue eagerly working through all the gaps between my fingers. My chin, my cheeks, my nose, my eyelids. "Thank you, Marcus," I said, pushing my forehead against his. "You good dog, you."

"Come on, Jules. Tell me why this wouldn't solve a problem for you. You wanted that horse so much, then you just stopped talking about it. I figured you gave up on it. Now Rick is offering to buy him. It seems like another stroke of good fortune. First the co-op buys you Mickey, now Rick wants this horse of Amanda's? Horses and buyers are falling into your lap—"

"I don't want *someone else* to own him! I didn't want someone else to own Mickey, either, Pete. I wanted him for *me*. And now I'll never be able to afford Mickey for myself, unless they give him to me when he retires, but at least *this* horse could have been mine."

Pete blinked at me. "But it's much better business to have someone else own the horse. That's why everyone does syndicates or finds good ownership teams. You *know* this. You've always been hunting good owners."

"That was before."

"Before what?"

"Before the co-op! Before the kids and the lessons and the coaching and the camps. When I was just riding professionally, that was one thing. But I'm someone different now. My day isn't just all riding, all day long. I have lessons to teach, I have their horses to school." I sighed.

"I can only fit a couple of horses into my day. I want them to be *mine.*"

"I'm sorry," Pete said. "I didn't realize."

He sat down on the bed next to me, and took my hands in his. His fingers were cold. The air conditioning was on full-blast, I thought. That was why they were so chilly.

"I don't know the right thing to say to you anymore," he said.

I leaned my head against his shoulder. "Come on, Pete," I muttered. "No one ever could."

CHAPTER TWENTY-EIGHT

September in Central Park: golden leaves, wet grass, slanting sunlight, and million-dollar horses living in tents.

The four-legged athletes of the Central Park Horse Show were all settled in by the time we arrived, munching hay in the tent stables at the Rumsey Playfield. From the name, I'd expected slides and swings, or a soccer field, but instead, the stables had been pitched within a large, brick-enclosed ring which could have been a riding arena.

It was, in fact, home to a summer concert series. The last show of the season had been last week, Evan told me, smiling like he'd performed the gig himself. There were still cigarettes ground into the sand where the audience had ignored the park's smoking prohibition, and one groom found a guitar pick while she was cleaning her horse's stall.

The stables were a strange little island of normal life (to me) inside a vast ocean of humanity and cars and dogs (so many dogs!). On Wednesday evening, the shadows casting premature twilight over the park, a yellow cab dropped us at a Fifth Avenue park entrance. We had already checked in at the hotel, and Pete had stayed behind to rest for the next day. Lacey and I walked through the park, dodging hounds of every AKC description, until we spotted Evan standing beneath a street lamp, hand raised in welcome.

Alone among all of us, Evan seemed to be in his element in the city. Here, unlike in Ocala, his English countryman style could be shown off to people who knew who had designed his coat and his trousers, and the women were not so jaded from dating jerk horse trainers that they could no longer appreciate a fella with a nice ass in a pair of Tailored Sportsmans walking down Fifth Avenue. And that's just what the arena eventing team did, once we'd met the grooms who had escorted our horses here, and checked our horses' hay-nets and water buckets for ourselves: we walked south under glowing street laps, stumbled out of the park at Grand Army Plaza, our eyes tracing the French Renaissance hauteur of the Plaza Hotel rising above us, and marched in a close group past the flagships of Fifth Avenue, dressed in breeches and boots like a misplaced fox hunt.

Horse-crazy little girls tugged at their mother's hands and pointed. As we stood at crosswalks, waiting with the other tourists for the lights to change, passersby of both sexes let their eyes wander over our outfits at leisure. Locals flooded past us, pouring into cross-streets at the slightest gap in traffic, too impatient to be impressed with us, with their surroundings, with anything anymore.

The afternoon had been cool and gray, with a pearly sky hanging low over the Manhattan towers, and now the lights from the city were pressing back against the clouds, the skyscrapers trying to shrug off their wet blankets. I spotted the sculpted peaks of the Chrysler Building in the distance and tried not to gawk, but it was hard to keep my head down when everything around me had come straight out of a movie. I slowed my steps at the tiny window displays outside Tiffany's, peering into their sparkling depths. A security guard stood silently at the door, looking at no one and seeing everyone.

Pete had been waiting for us at the hotel, and he was in the bar when we arrived, at the center of a group of riders. Evan pushed through the brass-framed revolving door ahead of me and beckoned for me to follow with that delighted grin. I smiled back, because his enthusiasm was contagious and the city was thrilling, and when I looked ahead again, Pete was watching me, the slightest of frowns on his face. I winked at him, not letting my smile falter, and watched his lips relax.

The other riders were from the show jumping and dressage disciplines, along with a few members of my own arena eventing team who had arrived earlier in the day. They were wearing every sort of outfit, their wardrobe apparently dependent on when they'd arrived and what discipline they'd devoted their lives to. Most comfortable, and best adapted to their surroundings, were the women lounging against bar stools in deceptively casual summer dresses, sweaters shrugged over their shoulders. They were from the dressage team, and every one of them had the red lipstick and pearl earrings one would expect of the riding world's designated queens. Evan whispered that they'd all come in yesterday, and were enjoying New York with the same devotion they put into their pirouettes and tempi changes. I wished I could be that brave, but I wasn't sure I was ready to go back out the door without a tour guide at my side. Those teeming streets were like nothing I had ever experienced, and I suspected that I didn't have the smarts necessary to navigate them on my own. It would be like opening Dynamo's stall door and expecting him to figure out Central Park alone.

Except Dynamo would probably have enough sense to stop at the first green meadow he found, and just stay there chowing down. Whereas I would walk past a dozen cafes looking for one that didn't look too intimidating, and get lost for my trouble.

"Jules!" Pete called, straightening up from the low chair he was lounging in. He beckoned, casting a dark glance at Evan as he did so. "Come and tell me everything."

"Hey," I said, sliding on the arm of Pete's chair and leaning down for a kiss. His lips were cool. "What have I missed?"

The chair's fat arm was over-stuffed and covered in slick, glossy leather. I had to push one leg hard against the tiled floor to keep my balance on it.

"Nothing much," piped up my fellow eventer Ellen O'Brien, looking up from the chair next to Pete's. She was definitely not on her first martini, but I'd seen Ellen put away the complimentary beers in the hospitality tents before, and I wasn't surprised she was taking advantage of the comped bar tab tonight. "Pete here was just telling us about your lunatic asy-sy-a-sy,"—she paused and frowned —"your crazy barn," she managed finally, then grinned triumphantly. "That's a hard word! Don't laugh at me, guys. That's a hard word."

Maybe she was a bit more sloshed than I'd thought. "What's crazy about my barn?" I asked, glancing down at Pete, whose ears had turned red. "I have two dozen kids running around at all hours, but you guys all told me that was normal. Teach lessons, you said. Be a coach, you said. It'll bring in the bucks, you said. Well, here I am!"

I stood up and did a little spin, showing off my sponsored ensemble. For once, from the little gray slouch cap on my head to the polished field boots on my feet, I knew that I looked good—as good or better than anyone else in the bar, even if you included the non-equestrians in the sample. I was wearing the best of Rockwell's fall line, with a beautiful pale blue top and dove-gray breeches. For the event itself, I was going to debut a new blue-gray show coat, which I'd never ridden in before. I was thrilled to put aside the sober black coat I'd been jumping in for what felt like an eternity, and wear something trendy and modern. Sure, I'd never cared much what I'd looked like before, but I'd never been able to afford nice clothes before, either. It's amazing what a clothing stipend will do for your interest in fashion.

"Am I New York enough for ya?" I asked, and turned on my heel, sauntering over to the bar to order myself a drink. Something with liquor, a Manhattan-worthy drink, not just a beer. We weren't in Alachua County anymore.

The dressage queens leaned over while I was waiting for the bartender's attention. "Your team captain certainly is a cutie," one of them said, smiling to reveal perfect white teeth that seemed to match her pearl studs. "Why are you eventers always so damn attractive?"

"You're stuck with all the serious, cerebral guys," I agreed sympathetically.

"If they're not gay," the white-toothed woman said regretfully. "Straight guys just don't play in the sandbox."

"Well, you get that in all the disciplines," the other dressage queen said. She ran a hand through her short blonde hair. It was so white, I wondered if she was Scandinavian, Swedish maybe. But her accent was pure New Jersey. "Hunters, eventers, dressage, there's no one sport that's inherently gay."

I choked back a laugh.

"What are we talking about ladies?" The bartender arrived on the scene with an interested look, as if he'd been part of their conversation earlier and had been loathe to give it up.

"The good ones are gay," the blonde said, shrugging.

"I'm not."

"You ever ride a horse?"

"My sister's, when we were kids. I fell off and it stepped on my stomach. I never rode it again."

"You see, you used the word *it* to describe a horse when you definitely knew the gender," the white-toothed one said. "Very disappointing, Victor."

"It won't happen again," the bartender promised. "Although I don't remember if it—if *the horse*—was a boy or a girl. Stomped on me like a woman, now that I think about it. Had very good aim."

Through their laughter, I managed to order a vodka cranberry, the only liquor-based drink I could think of. Victor mixed it up for me, threw in a lime wedge, and gave me a conspiratorial wink, which at first I did not understand. When I'd wandered back to the group and taken my first sip, I realized, around my coughs, that it was because he'd poured me a double.

It proved to be the first of many. Eventually we all decamped and went to the restaurant the coaches had booked us for dinner, an Italian hole-in-the-wall back up near Central Park, where we crowded out the regulars with our wine and our bread and our enthusiastic attacks on swirling, slippery pasta. Why was it so hard to get it on my fork? I wondered at one point, before someone filled my glass again and I renewed my assault on the bread basket. Whether we were there to carb-load or to bond as a team or the restaurant had simply offered the best group rate, the end result was the same: we tumbled into cabs afterward and stared out the windows at the rain-slicked streets, the color from neon signs dripping from the buildings and pooling on the pavement, slowly slipping into a trance that would see us all the way up the elevators, into our rooms, and straight into our beds.

CHAPTER TWENTY-NINE

Thursday morning, the rain was still falling, and we climbed into cabs for the short ride up to the stabling in a fog of headaches and exhaust fumes. The city was wide awake despite the early hour, the cafes humming with life and endless lines of cabs and buses splashing through puddles. The sidewalks of Fifth Avenue teemed with black umbrellas, which looked like so many busy beetles when viewed from high up in the hotel, but at ground level were revealed to be high-speed weapons threatening to take out the face of anyone who didn't duck out of the way quickly enough.

"I'm not sure umbrellas work with this many people," I observed as the cab ground its way north, windshield wipers slapping rhythmically.

"Nothing works with this many people," Pete growled. He'd been bad-tempered all morning, barely speaking to me in the hotel room as we'd dressed around each other.

"Are we fighting? Remind me."

"We're not fighting."

"Really?" I turned to him. "Then can you adjust your tone when you speak to me, please? I did not create this traffic."

"It's not the traffic," Pete said sulkily. "It's this whole damn city."

"Then get out and yell at the city," I suggested, "and stop taking it out on me. I asked you to come along to be supportive, not stress me out."

"Of course," he agreed, looking out of the window. "I am here to be your support."

Something in his words struck me as insincere, but I decided to put it out of my head and concentrate on the morning to come. I had two schooling rides to get Dynamo right in the park arena. One today, one tomorrow. Then, Saturday night, the show went on, rain or shine. There would be no second chances. If Dynamo hated the city as much as Pete apparently did, I'd just have to put him together as best as I could and remind him that we were both professionals. But the truth was, I needed nothing less than perfection this weekend. Not a tall order at all, right?

The cabs weren't allowed onto the park road where the stable tents were, so we had to get out at a nearby cross-street, cross Fifth Avenue, and walk into the park. Dogs ran unleashed, splashing in puddles, and toddlers in rubber boots followed suit while nannies sighed and dog walkers laughed. The park was nearly as busy as the streets outside;

I turned to watch a Border Collie rocket after a Frisbee and was nearly taken down by a very serious-looking jogger.

Pete, still on crutches, had put on a long waxed raincoat courtesy of Rockwell Bros. and was looking very *Man From Snowy River*. I told him so, and got a grimace for my trouble. So, today's going to be fun, I thought.

Lacey was already at the barn, the grooms having been brought up on a van early in the morning to take care of their charges. She was sitting on a bale of hay when we came into the barn, talking to a groom with a purple pony-tail and an arm's worth of unicorn tattoos. Sort of a more bubbly version of Lindsay, I thought, offering them both a good morning. I had brought Lacey coffee and handed it over, wishing I had more, but the other groom excused herself, saying her rider was probably here, too.

Lacey took a deep gulp of coffee. "Oh, that's sweet," she sighed. "Thank you." Lacey preferred her sugar with a side of coffee, and was the first to jump on every gimmicky new flavor the cafes came out with. "What *is* this?" she asked after a second deep dive.

"Maple toffee," I said, my teeth aching at the mere thought. "It's the latest and greatest in dessert for breakfast."

"Bless," Lacey said. "Oh, Dynamo's just fine," she added, waving at the stall behind her.

Dynamo was nostrils-deep in a flake of alfalfa, his coat shining from an early morning grooming. He glanced up at me when I leaned over the stall guard, blew a snort in greeting, and then went back to his hay. "Thank you for taking care of him," I said. "Lindsay really wanted to come, but I felt more comfortable letting her help Haley's working student with the barn, than bringing her to the city without her parents."

"She's too young to be let loose here," Lacey agreed. "Plus, I'm afraid once Lindsay discovers the big city, all those horse-girl dreams are going to get knocked right out of her head."

"You think? I don't know. She's pretty devoted to the barn. She hated you when you came, you know. She wanted to be my barn manager, or my groom, or anything that made her my right-hand man."

"I know, but there's something about Lindsay that's hungry for more than mucking stalls and dumping grain."

Pete had settled down onto the hay bale Lacey had vacated. He nodded at her words. "I think Lindsay has some wild years ahead of her, but she might come back to horses once she gets it out of her system."

I hated the idea of Lindsay leaving. We'd had a few conspiratorial chats about what she'd do next year, after high school graduation, and most of them had revolved around taking classes at the University of Florida in Gainesville to please her parents, and spending every spare moment at the barn as a working student, plus maybe bringing up a new horse to be her eventer after William retired—possibly an off-track Thoroughbred. "Let's think about today instead of next year," I decided. "Our schooling window is coming up, so we'd better think about tacking up and getting over to the arena."

Riding through Central Park was the strangest sensation of my life. All around me, the city rose up in granite and steel —there was no way to miss it, or forget it was there, even in the most thickly wooded sections we rode through. The pathways were more elegant than anything I'd ever seen in a park before: black iron fences, stately lamp-posts, noble statues. We rode down a park drive which led us towards the imposing barricade of skyscrapers at Central Park South. As the buildings grew higher and higher, I felt as if we were descending towards a tunnel, as if we'd have to find our way down beneath those massive buildings, and if I hadn't been so busy trying to keep Dynamo focused and avoiding a spook on the rain-slick pavement, I might have felt a little panicky. It was just so *different*.

We turned off the main road before we had to navigate the roads between those skyscrapers, though, and instead meandered along a charming footpath, until we suddenly came around a corner and found the Central Park Horse Show laid out before us. The grandstand wrapping around the arena felt reassuringly *real* compared with the strange surroundings of city buildings and city people and all those beautiful, manic, city dogs. Dynamo blew out through his nostrils and quickened his pace, finally realizing why he was here. *Ah, a horse show!* I could hear him thinking. *Now, that makes more sense.*

A few police officers sat on dark horses near the arena

entrance, smiling and waving at us as we rode up to the steward and got our permission to enter. Their horses snoozed, ears waggling at half-mast, hardly noticing as the new show horses paraded in and out of their personal space. Even the horses were different in the city, I thought. Nothing in New York was like its counterpart in the real world.

The million-dollar footing in the arena was smooth under Dynamo's hooves, even in the places where puddles were threatening to take over. There were no jumps loaded in yet, but a few plain standards and poles had been set up to allow us to get some jump schooling in. Evan busied himself setting fences and schooling riders one at a time over them, building a tall vertical and a wide, boxy oxer side-by-side. It felt like the warm-up at any show, except for the sounds of sirens and car horns and general din that seemed to permeate every moment of Manhattan life.

"The constant sirens were making me nervous at first," I said to another rider as we sat side-by-side, waiting for someone else to jump. "I thought there was a bombing or something. But I guess that's just the way it is here."

"Nonstop emergencies," he agreed. "This must be an exhausting place to live."

Both of us nodded, as if we didn't lead exhausting dawn to late-night lives as horse trainers.

"Are you going out to see some of the city this afternoon?" he asked.

"Is that a better idea than hiding in my room with a

pillow over my head? Because that was my first plan."

He laughed. "You have to get out there. At least for a couple of hours. See another version of life."

"Are you coming out with the team this afternoon?"

I looked up from the shavings where I was kneeling, adjusting the wraps on Dynamo's legs. Evan was leaning over the stall guard, his expression chipper despite the sound of rain falling on the tent above our heads. "Where are you going?" I asked, knowing Pete wouldn't be up for anything too physical.

"Oh, all over the city. I've got a whole itinerary mapped out, the full tourist treatment. Chinatown, Times Square, Rockefeller Center—we're going to see it all. Who knows when we'll have a chance to come back?"

"Sounds fun, but really tiring. I'd better not." I turned back to Dynamo's bandages, hoping to hide my disappointment. I couldn't help but want to spend more time with Evan, feeding that beast inside that still found his smile electric and exciting, because once this show was over, so was our training together. There would be no excuses to get coffee or talk horses when he was back in Ocala and I was back in Alachua County, an hour's drive and a world apart. I knew that was for the best, but it didn't mean I had to like it. "Maybe Pete and I will do some sightseeing on our own," I said, tucking the Velcro into place, then adding a bandage pin, the way my racing friend Alex had once shown me, for maximum security. "There are probably some places on his list to see."

"Pete's leg might be worn out from this morning," Evan suggested. "If he can't make it out, come with us."

"Okay," I agreed. "Thanks."

"You know, you don't have to avoid me. I can behave myself." Evan was whispering now, leaning into the stall, his expression serious.

"I know, Evan. But thank you for saying so."

He nodded, turning away with a little wave. I watched him go off down the aisle. The sooner he's out of my life, the better, I told myself. Even if it would hurt like hell at first. Infatuations were a pain in the ass.

I'd finished straightening Dynamo's bandages when Pete arrived, settling down on the hay bale outside the stall door with a low sigh that was half a groan in disguise. "Are you alright?" I asked, coming over to the door.

He was looking at his leg in disgust, as if the continued presence of the fracture was a personal affront to him. "Fine, I suppose. And how is Mr. Dynamo?"

"Cleaning up his hay like a Dyson," I said, ducking under the stall guard. I settled down on the hay next to him. "Do you want to go out and see some sights? The team is going on this whole tourist thing."

"The team? I'm not invited on that."

"Of course you are," I protested. "You're part of my team."

"You wouldn't bring Lacey," Pete pointed out, correctly.

"You're not my groom. That's not the same thing at all."

But I could see his point. A team outing was not a place to bring spouses or significant others. "But actually, I wasn't going to suggest we went with them. We could, I don't know, pick a couple of things to see and get a nice dinner..."

Pete looked at the ground, and I could see he was tired and sore. I regretted my words at once; Evan was the one putting the idea in my head that we had to go out, had to see the city. I started to speak again, to tell him it was fine, but Pete was already nodding. "Let's do that," he said. "We're actually really close to the Met—let's go there, and then see what we feel like doing next."

"Okay," I said. "If you're sure."

Pete smiled and then shrugged, the ultimate *who knows, who cares* combination. "Let's go get cleaned up, then."

Pete sat on a bench while I wandered the arms and armor room at the Met, studying the steel-plated warhorses. The museum was a maze of antiquities, and at first we'd found our way into the Egyptian room instead of the medieval galleries everyone had told us to go see, so by the time the world around us had shifted from pharaohs to knights, Pete was looking exhausted and my own feet were starting to suffer from too many miles of marble tiles. After a few minutes, I found myself on the bench next to him, flexing my toes inside my clogs.

"These aren't museum shoes," he said eventually.

"It was these or my sneakers, and I didn't want to get wet feet and end up with blisters before the show."

"Fair point."

We looked at the model horses in silence.

"This is weird for me," Pete said, so low I had to duck my head towards him to catch his words.

"What is? Being in New York?"

"Being on the sidelines. Watching everyone else warm-up for this huge show. Watching Evan boss you around."

I looked down at my clogs, the mud clinging to the toes. "This isn't about Evan, is it?"

"It is a little bit. I can't help that. He shouldn't have gotten further than me. He shouldn't be the coach out there. Just because his father is sick, he asks to be put in charge and they hand it to him?"

I smiled sadly. "Pete, you and Evan are both eventing aristocracy. You're both where you're at because you came from eventing families. When are you going to realize that? He's not your enemy. He's just another rich horse kid, and you're mad because he's still rich and you're not anymore. It's worse because you're not riding, but you're going to get out there and destroy them all this winter. Just wait. Just wait and see."

Pete didn't say anything.

The horses in front of us marched towards battle in lockstep, hooves frozen in mid-stride, draped in metal from nose to tail.

I took his hand, squeezed it.

"You're going to be *fine.*"

After a moment, he squeezed back.

Little triumphs, I thought.

CHAPTER THIRTY

One last warm-up, one last chance to feel out the ground and the light and the sound, and then the show would be upon us.

As Dynamo and I stood waiting at the in-gate, the steward keeping rigid time as everyone wanted their turn at a ride in the arena, a little rain shower began, the drops pattering on my helmet. I was happy I wasn't wearing my new show ensemble yet. The elegant jacket had been carefully hung up, wrapped in plastic and zippered inside a monogrammed garment bag, in the nearby tents set up for the horses and riders performing tonight. With the full stabling so far away, they'd moved the event horses down to day stalls near the arena for the evening. After the competition, we'd take them back up to the main stabling for the night, and tomorrow, the jumpers and dressage horses would come down for their shift.

Pete was nearby, leaning against the fence, still covered up in the oilskin coat he'd been wearing for the past two days, trying to keep his leg dry. He'd been detached and cool with me, but he'd been helpful—when Evan wasn't nearby. The moment the team coach appeared by my side with a tip or suggestion, Pete retreated, disappearing into the crowds of spectators who had come for a peek at the country's top horses, and I hadn't been able to keep track of him all afternoon. It was nice to see him now. I nudged Dynamo closer to him.

"Pete," I called, "what do you think of the approach to the sixth fence?"

Pete glanced at me, then squinted through the raindrops at the fence with the 6 sign leaning against it. The obstacle was a brightly painted barn-shaped box, built to enormous proportions, with a few wooden chickens pecking at the dust in front of it. It sat at a slight angle just about six feet from the arena rail, so there was no way to ride a truly straight line to it—something challenging for a fence of that size and shape.

"Take five from this angle," Pete said finally, gesturing at the floral concoction a short distance away, "and then gun for three strides to the arena wall, turn left, and lock in. You'll have enough time to balance up for it if you get that turn in time. Think you can manage it?"

"Do you?" I smiled at him, a peace offering. *You're my coach here.*

"I know you can," Pete said. "Take him past it one time

in this warm-up, to give you both a look, but I know you can get the distance."

We weren't allowed to jump the fences during the final warm-up session; we were just getting the horses used to the delirium of seeing a cross-country course in an arena surrounded by grandstands and skyscrapers. A fly-by of the fences to come was a bonus we didn't usually get in this game, and everyone was trying to take full advantage of it during their scheduled warm-up rounds.

A middle-aged man in a gray suit was making his way towards the in-gate, a young woman holding an umbrella over his head as they picked through the muddy puddles. He looked up at me and smiled as if we knew one another. I smiled tentatively in return. Which rich person was this?

"This is the mayor," the woman said brightly.

"Of New York?" I asked, leaning down to shake his hand.

"That's what they tell me," he said cheerfully, his grip light on my gloved hand. "Good luck out there. Where are you here from?"

"Florida," Pete answered for me. A bid to be noticed, I thought, feeling guilty, although it wasn't my fault Pete was grounded while I was mounted.

"You're here together?" The mayor shook Pete's hand as well, looking interested in our backstory.

"We are," Pete said after a pause. "We are partners. But *she's* the one with the big horse right now. This is Jules Thornton and Dynamo."

The mayor smiled broadly. "My niece loves you!" He

exclaimed. "Wait until I tell her that I met you. She rode at the Winter Equestrian Festival last winter. Maybe you saw her?" The mayor rambled on a bit about his niece's barn and trainer. It was painfully clear she was a hunter rider and never would have heard of us, but to the mayor of New York City, we were all just people on horseback wearing funny hats.

"Maybe we did," I said, when it became obvious Pete wasn't going to lie to make him happy. "We'll look for her this winter."

"She'll love that."

"Jules?" Evan called. "You're up!"

I felt a sudden rush of butterflies. I looked around to find Evan and give him a wave. When I turned back to Pete, he was looking at me, his jaw tight.

"I'm going to do my round, Pete," I called, trying to sound normal.

Pete nodded grimly.

I gathered my reins and blew air through my lips, waking up Dynamo, and we went trotting into the arena, leaving all the insanity on the other side of the gate.

Evan was the one who caught us on the way out of the arena. I had been looking for Pete, but one glance at Evan's shining smile and I surrendered Dynamo's reins to him.

"He looked lovely out there," he told me brightly, clutching at the reins as Dynamo pushed at him. "Ride him just like that again tonight and you'll clinch the win. And I don't just mean the team win—I mean the whole shebang."

The whole shebang was what I wanted—that was the big check, that was Confident Liar coming to my farm on a truck, wholly mine and no one else's, forever and ever.

Dynamo, still worked up from galloping around the arena, started eyeballing the gathering media trucks. He spun around Evan, tugging at the reins. Evan let go and stepped out of the big horse's way, but he stayed close to us, keeping his eyes locked on mine. All at once, I felt that magnetism of his again, the way his gaze bored into my thoughts, the way my skin tingled at his nearness. The worst part was that he knew it: he knew that I was keyed up and thrilled and above all hungry, and he wanted me to turn that hunger towards him. He knew exactly how vulnerable I was to him at this moment, and he was encouraging it. He'd told me he was safe, but he wasn't.

I flushed with the realization, feeling both angry and flattered. I wasn't used to being the object of such a determined chase, so despite Pete's words from months ago, that Evan went after women all the time and left a trail of destruction in his wake, an idiotic part of my mind was preening with the attention. I didn't want to be one of Evan's conquests, of course, and yet he'd given me the impression, probably perfected over the years on dozens of women but no less enticing when directed at me, that I was the *one* he wanted, that everyone else had been a lead-up to me. After all, I was Jules Thornton, the star of the US Arena Eventing Team, poised to clinch the individual title at the arena eventing championship in beautiful Central Park, Manhattan—*I was the girl everyone wanted to be seen with*, and Evan should be so lucky as to take me back to his hotel room.

Dynamo flung up his head, slinging foam from his bit through the air, and I pushed him away from Evan before one of us got hurt. I knew it was only a matter of time before that happened.

I walked Dynamo in a circle on the grass near the parked news vans and tried to collect my thoughts. One thing was certain: I had to force myself to stay away from Evan. There were perfectly good reasons to explain away my attraction to him, but knowing the cause didn't mean I could just switch it off. I was high on adrenaline and nerves, a cocktail of terror and anticipation that could only lead to bad decisions if my energy wasn't totally channeled towards the challenge ahead.

I had a few hours to kill before we came back for the event, and in that period I just had to steer clear of Evan, keep myself busy, keep my brain occupied—then, after tonight, after I'd won the big check and the fear was gone and I could think clearly, then everything would be fine again. It would be over. We could move on.

"Watch out, lady!" A panicky guy in a raincoat, holding a spool of heavy black cable, held up his free hand. I'd ridden Dynamo right into the area where they were setting up more hospitality tents for the glittering VIPs who would be in the audience tonight.

I spun Dynamo around and looked around for the best way out of the growing crowd of spectators and media; I wanted to get him back to the stabling and cleaned up so that he could rest for the afternoon, and so I could put some distance between myself and Evan.

Suddenly Pete was standing in front of us, his face stormy, the rain dripping from the hood of his coat and onto his nose. I noticed for the first time that his habitual tan had faded. He'd probably been losing it during all these weeks he'd been sidelined by his broken leg, but it hadn't become clear until we were here in this wet city, where the pavement and the granite and the steel drained the color from everything real and good.

I reined back Dynamo, and though at first he teetered back and forth, shifting his balance as he tried to decide how naughty he should be about it, the excited horse finally stood still for longer than five seconds. Pete came closer.

"What was that about?" Pete asked, his voice tight.

"What was *what?*" I asked, but I already knew, and my heart was sinking. He'd seen all those quick looks I'd exchanged with Evan today, and he was no fool—he'd seen them before. But how to convince him that I was fighting it? That I was keeping well away from Evan until this was over? That it meant absolutely nothing? That it was all just nerves and passion welling up in me until I couldn't see straight? That if he'd stop pushing me away, I could direct all this terrified energy at him, instead?

I didn't know how to explain it in words, though. I didn't

know how brains and attraction worked. I knew how to train horses. That was it.

Everything else in my life was catch as catch can.

"Pete, help me take Dynamo back to the stabling area. I'm totally flustered. I can't think straight."

"You should know that Evan is telling people that he's inviting you to move to Aiken at the end of this," Pete said, his words tumbling out in a staccato rush. "That he wants you at the team trainings there all winter, and since they're not in Ocala this year, he'll make room for you at his farm. What did you tell him? Are you leaving?"

My jaw dropped. Of all the accusations I'd been steeling myself for, this was not the one I had anticipated. "I don't know anything about that," I managed to gasp. "Why would he say that to you?"

"He didn't say it *to* me," Pete admitted. "We're not exactly on speaking terms. As you know. But he made sure it would get back to me, I can assure you."

"I don't think it's true," I said, picking up the reins and circling Dynamo again as the horse pulled on me, wrenching at my shoulders with his strong neck. "He would have said something to me. Team training?" My voice caught. Crazy words began to bubble up in my brain. *The US team. International competition. Kentucky. Burghley. The World Cup. The Olympics.* It was all so close I could almost feel the weight of the medal around my neck, the cold metal pressing against my chest. What kind of substitute would it make for real feelings?

"I knew things were falling apart, Jules, but this isn't how I saw it happening," Pete said, his fierce tone jolting me back to reality.

"Things *aren't* falling apart," I cried. Startled, Dynamo ducked his head and tried to bolt; I snatched back on the reins, ignoring his protest as he flung up his head, gaping his mouth. I turned my head to keep Pete from disappearing again. Somehow, I thought that if he escaped my sight, I'd never see him again. "How can you say that? I have been waiting for *you*—I have been waiting for you to figure out what you want, so that I can help you get it! I told you to figure it out, Pete, but I never gave you an ultimatum, and I never even hinted that I might leave, so why would you believe that?"

"It's what you want," Pete said simply, and for the first time I saw the sag of defeat creep into his tense jaw. "Evan's offering you what you've always wanted."

"No, he's not," I protested, but I knew Pete was right, and it was a silly thing to pretend, even for a moment, that it wasn't. This was Evan's moment on the mountaintop, I realized. He was the devil, offering me everything I'd ever wanted. I just had to give him what *he* wanted.

And give up Pete.

I swung my leg over Dynamo, sliding down to the muddy grass, but Pete backed away from me, his limp pitiful to behold. The rain had stopped while we'd been arguing, and the sun was suddenly emerging as if summoned by a shaman, the clouds parting in the most theatrical way imaginable. Suddenly, all around us, New York sparkled, a city of a million, billion sheets of glass held in place by steel and brick and granite and iron, a canyon of sand melted into structure, and we sat helpless in its bowl, our faces dusted with its golden reflections. Pete's chin came up, and his jaw squared again, as if the sun was just what he needed to back him up, an ally sparkling right out of our Florida life.

"Put yourself first, Jules," he said firmly. "That's who you are. I've always known that about you, and I accepted it. I've never expected you to change."

So he was just going to make that decision for me, was he? He was going to stand there and tell *me* that I was too self-absorbed to stay with him, that I would never make a sacrifice for him? I drew myself up and ran at him, my fists clenched at my side. Behind me, Lacey had appeared and was drawing Dynamo away, back into the tent where he could be groomed and braided and prepped for his biggest moment yet. I let him go, be led away, because I was the rider and she was the groom, and when I didn't have to fit every single aspect of horse care and training into my life, I had room for other things. Even the things that made me hurt and rage. I had room for all of them because I *wanted* them. I wanted all of life.

"You don't get to make this call for me," I hissed, rage coursing through my veins and making me tremble. I clenched my fists tighter so that my hands wouldn't shake. There was no time to look vulnerable. This was a moment for a warrior, not a lover. He'd turned away from my love, time and time again this summer, making himself out to be too damaged, too disappointed, too downtrodden to be present emotionally. And so here we were. "You don't get to snap your fingers and end everything we've got, and blame it on *me*. This is *your* doing, Pete Morrison. *Yours!* I have *waited* for you to get yourself together, to figure out your horses and your life, and you have *refused!* So while my life was actually coming together, you just got resentful. Well, *fuck you*, Pete. *Fuck you* for not being here for me, and coming up to me spreading rumors, like I ought to be ashamed that someone has recognized my potential. You should have walked up to me and told me what good news you had, not treated me like I was plotting behind your back."

Pete's response at first was stunned silence, and a quick sliding of his eyes from side to side, and I realized we had an audience, that the moment the sun had emerged, so had the guests and media and early-arriving spectators from their pavilions and vans, and that dozens, maybe hundreds of people were watching us in riveted silence. It crossed my mind that this was a hundred times worse than the day Lacey and Becky had fought at the Sunshine State Horse Park, and that incident had followed me for months, if not years. This could be the end of whatever Evan had been planning on offering me, if that story was even true.

But all of that was secondary now. I focused all of my anger on Pete. This was a fight that had be fought, finally, after months of skirmishes. It ended now.

Oh, how it ended now.

"If that's how you feel, maybe this Aiken thing is just really good timing," Pete said, his voice low, foiling the crowds who were straining to hear our lover's quarrel.

I turned away so that he wouldn't see my face twist in pain. It was like a knife to the gut, and I'd never thought Pete would be the one who would stab me.

When I looked back, unable to stop myself, he was already limping away.

CHAPTER THIRTY-ONE

There was a knock at the hotel room door.

I was still sitting in shock, looking at the empty spot in the bed beside me, with the sheets pulled up to my chin, and yet my mouth stupidly called: "Come in!" as if I was expecting room service or a package from the front desk. The doorknob rattled, and I realized it couldn't be a member of the staff at the door, who would have entered with their own key... and even if it had been, they wouldn't have been able to get past the chain latch.

"I'm coming," I shouted, jumping out of bed and pulling the hotel's white plush robe around me, hoisting the thick collar high around my neck and drawing the belt tight. Just in case... just in case.

I peered through the peephole and saw Lacey standing in the narrow hallway, glaring impatiently at the little bubble of glass as if she could see me through it. A sigh shuddered through my lungs, so deep it seemed to have begun at the very soles of my feet. *It's only Lacey.* Who had I expected? Evan? A serial killer? Misdirected pizza delivery guy?

Pete?

Lacey came inside as soon as I opened the door, casting a critical gaze over my robe and bare feet. She was fully dressed in jeans and paddock boots, a gray hoodie zipped up to her throat. "I thought you wanted to come to the barn with me this morning," she said, "to see how Dynamo came out of the show."

"Did I? Did I say that?" I tried to remember the night before. I'd been so tired, after the show and the fanfare and the search for Pete. I couldn't recall what I'd said to Lacey, or to the press, or to the mayor of New York, or to anyone, for that matter. It had all happened without me, somehow. The best moments of my life to date and I'd missed them. "I just need a few minutes."

"No, it's fine. Stay here, get yourself together. I'll go feed and check his legs. Meet you up there later." Lacey turned to leave, not bothering to hide her irritation.

"Stop!" I put my hand on Lacey's shoulder. I felt an intense terror at the idea of being left alone again. "Don't go without me, please. I'll be ready in ten minutes."

Lacey studied me for a moment. "Fine," she said finally, with the air of granting a huge favor. "I'm going to go down and get us some coffees. I'll be in the lobby."

"That's perfect," I said, letting her go, although the truth was I would have preferred she stay with me while I ran cold water over my face and brushed my teeth and pulled on my jeans and paddock boots. What might happen to me while she was gone? What if she disappeared, too? The dread pooling in my stomach was nauseating. "Get me a banana, please," I called as she went down the hallway, and she waved a hand in response.

I retreated back into my room as Lacey disappeared around the corner, heading for the elevator landing, and nearly had the door shut on her and whatever bogeyman was out there waiting to frighten me when I heard my name.

I paused.

"Jules? Are you there?"

It was Evan.

I should close the door, I thought. I should close the door and lock it. Put the chain up. Get back into bed and hide under the covers.

Instead, I waited.

Evan's face appeared around the half-open door. "Did you just get up?" he asked. He was dressed and ready for the stables, if the stables had a formal dress code which called for pressed tan trousers and polished jodhpur boots.

I nodded. "I'm going down to the stables with Lacey," I said. "She's waiting for me, I have to hurry."

"She can wait a minute, I'm sure. The cars will be coming around to pick everyone up, one will wait for you guys."

The cars? I wondered what I'd missed last night, if there'd been a team update on horse care schedules while the dressage and jumpers took their day in the spotlight. We started shipping out tomorrow morning, but we'd need room to hand-walk and graze our horses today. Maybe the park people were insisting we got that done early, before the crowds of New Yorkers and tourists descended upon the park for a sunny Sunday out.

"I have to go," I insisted, and started to push the door closed.

Evan put his hand on the door and held it open.

He was surprisingly strong—or maybe it wasn't a surprise. He was a horseman, too, after all. "Just let me talk while you get ready."

I was wearing only the robe; my show clothes, my white breeches and my lovely blue-gray riding coat, were tossed over the chair by the window. I vaguely remembered pulling them off and flinging them aside before I'd crawled into bed last night, exhausted beyond all measure. I glanced back at them, then shrugged and let Evan into the room. "I'm changing clothes in the bathroom," I warned him, choosing my words to make it sound like I was wearing pajamas under my robe.

"Fine," he said. "Of course."

And then he started talking.

He told me I was a star in the making, a diamond in the rough, a champion on the cusp of greatness. He told me he could get me the best owners in the sport, top horses with stunning sport bloodlines, experienced horses who were just looking for the ride to take them to the top. He told me everything I'd ever wanted to hear.

The bathroom door was open a crack; he leaned back just outside the door, his head tipped against the wall, and talked while I cautiously dropped my robe and pulled on underwear and socks and a bra and jeans and a navy blue polo shirt with a Briar Hill logo stitched on the chest. Occasionally, I saw his hand wave past the half-inch of space between the door and the frame as he gestured to no one, making some argument about the infancy of my career, the endless triumphs of my future.

"Aiken," he said as I pulled my hair back in a tight pony-tail. "We're wintering in Aiken this year, and I think you should be there."

You're not going to Aiken, I told my reflection silently, looping the elastic around my fingers, pulling them free, smoothing back loose hairs from my forehead. *You're not going anywhere with him.*

"There's a World Equestrian Games next summer and I'm not making any guarantees, but you could be a strong contender. All we have to do is keep Dynamo going, and I have a full range of therapy options up there to do it. And then in a couple of years, on bigger and better horses, you'll have no problem qualifying. But you have to start now. Today. There's no time to waste. Eventing's a sport for the young."

I brushed my teeth laboriously, fitting the bristles into every chink of my mouth, and considered what a strangely false statement that was. Eventing was a sport for the middle-aged, even the old. The elder champions of our sport were in their sixties. The thing about eventing was that you could never, ever master it. You could only get better. You could only try harder. You could only ride with more grace, and softness, and empathy. Eventing was a sport you aged into, skills strengthening and sharp edges smoothing over the decades, like wine mellowing in a cellar.

I spit toothpaste into the sink. Evan went on talking, about wasted chances and misspent youth, and how I didn't have a second to lose.

I thought about Pete's grandfather.

Pete had once said that the best ride of the old man's life had come just weeks before he died.

I pushed open the bathroom door, and Evan jumped aside, startled.

"Are you ready?" he asked, reaching for the door handle.

"Meet me in the cafe next door," I said. "Get me a medium latte with three shots. I have to get a couple things and I'll be right down." I moved to the dresser, started picking up things that were still plugged in: my watch, my phone. Evan hesitated. "Go! I'll be right down."

He went out the door.

I texted Lacey: *get a cab out front and lmk when it's waiting.*

When we finally got to the stables, people were already buzzing around outside. Grooms were lugging muck tubs to the dumpster nearby, riders were watching horses trot up in front of the tent, and a few hangers-on were drinking coffee and chatting in clusters nearby. Outside the stone walls of the enclosure, New York jogged and cycled and strolled by, not one in ten looking to see what the circus had brought to their town this time.

Lacey was looking over her shoulder every few steps, but I was confident we'd put at least a few blocks between us and Evan. How long would he wait in the cafe next to the hotel, while my latte cooled in his hand? Hopefully at least ten minutes. Hopefully I was worth that long to him.

"Can you wait out here for a moment?" I stopped Lacey outside of the tent entrance. "Text me if he shows."

"You mean Evan or Pete?"

"Evan," I said. "I have a feeling I know where Pete is."

And there he was, leaning against Dynamo's flimsy stall wall, watching my big chestnut pull from a freshly-filled hay-net. They'd gotten close last year when Pete was competing him, and it only made sense that when the rest of the world was failing him, Pete would come back to a horse he knew and trusted.

He was wearing last night's clothes, and his face was weary, lines of exhaustion etched into his cheeks and around his eyes. But he straightened his shoulders when he saw me.

"Jules," he said, keeping his hands at his sides, a formality I appreciated. If he'd thought we were on touching terms, as if nothing had happened, I might have had to murder him, and that would be hard to explain to the police and our sponsors. "I—I'm sorry about yesterday."

I leaned over the stall guard and gave Dynamo's neck a rub. He was warm and firm and real—the only rock a person could ever need. "Thank you," I said, my voice cool. I had years of experience in pushing down my emotions, and I was grateful for every painful day of them now. I was furious with Pete—furious and desperately relieved that he was fine —but detachment was my only defense, the last line I had before I lost it completely. And I needed to let Pete find his way out of this on his own.

I wasn't going to simply forgive him with just an apology, and I couldn't simply walk away. We would have to find a middle ground.

Pete tugged at the sleeves of his coat. "I've been— drifting," he began, his voice hesitant. "I've been following you because I didn't know what else to do. But—it hasn't worked. You've gone places I couldn't follow. And," his words began to rush, as if he was ashamed to say them, or ashamed at what they signified, "you're so sure of yourself, you're so confident, that when you make a move it feels crazy not to follow you, even though I don't know if that's my path, and I just—I just started to feel like I was going crazy, like I didn't know my own mind. Cobbling together a day with rides here and there, going back to Amanda's barn, avoiding you, avoiding teaching the kids, then feeling bad and doubling back to do *more* with them..." his voice trailed off and he tugged hard at a seam on his cuff. The thread came out in his fingers, a zigzagging line that drifted towards the dirt at our feet.

Two grooms floated by, deep in conversation about the day's dressage competition. In my pocket, my phone buzzed, and I knew Evan was coming, but there was nothing I could do but let Pete try to finish. I felt a throbbing fear in my stomach. What he was going to say next—

"I have to go away for a little while," he said. "Not because of us, because of me. Because I'm a disaster now and you're—you're settled. You can go to Aiken or you can stay in Alachua and either way, you're going to come out on top. But I don't have your confidence. I thought I did, but it was just because of who I was told I was. It wasn't because of *who* I was."

"Oh god," I said, because I was out of words, and all I wanted right now was an all-knowing deity to help me make sense of what was happening. "Oh god."

"I love you," Pete said helplessly. "I don't want any of this."

"I love you," I said, tears choking my voice. "Don't do it." And I threw myself against him, hardly noticing when he rocked under my weight, leaning on his good leg to hold him upright, realizing only afterward that I could have hurt him, and what an apt metaphor for our relationship that was.

We flew home the next day, having loaded Dynamo onto one of a succession of horse vans which drove up the East Drive of the park to pick up their million-dollar loads and start heaving them all around the country. Some of the vans were going where we were, to JFK airport, with horses who were shipping off to Europe, bound for competitions held under the stern glares of manor houses and castles. I remembered when Pete had gone to England and I had been told to stay behind, left unwanted in Florida, and I thought about how strange life was.

Lacey was sitting a few rows behind us, the team not having spent the extra money on plane tickets with previously assigned seats, and I missed her calming presence as the plane rose through the air and pitched, gently at first and then with increasing insistence, over the city and towards the Jersey shore. I didn't fly often and I found myself gripping the armrests with white-knuckled strength. Then there was a warm hand on mine. I looked up at Pete and he smiled reassuringly.

He still looked tired and I thought he might look that way for a long time. His leg was nearly healed, his physical therapy was scheduled, and yesterday he had talked to a few different riders about winter season jobs. One was in Wellington. One was in California. None were in Ocala, or in Aiken, for that matter.

"But I'm not going to Aiken," I told him, when he explained why he wasn't considering the South Carolina town. "I have my kids to think about. *You* should go up there, show them all what you've got." Aiken's eventing scene was every bit as happening as Ocala's. If he just needed to step out of my slipstream for a while, I thought that was the logical choice.

"Not with Evan and the team you just competed with at every event in the area," Pete said. "I need to disappear for a little while. I need to just think about my riding, and sort out my goals, and not let anyone else feel like they can put me on notice."

I didn't quite understand, but I thought I almost understood, and that had to be enough. "And then you'll come back," I said, as I had said twenty times since yesterday morning.

"I'll come back," Pete promised. "And I'll get my book written. Did I tell you I was writing a book about dressage for eventing?"

"No," I said, pretending to be astonished. "Are you really?"

"I am. You'll love it. Seriously, Jules. I'll come back better than before. All of my problems sorted out."

We both knew that was a ridiculous sort of optimism, but at the same time, his plan was a good one. Some fresh perspectives, some fresh riding insights, and someone to tell him what to do for a little while. A quiet place to ride someone else's horses by day, and write about dressage by night. Sometimes, you could be your own boss for so long, you forgot what you wanted to do.

Or you could be given so much, you'd never learned how to go out and earn it for yourself.

CHAPTER THIRTY-TWO

"He's kind of a plain bay," Lacey said, watching the horse walk around the paddock. "Maybe I didn't realize how plain he was before."

I punched her in the arm. "You just shut your mouth. He's gorgeous. Everything you could want in a horse with a plain brown wrapper. That's a plus for you, because there's less white to scrub before shows."

We had brought home Confident Liar an hour ago, and had just turned him out in the little paddock behind the house, where an oak tree sheltered the thin grass with the kind of deep shade most animals craved on a September afternoon in Florida. A few white ibis had gathered beneath the tree, poking their long red beaks around the gnarled roots.

"He's looking at the birds," Lacey said. "That's kind of funny."

"He *is* watching them," I agreed, watching the horse's muscles tense. "And not in a good way, if that makes sense?"

Confident Liar squealed and plunged forward, his long legs eating up the handful of strides between him and the birds. They scattered upwards and hit the sky with black-tipped wings flapping furiously, but only just in time. The horse trotted around the tree, his neck arched and his ears flattened, before he shook himself off and got back to grazing.

"Oh, what the fuck," I said, and put my fist in my mouth, biting down on my knuckles.

"So he hates birds," Lacey scoffed. "Maybe that's all he hates?"

I watched the horse of my dreams pull ferociously at the grass. He had a lot of attitude—I'd already known that, long before that happy moment when I'd called Amanda and told her I was ready to make an offer. I'd looked forward to a horse with some sass. But after seeing that bizarre episode... well, I couldn't help but wonder how much I didn't know about Confident Liar.

Pete came out to the barn a short while later.

"Everything's packed," he said, throwing himself down onto the office couch. "It's just a question of waiting for the truck now."

I had been pretending to work on the fall lesson calendar, but now I could throw aside the sham and just devote myself to worrying about Pete's imminent departure.

He was driving to California once Rogue and Barsuk were on their way, an act of craziness I could barely stomach. I wanted him to fly, but he said he needed his truck and everything he could pack into it too much to leave it behind. I'd asked him to hire a driver instead, someone who did this sort of thing regularly, but Pete insisted he could manage.

What he didn't consider was how it would make me feel. It was bad enough he'd chosen the job in California, but now I had to worry about him driving cross-country for four days, as well. My stomach was already a wreck, and I knew I wouldn't be eating much beyond crackers and ice cream for the rest of the week.

Luckily, it was an off weekend coming up—no events, no horse shows, and I'd told the kids they would need to be an extra help to Lacey all week long, because I was going to be a walking disaster.

"Has Lacey started packing up her apartment?" Pete asked, as if nothing crazy was happening, as if our lives weren't being completely upended.

I shrugged. "We're going to take the trailer down there in a few days and get everything, so I guess so. She's bringing a suitcase up this evening, to get settled in."

"I'm glad she's moving in while I'm gone," Pete said, and the way he said it made me think he really did plan on coming back.

But when?

In six months, in a year? There was no plan. Pete had taken a job riding with Marissa Miller in California. He'd be getting on her young horses, taking on some of her intermediate students, and riding with her every week. Marissa had gone to the last Olympics and had come home with a team bronze, and competed all over Europe, with top-ten finishes at events like Burghley, Badminton, and Pau. She was easily one of the sport's true up-and-coming riders, someone who would be around to accept the mantle when luminaries like Sir Mark Todd finally exited the stage. Riders like Pete and I, with occasional wins and a couple of good horses, were just hangers-on compared to her. My rational mind knew all of that, and knew those things added up into reasons why Pete's decision was the right one. When in doubt, sign on with the very best trainer you can find.

If only she wasn't so far away!

I put down my pen and closed my planner on top of it, giving up all pretense of work. I looked at Pete, stretched out on the old threadbare sofa. *Leaving*, I thought with the same sense of disbelief I'd had for weeks, ever since he'd made up his mind to take the job. *He's really leaving.*

Pete opened one eye, arched his eyebrow at me when he saw me staring at him. "It's not forever, love," he said gently. "You know that, don't you? You know."

"I know."

There was a pause, but not quite silence: we were in the barn and no barn was ever silent for long. A horse was led down the aisle, shoes ringing on concrete. A songbird trilled from a rafter. There was a sharp whinny as someone registered the missing presence of a friend.

"You're going to come back a better rider than me," I said finally, tossing him a sardonic grin, "and I'm going to have to make your life miserable to make up for it."

"As if," Pete said, hopping up from the couch, "I wasn't already a better rider than you."

He was out the door and pelting down the aisle before I could get out from behind my desk.

I caught him just outside the barn, laughing; he caught my fist when I swung it as his upper arm and pulled me close for a kiss that began fierce and hot, and ended long and sweet. "I love you," he told me, in a voice that brooked no argument, "and I'll *always* love you, and I'm coming home when this is over."

Pete hit the road after the horses were loaded and gone, and I retreated indoors to cuddle with Marcus and let myself cry for a while. I wasn't alone for long. I'd barely gotten my nose good and stuffed up when I heard the sound of children in the barn, which meant the after-school drop-off had begun.

It was a gradual process. Lindsay ferried over the kids who went to her high school, but they often stopped for fries and soda before they got here. The first arrivals were usually a few kids from the middle school, who got a ride together with one of their moms, who worked from home. Leah had convinced the school board to add an afternoon bus stop at the foot of my driveway, so whoever couldn't get a ride in an actual car still had a way to get here. The bus kids had a disadvantage, though; they would arrive later than the others, and miss some of the fun: the whispered secrets, the inside jokes, the bareback jousts and sneaky trail rides they organized when they thought I wasn't around to be the fun police.

Today would be a prime day for the kids to get themselves into trouble, since they all knew Pete had left and I'd be a disaster. Lacey hadn't yet come back from her apartment, where she was packing up her essentials ahead of her full move next week, so I dragged myself up from the couch, washed my face with cold water, and went out to the barn to oversee operations. I noticed Lindsay's car was in the parking lot already, and I hoped I hadn't arrived too late to stop any ill-advised pony shenanigans.

I turned into the barn aisle and stopped cold, shocked.

Lindsay, standing on a ladder's top-most rung, turned around. "Damn," she said. "You weren't supposed to see this yet."

"It's okay," said Jordan, who was holding the ladder steady. She handed up a length of string and what looked like a handful of rainbow triangles. It took me a moment to realize that they were party decorations. "We're almost done."

I looked around in astonishment. The barn entrance had been looped with wreaths and tiny white lights, strung along the tops of the first few stalls and across the center aisle's rafters. A banner hung from the center: *Good Luck Jules!*

"What," I said blankly, turning from smiling face to the next. It seemed that the entire crew had arrived while I'd been in the house, sobbing luxuriously. And then, emerging from the tack room behind them, I saw Lacey, a big sheet cake in her hands.

"I love this," I admitted, "but I am a little confused."

The students parted for Lacey, and she handed the cake off to Maisey as she came up to me. "Everyone made a fuss for Pete over the weekend," she said, "and now it's your turn. You have new horses to ride and compete, you're fresh off the big win with the eventing team, and the fall season is about to begin, so this is a good luck party for *you*, Jules. We're all rooting for you." She put her arm around my shoulders as she turned to face the students. "Three... two... one..."

"You've got this, Jules!" everyone crowed, more or less in unison. Then they burst out laughing, Maisey nearly dropping the cake in the process.

So we ate cake and drank Hawaiian Punch out of cans, and let the horses lick the icing from the paper plates, and no one put away the ladder so it was in all of the pictures that Lacey took, reminding us, forever, or at least once a year when it popped up in our memories, that I'd walked into the barn while Lindsay was finishing up the decorations for my good luck party.

CHAPTER THIRTY-THREE

I was climbing into bed for the night when Pete's video chat showed up on my phone. I smiled, pulling the sheet up—the October night was cool, following our first chilly cold front of the year—and answered the call. It was our nightly routine. Even if we just talked for a few moments, it was enough.

There was a spectacular sunrise illuminating the sky behind Pete, and his face was shadowed, the phone's video camera struggling with the lighting. "Those California sunsets," I said, shaking my head. "Such show-offs."

"Almost as good as Florida sunsets," Pete sighed, "but not quite."

"So, this weekend, huh?"

"This weekend. Oh my god. I'm riding five horses, and helping Marissa's groom out as well. It's going to be exhausting."

"I know the feeling. I'm riding four, and I have six students riding."

"Thank goodness you started splitting them up between events," Pete said. "It means more weekends competing, but at least you aren't trying to manage a dozen at a time."

"I need a working student, like, a formal arrangement," I said. "I'm thinking Lindsay. It's time. But I might look for someone full-time for weekdays, too."

"Growing by leaps and bounds," Pete said. "And how is the new horse?"

"Con?" I considered his question for a moment. How *was* Con? The bay horse I'd brought home from Amanda's last month was a handful, that much was certain. No one was allowed to touch him but myself and Lacey, and I'd put him in the very end stall, to keep him away from the activity centered around the middle of the barn, the entrance, and the parking lot. Still, he'd managed to scare Julia out of her mind one day when she'd gone into his paddock to look for a bell boot her horse had lost out there the day previously, and he'd lunged after her, ears pinned and neck stretched out like a snake's. She'd run for the fence, screaming blue murder, and clambered over the boards with impressive agility... but no one had been in much of a hurry to go near him again. "He's working well," I said truthfully. "He moves like a puma."

"Still a psycho, huh?"

"I don't think that's going away anytime soon. But we'll figure it out." I paused. "I'll figure it out. But it's going take a while. Rick would have had a fit if he'd bought him. Thank goodness I beat him to it."

We both wished Pete was around to help with Con, but neither of us would say it out loud. That was our agreement: to accept that Pete would come back when the time was right. When things were sorted out. Whatever his things were.

"I'm convincing Jordan to start looking at horses," I said eventually, trying to think of barn gossip to share with him.

"Oh, finally?"

"I know. She's dedicated to poor old Sammy. We'll find something for him to do. But she needs to think of herself, and moving up."

"Don't teach them to be ambitious, Jules. You'll wreck them if they all turn out like you."

We laughed. Jordan was many things, but she was not a mini-Jules in the making. Then I yawned. "Pete..."

"Bedtime, is it?"

"I'm sorry. I wish I could talk more, but tomorrow we have to prep for the event and I have to ride everyone by noon and—"

"Don't apologize. Get some sleep. Text me tomorrow."

"I will." I smiled at him, and he smiled back, and we held that for a moment, just two silly lovers soaking up each other's smiles. "I love you," I said finally.

"I love you, Jules."

ACKNOWLEDGMENTS

When I decided to send Jules to the Central Park Horse Show, I did some preliminary research and came away with more questions than answers. The competition there has changed frequently, sometimes at the last minute, and arena eventing has had a very interesting team format in that venue. I played with it to match what I needed. I know Central Park very well, having spent many years both as a park patron and as a member of the New York City Parks Department's mounted patrol, but I left right before the first horse show, so the show details in *Forward* are more imagined than usual.

Writing *Forward* came at a very precarious and exciting time in my life, and I owe it all to the readers and supporters who have stood by my work, contributed to my monthly care and feeding, and who have continued to ask for more stories, as quickly as possible. No one wants to lose their job, even when their job has stopped making them happy, but I was lucky enough to have these books and these readers to give me a somewhat softer landing than many.

I couldn't have done it without the support of my Patreon member Patrons, who help fund my writing from month to month, and also read my first drafts, give me incredible feedback, and encourage me through tough weeks and dry creative spells. Having you in my corner has been simply amazing—both really tough, because I know you're waiting for new chapters, and really inspiring, because I know you're waiting for new chapters! Much love to each of you: Zoe B., Emily J., Heather W., Kaylee A., Rachael R., Dana P., Kath, Liza S., Barbara H., Rose T., Sarah S., Ann B., Diana A., Emily N., Jenny B., Sandra G., Megan D., Cindy S., Claus G., Kathi H., Jennifer, Tricia J., Cheryl B., Brinn D., Rhonda L., Amy J., Orpu, Liz G., Christine B., Lindsay M., Mary, Cyndy S., Karen M., Mara S., Kathy G., Carolyn B., Kathi L., and Kim K.

You can join this special group of people at patreon.com/nataliekreinert.

I'd also like to say thanks to my old boss, Simon, who asked me, over a pint of Guinness in a touristy Kensington pub, why I didn't write novels full-time. I stammered some reply brushing off the idea, but his question was valid and it didn't leave me until the day I decided I was, in fact, going to write novels full-time. I hope we have another Guinness in London sometime soon, so I can thank him in person.

And thanks to Jess, who keeps me in horses and doesn't

freak out every time I decide we should revamp her business model. We'll build a world-class equestrian center yet!

But the biggest thanks of all goes to Cory, for not fainting when I said I was going to write novels full-time. Everyone deserves a person like him in their corner, but hardly anyone gets them. I just got lucky.

ABOUT THE AUTHOR

Natalie Keller Reinert grew up with horses: first riding hunters, then discovering eventing with a green off-track Thoroughbred named Amarillo. Never one to turn down an adventure, Reinert has started and galloped racehorses, groomed for Olympic riders, worked in the New York City Parks Department mounted patrol, and so much more. Today Reinert lives in Orlando, Florida with her family.

Reinert has been a finalist and semi-finalist for the Dr. Tony Ryan Book Award, awarded for horse-racing literature, with *Turning For Home* and *Other People's Horses*.

For more information and to keep up with new projects, visit NatalieKReinert.com. You can also follow updates on Twitter at twitter.com/nataliegallops and on Facebook at facebook.com/NatalieKellerReinert. For unpublished works and to read upcoming novels as they are written, please visit patreon.com/nataliekreinert.